07.

010

1

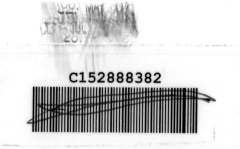

C152888382

USAAF
FIGHTER STORIES

USAAF FIGHTER STORIES

A NEW SELECTION

Ian McLachlan

SUTTON PUBLISHING

First published in the United Kingdom in 2005 by
Sutton Publishing Limited · Phoenix Mill
Thrupp · Stroud · Gloucestershire · GL5 2BU

Copyright © Ian McLachlan, 2005

All rights reserved. No part of this publication may be reproduced, stored in a retrieval system, or transmitted, in any form, or by any means, electronic, mechanical, photocopying, recording or otherwise, without the prior permission of the publisher and copyright holder.

Ian McLachlan has asserted the moral right to be identified as the author of this work.

British Library Cataloguing in Publication Data
A catalogue record for this book is available from the British Library.

ISBN 0-7509-3361-5

Typeset in 10.5/14pt Garamond 3.
Typesetting and origination by
Sutton Publishing Limited.
Printed and bound in England by
J.H. Haynes & Co. Ltd, Sparkford.

For Sue – my Mustang Mk III – still enduring despite the flak.
I hope we make 'mission accomplished'.

Contents

Preface

These words are being written on 1 January 2005. Today, the world is reeling from a natural disaster taking over 150,000 lives. Sixty years ago, before many readers and I were born, mankind was reeling from a self-inflicted disaster – the Second World War. That epic tragedy cost millions of lives; it was an enormous loss of human potential and a diversion of resources; the war effort was immense and few families unaffected. Today we are living with another self-inflicted war: the war against terrorism. Again, it induces fear, quite apart from once again diverting resources. As during the Second World War, democratic nations need to unite to fight terrorism as they are uniting to give aid to those afflicted by the massive tsunami. There are personal stories of courage emerging from the fight against terrorism and from the struggle to survive and rebuild after the tsunami. This has always been so whenever man is in conflict, whether with a mortal enemy or with the elements. This book contains personal stories from sixty years ago and includes accounts of man's struggle against himself and against the forces of nature. It touches on just a few to represent the many. The common denominators then, as now, are courage and care. The courage is that needed to fight for democratic freedoms; the care is that of free nations finding the resources to aid those afflicted by tragedy, whether that tragedy is subordination, murder and torture beneath a tyrannical regime or one of the many masks worn by terrorism.

The young men whose stories feature in the following pages took up arms to preserve democracy in their own nations and to see it restored to others. Those who perished made the ultimate sacrifice to make the world a better place for their children. The survivors, now fast dwindling in numbers, earned our undying gratitude. Those of us who succeed them should be grateful that they fought for our freedom and do what we can to preserve that legacy and share the benefits bestowed upon us.

Ian McLachlan
Suffolk, England, 1 January 2005

Acknowledgements

My wife Sue deserves to be first in the list of people who have helped make this book possible. I commenced it at the same time as starting a new job for a book wholesaler. Unfortunately, in the long run the job did not work out, and I hope the book will do better. Sue supported me through both, enduring not only my commitment to the 'day job' and the disappointment and ingratitude of redundancy but the prolonged hours alone while I endeavoured to complete this new selection of *USAAF Fighter Stories*. She has given this support because she endorses my belief that the young men herein, who represent countless others, deserve to be recognised. We have shared touching moments when family members and friends of the fallen have, through the research, gained greater knowledge of loved ones lost during that titanic struggle. Even though it is now sixty years ago – we should still say, 'Thanks Yanks'.

There are other historians and researchers who have adopted this spirit and generously provided their research material so that stories they have worked upon so hard for so long can be expressed. It is my privilege to be the outlet for their efforts; any errors or omissions are mine. I hope the result meets with their approval and reminds us all of the enormous loss when a fighter fell from one heavenly vault and took its pilot to another. Many of those who survived have also since soared into that realm, and publication has been too late for them to see the end result of the research and correspondence. My acknowledgements are posthumous, but I hope the book will perpetuate their achievements.

Having encountered the book industry from another aspect, I have discovered more about the difficulties of getting into print, the competitive forces surrounding an author's cherished work and the ruthless behaviour of some in the book world. The team at Sutton Publishing flew escort for this flak-damaged author and helped restore my faith in some members of the book industry. I cannot thank them enough for their support, perseverance and patience: Hilary Walford, Jonathan Falconer, Nick Reynolds, Helen Holness, Nazia Achmed-White and the many others who keep their aviation range airborne.

Having earlier acknowledged Sue's support, I have also to thank other members of my family whose invaluable help and advice ensured this new selection of *USAAF Fighter Stories* finally emerged from the hangar: Bethan McLachlan, Rowan McLachlan, Jake Balls, Maddie Balls, and Gordon and Kenneth McLachlan.

I am also indebted to the following organisations and individuals for their support. Without them, there would be no book and the stories would have been lost. They have generously shared their research material and memories to ensure the achievements of the young men who flew USAAF fighters are acknowledged.

100BG Memorial Air Museum, 390 BG Memorial Air Museum, Air Forces Escape & Evasion Society, Alan Hague, Alan McLachlan, Albert E. Scott, Alice Cooper, Andrew Height, Anthony Chardella, Arthur Beech, Aviation Research Group, Barbara Pleasance, Bill Bankston, Bill Gadd, Bill Varnedoe, Billy Buck, Bob Collis, Bob Dunnett, British Aviation Archaeological Council, Buddies of The Ninth Association, C. Thomas Bendorf, Carol Lochhead, Char Baldridge, Chris Gotts, Christine Armes, Cliff Bishop, Colin Lee, Craig A. Fuller, Dale Larrabee, Dan Engle, Danny Morris, David C. Crow, David Wade, Denis Kilcommons, *Huddersfield Examiner*, Dennis B. Rawls, Derrick Knowles, Donald L. Caldwell, Donald McKibben, E. Scott Mackey, East Anglian Aviation Research Group, East Anglian Aviation Society, *East Anglian Daily Times*, *Eastern Daily Press*, Eddie Malo, Eighth Air Force Historical Society, Eugene F. Britton, Finn Buch, *Flypast Magazine*, Frank M. Stillwell, Fred Vonderlage, *Fremont Tribune*, Fremont W. Miller, Garry L. Fry, Genevieve Samson, Gordon McLachlan, Graham Cross, Harry Baker, Ian Hawkins, Ivy Moss, James R. Starnes, Jeff Carless, Jeffrey L. Ethell, John Betts, John A. Hey, John Harris, Joseph A. Kuhn, Ken Fish, Kenneth McLachlan, Kent D. Miller, Lancashire Aircraft Investigation Team, Larry Ksanznak, Leslie Brody, Library and Archives Canada, Lucius Foster, Marc L. Hamel, Martin Sheldrick, Martin W. Bowman, Martlesham Heath Aviation Society, Maurice Hammond, Merle C. Olmsted, Mick Tipple, Mike Bailey, Mike Harris, Nick Wotherspoon, Nigel Beckett, Norfolk & Suffolk Aviation Museum, Pat (Ksanznak) Lynn, Pat Everson, Pat Ramm, Patsy Feather, Paul Evans, Paul Thrower, Pauline Bird, Pete Snowling, Pete Wilson, Peter Claydon, R. Whipps, Rémy Chuinard, Rex Webster, Richard C. Penrose, Robert H. Powell Jr, Roger A. Freeman, Ross Smart, Roy Mitchell, Ruth Skye, S.E. Harvey, Sam L. Sox Jr, Simon Dunham, Stan Bishop, Steve Gotts, Tammy Real-McKeighan, Terry Hobert, *The Advocate*, The Fighter Collection, *The Record*, Thelma Jones, Tim Power, *Halifax Courier*, Tony Jeckells, Tony North, Trevor Elam, William R. Beyer, www.AviationArchaeology.com.

CHAPTER ONE

Mid-Air Collisions

In the congested wartime East Anglian airspace, mid-air collisions occurred with tragic regularity. Hundreds of aircraft might be funnelling out of or into that bulbous protrusion forming the east coast of England, the country's closest landmass to Germany itself. True, the comparatively flat terrain was ideal for establishing aerodromes, and they sprang up like mushrooms in a competition between the country's dual need for crops and combat bases. As the airfields proliferated, so, too, did the hazards of round-the-clock aircraft movements, which climaxed during 1944–5. A normal day would see over 2,000 operational

During March 1944 the 352FG bade farewell to its Thunderbolts. Aircraft of the 486FS prepare to take off. Ground crews now had the long, anxious wait for the safe return of their aircraft and pilots. *(352FG Association)*

aircraft movements over the region, with RAF operational and non-operational activity plus USAAF bombers becoming airborne, soon to be followed by fighters in relays of protection for their 'big friends'. The busy skies required coordination, with timings, altitudes and territorial separation becoming logistical juggling acts for hard-pressed planners and air traffic controllers. It is thanks to their skills and those of the aviators that there were not more losses through mid-air collisions. When crashes or collisions occurred, casualties were not always restricted to those unfortunate souls in the machines. People in the communities below stoically accepted this threat, for they knew the risk to them was slight and the men struggling to get airborne in often appalling conditions were doing so on their behalf.

One such day drearily drizzled into existence on 8 March 1944 over USAAF Station 141 at Bodney in Norfolk. This breckland base was home to the 352FG, which comprised the standard three squadrons – the 328FS with the 486 and 487FS, all, until now, operational with Republic's redoubtable P-47 Thunderbolt. Today would see the beginning of change mixed with misadventure and death. The change was the operational debut for the 352FG of its first North American Mustangs, now nudging the portly P-47 aside to establish grazing rights on fighter bases throughout the region. In time Mustangs would supplant the rugged Thunderbolt almost entirely, but 8FC was still foaling its herd, and the 352FG had waited patiently. The 357FG and the premier 4FG, with its legacy and love of the nimble Spitfire, had welcomed the similarly sleek if temperamental new P-51. The 4FG had never settled with the Thunderbolt and were delighted to see the return of the Merlin in their new steed and, above all, the advantage of the increased range it offered. Other groups soon followed, and the first Mustangs designated for the 352FG touched the airfield's turf on 1 March. Conversion commenced immediately, but the exigencies of war allowed no respite during this process, and the maximum effort called for on the 8th saw the unusual combination of a mixed P-47 and P-51 force. This created some planning problems, because the range and fuel consumption figures differed between the types.

At briefing that morning, it made sense to specify the order of take-off, with the higher endurance P-51s going first and the P-47s following. Their role would be to cover the B-17s and B-24s during the bombers' return from attacking the VKF bearing factory at Erkner in Berlin. All told, the 352FG despatched fifty-seven fighters that day, but the cloudy, crowded skies would cause more casualties than actual combat.

With its mixed contingent of seven Mustangs and sixteen Thunderbolts, the 486FS took off first. Visibility below cloud gave the ascending pilots some 3–5 miles, but their initial assembly was compressed beneath the cloud base at some 700ft extending to 3,500ft. This created a layer of patchy density some 2,800ft deep and meant plenty of time in poor or non-existent visibility for things to go wrong. Following closely behind the Mustangs, the first 486FS Thunderbolts lifted off and were soon trailing the P-51s as they gathered in multiples of four for a squadron ascent through cloud.

As they entered the overcast, 1/Lt Stanley G. Miles was adhering to standard procedure and concentrating on his flight leader, who would fly instruments for them both. So dense was the cloud that Stan found it increasingly difficult keeping his P-47, 'Bundle of Joy' in position. Quite how, Stan never knew, but he lost the wraithlike form of his flight leader; the

1/Lt Stanley G. Miles with his P-47D-5 'Bundle of Joy' – serial number 42-8490, PZ-S. They flew their last sortie together on 8 March 1944. *(352FG Association)*

other P-47 seemed simply to disappear. Stan barely had time to adjust to using his own instruments when his aircraft received a sharp jolt from astern and was instantly shoved into a steep dive. Within moments, the great Pratt and Whitney R-2800 Double Wasp stopped dead, as hydraulic fluid and oil spurted over Stan's windscreen. Stan knew he was now fighting for his life as the 'Bundle of Joy' dropped earthwards pulled by a dead engine. Robbed of any forward vision, Stan heaved back hard on the control column to recover from the dive. The largest and heaviest single-engined fighter built to that time, the P-47 had a renowned propensity for accumulating speed during descent and his 'Bundle of Joy' now seemed intent on burying its pilot deep into the East Anglian countryside. Unable to see directly ahead, Stan was spared the view of the earth rushing up to meet him as he burst out of the overcast, but the Thunderbolt's nose was coming up – would it be in time? Then, through his side window, Stan spotted a large airbase with 'a beautiful runway'. The P-47 was levelling off, but, with his engine dead, Stan now needed to convert the momentum of his dive into enough speed to reach the welcoming concrete. A flurry of decisions and actions crammed into his mind, but some 700 hours of flying experience had taught him how to handle emergencies. He could belly land – the P-47's rugged construction had saved many a pilot – but the thought of his fuel-laden fighter scraping along amid a shower of sparks – a giant match – persuaded him to try dropping his undercarriage. Instinctively, his left hand located the landing gear lever and he pulled it to 'down'. Without hydraulic power, the undercarriage now depended on its own weight to drop and lock; there would be no second chance. He felt the gear fall and, with relief, saw it had locked. Using his side windows, Stan judged his moment, and the wheels made firm contact, as one very relieved and joyous pilot rolled the 'Bundle of Joy' to a standstill. Stan had not taken the option of bailing out and only now discovered that he had not had the choice; his canopy was damaged and jammed shut. Luckily, personnel from the base were soon on hand, and, as they assisted him from the cockpit, he discovered his sanctuary was the 389BG Liberator base at Hethel. A small crowd now surrounded the 'Bundle of Joy' and Stan took stock. His prop tips were bent and the engine cowling torn and shredded away exposing the engine cylinders; the front end of his fighter looked naked. Later examination also revealed his engine oil cooler line had been severed, and the Thunderbolt was written off to salvage. Standing gratefully on terra firma and surveying the damage, Stan knew he had been lucky. Visible in the distance, three ominous columns of smoke smeared the horizon, and Stan, guessing their origins, wondered if those pilots had been as fortunate.

1/Lt Henry J. Miklajcyk was Red Flight Leader. For reasons unknown, 'Mike' Miklajyck was piloting a borrowed 353FG aircraft coded LH-Y instead of his favoured P-47C, 'The

In classic garb, posing for a PR shot, 1/Lt Henry J. Miklajcyk with his favourite aircraft, 'The Syracusan', a modified P-47C, 41-6531, PZ-K, the oldest P-47 in the 352FG. The panel beneath the cockpit honours the labours of his ground crew: Crew Chief S/Sgt R.H. Sprole; Assistant Crew Chief, Sgt C.C. Thomas and armourer, Sgt S.J. Lengieza. Miklajcyk became an ace with 7.5 victories before being killed in action near Halle, Germany, on 2 November 1944 in P-51D 44-13690, 'Syracusan The 3rd'. *(352FG Association)*

Syracusan', the oldest Thunderbolt in the 352FG. According to the Report of Aircraft Accident, Mike was using visual alignment with White Flight ahead to take his own Red Flight up through the clouds. In theory, this line of sight was like a lifeline linking one flight to another as they climbed, but this tenuous lifeline was about to be broken. Flying with Miklajcyk as No. 2 was 1/Lt Earl H. Bond in 'The Bid', while 1/Lt Donald 'Mac' McKibben was No. 3 in his 'Sneezy' and 1/Lt Edward Fahrewald was in the No. 4 slot. Flying conditions were dreadful, and Fahrewald was struggling with the contradictory sensations of vertigo. His mind became convinced that their flying attitude was wrong and he finally decided to try it alone, so he deliberately left the formation and continued a solo instrument ascent. This decision probably saved his life. Unseen by Mike Miklajcyk, Stan Miles had drifted from his position in White Flight and either had slipped back into the oncoming Red Flight or been run down by them. The jolt that sent Stan tumbling earthwards came from an impact with Miklajcyk's aircraft. The reaction from Red Flight was like a ten-pin ball making a strike. Mac McKibben 'suddenly became aware of the form of an aircraft where it shouldn't be', close above and to his left. The next instant there was numerous pieces of P-47 being thrown around. Hitting chunks of wreckage could be lethal, and Mac's reaction was instinctive as he pulled 'Sneezy' into a sharp, climbing turn, away from the spill of debris. This tumbled the gyro in his artificial horizon, rendering the instrument useless. With no horizon, real or artificial, Mac quickly decided there would be no time for any recovery if he hurtled out of the

overcast heading straight down. His only option was to jump. Opening the canopy, he discarded his helmet, disconnected his seat harness and hauled himself out into the slipstream. Halfway onto the wing, he was snagged by the oxygen hose that he had forgotten to unplug. Ripping his oxygen mask away, Mac continued out onto the wing and leapt clear, perilously close to the ground. Tumbling through the air, he tugged his ripcord and must have been inverted when the parachute snapped open. The crack as it abruptly arrested his descent whipped him upright with such force that the escape kit inside his jacket flew out and smacked him in the eye as it ricocheted off his skull. Now clear of the overcast, smarting from the blow and feeling sore from the

1/Lt Donald 'Mac' McKibben and crew chief Luman Morey pose with 'Sneezy', P-47D-15, serial 42-76323 PZ-Y. 'Sneezy' would soon make an unwelcome appearance in the village of Hapton. *(352FG Association)*

wrench on his anatomy, Mac had little time to take in his surroundings. Beneath his feet he saw the wreckage of 'Sneezy' burning in a field very close to a hamlet and church; then, with the ground fast approaching, he tugged at his risers to avoid a country road and thudded unceremoniously into a marginally softer ploughed field. Other than the shiner he would get from the blow off the escape pack, Mac was uninjured. As he sat up, a charming English lady emerged from one of the nearby cottages and offered him the traditional British solution to any crisis – a nice cup of tea! Mac must have felt slightly embarrassed by such kindness considering that burning fuel from Sneezy had now set light to the thatched roof of a nearby dwelling and trees in the pretty little churchyard were also burning, threatening the church itself.

Mike Miklajcyk had been concentrating on the ascent and had no time to avoid the other aircraft looming into his path. He, too, had wisely taken to his parachute and survived, later becoming an ace with the 352FG. He scored 7½ victories before being shot down during November 1944, and, on that occasion, he either delayed opening his parachute for too long or it malfunctioned and the gallant pilot perished.

Earl Bond had also taken violent evasive action and his aircraft might have been struck by debris. Like many pilots of the period, his instrument time was low. He had attained his pilot status during January 1943 and gained an instrument rating the following summer. However, of over 502 hours' flying experience, little was on instruments, and he had only

Red Two. 1/Lt Earl H. Bond, a pilot with over 502 hours to his credit, beams broadly from the cockpit of his P-47 'The Bid'. This machine, serial 42-8652 PZ-O, crashed at Braconash. Bond was killed outright. (352FG Association)

accrued 2½ hours instrumentation flying during the previous six months. Like Mac's, his instruments tumbled when he broke away from the collision. Whether he tried to make an instrument recovery or waited for a visual reference when he broke cloud is unknown. Earl Bond died instantly when 'The Bid' exploded on impact at the edge of a wood half a mile from Mergate Hall at Braconash. Four Thunderbolts had been written off and one pilot killed, but further take-off troubles for the 352FG were still to follow.

Following the unfortunate 486FS, the 487FS began its own ascent into the soggy skies and suffered its own misadventures. An understandably nervous 2/Lt William E. Fowler was on his first combat mission. With the surname Fowler, it was inevitable that his flying companions would nickname him 'Flaps' after the Fowler flaps used on some aircraft of the period and still in use today. As the pilots waited in the 487FS ready room that morning, Flaps was approached by his CO, Col John C. Meyer, who queried the neophyte's proficiency on instruments. Flaps, replying as nonchalantly as possible, commented that he had not thought much about it, but he had been given the usual training. In fact, Flaps could claim over twelve hours on instruments during the last six months, which was higher than some of the longer-serving pilots. Inwardly, Flaps guessed the question had a purpose and determined that he would stick like a limpet to whichever leader he was assigned. Shortly after, Flaps heard he would be 'Crowned Prince Red Two' – wingman for Maj John C. 'Curly' Edwards, who was leading the 487FS that day. An experienced aviator, Curly had over 1,700 hours flying experience, more than four times that of the rookie, but, interestingly, his instrument time was less than an hour in the previous six months.

Taxiing out, Flaps knew his position put him at the front of the squadron, and, catching the signal, he accelerated in place and lifted away neatly on Maj Edwards's port wing. Rank has its privileges, and Flaps was flying an earlier derivate of the Thunderbolt, a P-47D-2, serial 42-22492, while his CO had a more recent P-47D-11, 42-75513, but there was little variation in performance and Flaps followed closely behind Curly Edwards. He later recalled:

> After take off we entered the overcast, and the flying game changed. Visibility went from bad to worse. At times I couldn't see Edwards at all and it was like flying formation in a milk bottle. Most of the time all I could see was his wingtip . . . this would sometimes vanish. I eased over towards Edwards to try to keep his plane in sight as I was supposed to by flying visual on him and didn't want to lose him. My Lord, it turns out I was already close enough!

In fact, Flaps tucked in so close that his right wingtip settled gently on top of Curly's port elevator, and, for a while, neither pilot realised their aircraft were actually touching as they both eased upwards at over 140 mph. Unwittingly, Flaps was literally sticking to his CO, because airflow pouring from the trailing edge of Edwards's left wing went over his own tail plane and the starboard wingtip from Flaps's machine. This created a suction that bonded the interloping wingtip even more firmly in place. Concentrating visually on the rearmost 486FS flight ahead, Curly was initially unaware of the problem, but then, easing his control column aft, he found it seemed to stick. Perhaps a control cable had jammed? He pulled more firmly – still no response. The situation gave increasing cause for concern because his P-47 appeared to be suffering from stuck elevators and was not responding as it should. Exasperated and anxious, Curly now yanked hard back on the joystick and his P-47, breaking free, now shot up out of formation and, seconds later, burst out of cloud. It was like a diver shooting to the surface after being trapped underwater. Flaps popped up close by with the rest of the flight now also emerging. Realisation dawned as the sharp clarity of broad daylight revealed the evidence. Flaps could see Maj Edwards's ship had damage to its port stabiliser and the elevator had a serious kink that was definitely not a design feature. Flaps's own wingtip was damaged, and it was evident that neither aircraft could be considered combat worthy. Maj Edwards reluctantly relinquished command of the 487FS and ordered a somewhat chastened Fowler to descend with him – not too close – and return to base.

The subsequent investigation attributed half the problem to young Fowler and, in mitigation, half to the poor weather conditions. Under 'Action to Prevent Repetition', the Report of Aircraft Accident commented, 'Operational missions in this theater usually require groups to climb through overcasts on instruments. To keep control of the group it is necessary to take squadrons through overcast in close formation. Formation instrument flying is being practiced.' Interestingly, Maj John C. Edwards was on the Investigation Board into the incident. Decades later, Flaps Fowler recalled:

> We landed our planes, went our separate ways and, surprisingly, I have never talked to him about it since the event. Thinking back on it now, I shudder to think how close my Thunderbolt's big prop was to Edwards' cockpit . . . We were fortunate that it did not turn out to be worse in our squadron.

Prior to any combat with the Luftwaffe, the cost to the 352FG was now four P-47s destroyed with two more damaged and one pilot killed. However, they now had an opportunity to redress the situation when they rendezvoused with the returning heavies. 1/Lt Edward 'Pappy' Gignac was leading Purple Flight and had only just met the bomber force when he spotted a straggling B-17 under attack from astern by an Me 109. Alerting his flight, Pappy pushed his P-51 into a steep dive and went swooping down to intervene. As his Mustang powered vengefully into the attack, he saw further strikes on the crippled bomber, but his impending arrival now distracted the German pilot, forcing him to break off from engaging the bomber. The Messerschmitt rolled rapidly away then whipped up into a vertical climb. Closing too fast, Pappy throttled back hard and tried a short burst at maximum deflection as he shot past. His judgement was excellent, because Ed Heller, flying as Green Two, saw the Me 109's pilot parachute clear and watched the enemy fighter until it exploded on impact some 6,000ft below. Pappy, flying a borrowed P-51B, 43-7022, PZ-W, 'Little Rebel', knew its regular pilot, Al Wallace, would be both envious and pleased that it was his aircraft at least that had taken first blood for their new mount.

Not to be outdone, the P-47 flown by Lt Virgil Meroney took another scalp. He was leading Blue Flight to the rear of the bombers and had reduced throttle settings to cruise more economically and stay closer to the bombers at their altitude of about 20,000ft. At first, their escort duties were uneventful and seemed set to remain that way until shortly after Meroney had received orders for a return to base. Just then, three Me 109s hurtled out of the sun in a beam attack on the rear of the B-17 formation. Meroney called in the attack and poured on power to the big Pratt and Whitney as the German fighters broke away, rolling over and diving earthwards. It took a few moments for the acceleration to cut in, but then 'Sweet Louise/Josephine' ably demonstrated the renowned diving capabilities of the P-47, as Blue Flight tore after the fleeing enemy fighters. Gaining on them, Meroney selected the leading pair, ignoring the third, which had taken a different course. With his aircraft accelerating fast after the 109, Meroney was still some 1,000yd behind when two other Thunderbolts cut in from his left. This attack split up the pair of Messerschmitts, and the leader chandelled to avoid the new attack. The other two P-47s roared away after the second 109, leaving Meroney to manage the leader. Seeking to distract the German, he squirted a burst from 400yd, even though it was a 90-degree deflection shot. His intention was to dissuade the 109 from curving back to fire at the other pair of P-47s chasing the German leader's wingman. This action proved a suitable deterrent, and the Me 109 now put its nose down and streaked for the deck. German pilots never seemed to learn that nothing could outrun a steeply diving P-47, and Meroney closed to 300yd. The battle had taken them to tree-top level, and, dodging branches, Meroney snapped bursts at the Me 109 as it jinked to shake his aim. Some of his rounds registered, and the Me 109 suddenly climbed perpendicularly, perhaps hoping the P-47 would pass beneath and give an opportunity to escape or attack. Chopping throttle, Meroney followed into a vertical climb, and the P-47, shedding unwanted speed, still carried enough power and momentum to close in. From only 100yd, Meroney's guns hammered at the German, and, in an instant, the 109 was ablaze and shedding large pieces of its airframe. Increasing power and converting more of the momentum from his dive, Meroney now pulled alongside the burning enemy machine. As he sat off its starboard wing, he noted the fighter seemed to have an extra long and larger nose. The colour scheme was a standard slate grey upper surface and light blue beneath. The wings and fuselage bore the *Balkenkreuz*, but the American noted there was a dash in front of the fuselage cross with some black chevrons pointing towards the nose. Clearly this pilot was significant, and, with no room for chivalry in this form of combat, Meroney determined to finish him off. His opponent had now jettisoned his canopy and was clambering from the cockpit. Easing back, Meroney slid underneath to administer the *coup de grâce*, but was unable to bring his guns to bear before the German tumbled clear; his parachute popped open and then he was gone. The empty Me 109 rolled over and span to destruction. Pleased with his victory but regretting the pilot's escape, Meroney advanced power and 'Sweet Louise/Josephine' climbed to rejoin the homebound 352FG. In his Encounter Report, he speculated that the enemy aircraft had been a 'Messerschmitt 209', but the existence of this type on operations was mythical and propagated to some extent by the German propaganda machine.

Research by aviation artist Troy White tied this combat into Hauptman Klaus Mietusch, commanding officer of III/JG26, and it features in Donald Calwell's superbly researched

Flaming fuel thrown from 'Sneezy' set fire to thatch on the Moss family home in Hapton. This picture was taken by a 389BG photographer who incorrectly called the village Flordon on his caption. *(Simon Dunham)*

book, *JG26: Top Guns of the Luftwaffe.* The aircraft flown by Mietusch was actually an Me 109G-6, werke number 162032, coded Black 21. The other Me 109 destroyed was also a G-6, number 410743, White 5, piloted by Uffz Emil Kampen, who was killed in action. Mietusch survived but suffered injuries serious enough to keep him out of the fray for several weeks. Had Meroney managed to kill his adversary that day, several Allied lives would have been spared, because, returning to combat, Mietusch destroyed one B-17, four P-38s, a P-47 and a P-51, before the encounter with William Beyer described in Chapter 5.

The events of 8 March 1944 were also traumatic for several British civilians, and these incidents have been investigated by enthusiasts Simon Dunham and David Wade, plus others, and even a bit of genuine spadework by the author. The violent arrival of 'Sneezy' in the parish of Hapton was noted in Norfolk's Civil Defence War Diary as occurring at 1400, with the brief comment, 'Pilot safe. House and stack on fire.' Mr and Mrs Lemon lived in the village, and Jessie Lemon remembered hearing the sound of aero-engines overhead, then 'a loud clattering noise'. Her husband, Harry Lemon, was working at Hapton Hall when he, too, heard the din from above and immediately knew something was wrong. Seconds later an aeroplane came out of the clouds streaking earthwards and exploded on impact in or on the village. Alarmed for the safety of his family and neighbours, Harry grabbed his bicycle and hastened homewards. Drawing nearer, he noticed a parachute and watched the flier float down barely 100yd from the burning wreckage. Harry was pleased that the man seemed safe, but his anxieties for the community increased when he realised that burning fuel thrown from the fighter had ignited the thatched roof of the Moss homestead, and flames were spreading towards the church. Rose Moss had been caught in an embarrassing situation and now found herself imprisoned in the outside privy. Thrown by the force of impact, the Thunderbolt's propeller had landed in the garden and jammed against the toilet door. First frightened by the explosion, a distraught Rose could be forgiven for experiencing further panic when she discovered her desire for a swift egress thwarted. Luckily, Jessie Lemon realised her neighbour's predicament and managed to lever the offending propeller blade aside so a somewhat shaken Rose could escape. Eleven fire tenders attended the blaze, including some from the USAAF airfields at Hethel and Hardwick, plus the British National Fire Service. Although most of the Moss family's possessions were saved, firemen were unable to prevent the flames from spreading, and the cottage, once a public house, was destroyed when the building eventually collapsed. The haystack nearby also burned down, and only hoses played onto trees in the churchyard and the roof of the church itself prevented further destruction.

Miklajcyk's P-47 augered into a hedgerow between Wreningham and Flordon. Local farmer Rex Webster heard the aircraft overhead; then came a crash followed within seconds by three fighters spiralling out of the clouds. The anguished screech from each engine terminated in a trio of explosions in close succession and three black columns of smoke. Events were even more alarming for farmworker Philip Taylor, who was muck-spreading on a horsedrawn wagon when the collision occurred. His horses were accustomed to aero-engines, but then came a sound like 'smashing crockery' followed by the frightening arrival of a sizeable piece of

Rose Moss, seated, was the veritable old lady 'locked in the lavatory'. A member of the Red Cross, she was not actually that old at the time and is seen acting the part of an old lady in what seems to be a cameo created to show the Red Cross in action. *(Eastern Daily Press via Ivy Moss)*

aeroplane thudding to earth close by. The aircraft itself soon followed and blasted itself to pieces some 500yd away. Startled by the explosion, his horses were made even more jittery by the crack of ammunition cooking off amid the flames. Philip's brother Leslie was even nearer the crash site on Webster's meadow and initially ran towards the downed machine in case he could assist any distressed pilot. He was soon persuaded to retreat by random rounds zinging from the conflagration and passing far too close for comfort. Philip saw McKibben's parachute descending, 'like one of them thistledown seeds', but he did not see Miklajcyk land. Someone who did was John Griffiths, and the cocky youngster, an evacuee from London, was quick off the mark in cheekily asking the aviator for his parachute. Undeterred by the pilot's refusal, the lad later purloined a belt of ammunition from the crash site and stashed it in a cupboard at home. When his father later found his hoard, the boy's dangerous trophies were discarded in a water-filled pit at Flordon, where they may still rest. John also discovered McKibben's escape kit, but, if this still exists, its whereabouts are unknown; interest in acquiring items from these aircraft would be perpetuated many years later.

The events of that afternoon eventually merged into wartime and village history, but, during this process, the facts became indistinct, until the efforts of Simon Dunham and David Wade created some historical clarity. I feel justified in claiming limited responsibility, having encouraged both young men during their early endeavours into research and aviation archaeology. I handed my own meagre notes to Simon, not realising how much further his research would take our knowledge. He began fitting events together by first finding the crash sites. On 13 September 1990, I joined Simon and his team on the edge of woodland near Mergate Hall, Braconash. Evidence of Bond's crash could still be discerned by a cut in the boundary hedge and scars on nearby trees. The buzz of busy detectors soon had us digging enthusiastically, and bits from 'The Bid', serial 42-8652, coded PZ-O, gradually accumulated in a forlorn pile bearing no resemblance to the once-proud and powerful P-47. During the course of two weekends, Simon added various manufacturers' plates, an aileron trim tab in fine condition, parts from the Pratt and Whitney radial and the boss from the big Curtiss Electric airscrew. These and an assortment of smaller finds represented the loss of Earl Bond.

Two years later, David arranged the recovery of items from Mac McKibben's 'Sneezy', serial 42-76323, PZ-Y. Impacting onto a terrain of unyielding Norfolk flint, the fighter had disintegrated into countless pieces. Delving to a depth of 6ft, the group were rewarded with various artefacts, including remains of the instrument panel and gun sight, the undercarriage selector controls, plus some seat harness buckles. This site had originally been investigated by Simon, who picked up on the surface a folded section of cowling panel that, when carefully prised open, revealed part of the original nose-art. This was later sent to a very appreciative Donald W. McKibben, who returned to the scene of his 'crime' several years later and was shown around by Simon. Mac had an opportunity to apologise for the mayhem his arrival had caused in the community, but there were no hard feelings, because, following reparations by the US authorities, the burnt-out cottage had been replaced with a more modern dwelling.

Simon also arranged a dig on the site of Miklajcyk's crash in September 1999, and it was a pleasure for me to pull my rather ancient, army-surplus Forster detector out of semi-

Remains of Miklajcyk's aircraft pictured in 1944. Note what appears to be a piece of wreckage hanging from a tree in the background. This picture was incorrectly captioned 'Hampton Hall [sic] A/c No. 2486 PZ-H' by the 389BG photographer. Inexplicably, Miklajcyk was flying a P-47D-10, serial 42-75157 LH-Y, borrowed from the 353FG. (Marc L. Hamel via Simon Dunham)

The same site fifty-four years later. Like rabbits burrowing amid the brambles, Simon Dunham (right) and his team search for parts of the fallen fighter. Confirmation came with the discovery of a manufacturer's plate endorsed 'Airplane Mod. P-47D . . .'.

retirement. The location was in a rough area of scrubland at the end of a large sloping field just outside Flordon. The aircraft had hit a shallow, sloping embankment across a small stream, and the crash site was dotted with gorse bushes. Experience told me the acidic, sandy sub-soil was not conducive to the preservation of parts, particularly aluminium, and this was soon confirmed by the discovery of large patches of corroded aluminium crystals. Some steel fittings and other small components were found using the bevy of standard detectors, and Perspex from the cockpit also emerged jumbled amid fragments of engine casing. The Forster hummed happily over an inconveniently positioned gorse bush, thus creating a battle with barbs and roots until we found some pieces of engine cylinder and an identification plate confirming the type P-47D. Nearby, a stainless steel ammunition chute was stencilled to denote that it had fed the No. 1 gun on the starboard side. However, it was evident that the aircraft had not penetrated to any depth, and pictures later traced by Simon showed a relatively flat angle of impact. Irrespective of the fact that little emerged of the fighter ace's machine, a few items exhibited with pictures and a story board would recall the combination of bad weather, human error and pure misfortune causing mid-air collisions on a day so tragically typical in skies once densely packed with young men striving to do their duty.

CHAPTER TWO

Take-off Troubles

The most hazardous moments of any flight are those occurring during the transition from ground to air. There are many white knucklers among today's airline passengers who will testify to such anxiety as engine power pours on and the take-off roll begins. An enormous collection of components, laden with combustible aviation fuel, now seeks to make a unified departure from terra firma. Burdened by the requirements of its role, any aircraft is more vulnerable to malfunction or misfortune at this juncture, and it was no different during the Second World War.

Pilots knew the risks and trained for many eventualities during those critical moments when power thrust them past the point of no return and they were committed, come what may. Perhaps the worst malfunction was engine failure, and definitely so when you had only the one power plant available. This was indeed the stuff of nightmares, and one pilot confronting this horror was 1/Lt Charles H. Kruger of the 369FS, 359FG.

Charles had been one of the original cadre who took custody of their airbase at East Wretham from the departing RAF. He also witnessed the reality of war even before the 359FG became operational. A badly shot-up P-38 crash landed on the airfield, and close examination of the wreckage brought it home to him for the first time: 'This was for keeps, we had arrived.' During the weeks that followed, Charles's arrival was noticed by the Luftwaffe to their detriment when he destroyed one Me 109 and claimed another as

1/Lt Charles H. Kruger, 369FS, 359FG. Note swastika symbols denoting two victories over Me 109s. *(C. Kruger via Chris Gotts)*

probable on 15 March south-west of Hanover. He destroyed another on 19 May, and two days later aided in the pre-D-Day disruption of the enemy railway network by sharing in the destruction of several locomotives.

On 24 May, Charles prepared for take-off as usual in his mustang, 'Tojo-Peach Nancy June 3rd', so named because his ground crew wanted Tojo-Peach and Charles liked the comfort of his young daughter's name, Nancy, plus a sense of being spiritually accompanied by his wife, June. He had already used this combination on two P-47 Thunderbolts before the Group re-equipped, and his P-51 was the third incarnation. Officially, the machine was on Air Force inventory as serial number 42-106629 with squadron codes IV-E and had served Charles well with only one abort when the high blower of the Merlin's two-stage supercharger system had failed to engage. Today, his fifty-third mission, Charles was on the take-off roster for a routine escort mission. As he recalls: 'The aircraft I crashed was a P-51B-10 with full fuel, 2 drop tanks on the wings and an extra internal tank of 108 gallons behind the seat which made the centre of gravity unstable until this was burned off.' These detrimental handling characteristics were referred to in the handling instruction for the aircraft where it advised that, during take-off,

when carrying full fuselage tank, there is some pitching as aircraft leaves the ground owing to reversal of stick loads . . . When the fuselage tank is full, the aircraft is longitudinally unstable in all conditions of flight, and tends to tighten up in turns; until at least . . . 48 US gallons have been consumed from the fuselage tank. No maneuvers other than very gentle turns should be attempted . . .

Charles continues:

I was a Captain at the time, leading D Flight taking off on a target support mission to escort the bombers over Berlin, intercept was about Peenamunde [sic] to Berlin then take them back until other fighters picked them up. We were supporting the 3rd Division's B-17s that day.

The Group lined up on the field, using it on the diagonal, in echelon formation – 4 taking off at a time in Flight formation, thus line up 12 deep. Four planes lifting off, four on the roll and four starting the roll. We were to assemble under the overcast going up through as a unit, each Flight stacked down and the Flight Leader flying on the Flight slightly above and ahead. In other words everyone flew visually on the Lead plane by tucking it in tight and not using your instruments, flying visually on the plane on your wing, if in the Flight, and the Flight Leaders flying on the Flight above. In this way we would break out on top with all 48 planes in formation and not scattered. The bombers had taken off hours before, we flew a straight intercept course to intercept the bombers at a pre-determined position.

On this day I had just retracted my wheels when I had a power failure and all the instruments went out, electrical circuits, radio, and I had huge amounts of oil coming back over the windscreen and side windows . . .

Charles was in serious trouble. A P-51 pilot typically commenced his climb when 150 mph had been reached, but Charles now had no way of knowing his air speed, and, as he was almost blinded by oil over the canopy, his flight attitude was hard to gauge, so he was in danger of stalling and plunging to destruction. In a perverse sense, the additional fuel in his wing tanks reduced the instability created by the fuselage-borne fuel load, and pilots were warned that jettisoning the wing tanks with fuel in the fuselage tank created an abrupt change in trim and decreased the aircraft's stability. This whirled through his mind. He was only 100ft high and knew the Merlin had only moments left to run, having suffered such a massive haemorrhage of oil.

I prepared for an emergency landing. I could find no place to drop the wing tanks or land. I attempted to land in the area between the tower and the planes taking off. I was at critical airspeed and in a tight turn to get back to the field. On the approach I attempted to drop the wheels, which apparently went down and I am not sure they locked. On the approach I had a red flare but at that point the engine was gone so I attempted a dead stick landing. I had the area perfect but, in the take off, much dust was raised and when I pulled the plane into a full stall for a short field landing I felt it drop.

I thought I was on the ground but I was too high as the dust and oil had caused me to misjudge my height. I caught fire on impact, the wing tanks first as I could see the flames following me in the rear view mirror. The plane ground looped out of control and broke in

'I could not get out and I was sitting in a sea of flames.' A fire-fighter foams the blazing wreckage of 'Tojo-Peach Nancy June'. *(C. Kruger via Chris Gotts)*

Charles recovered in time to fly on 6 June 1944 – the momentous D-Day, during which he logged 10 hours 50 minutes. Note hastily applied black-and-white recognition bands have obliterated the fuselage coding. *(C. Kruger via Chris Gotts)*

half, causing the exposed 108 gallon tank behind the seat to rupture, filling the cockpit with fuel. Everything exploded at that time, gas oxygen etc. I had been thrown into the gun sight by the force of the impact and my flying glasses were thrown loose. I was knocked out for some period of time and I was burning when I came to realize what had happened. I pulled the emergency release on the canopy but it had jammed on impact. I could not get out and I was sitting in a sea of flames. I remember pulling back over my eyes the flight goggles and then I slightly remember the crash crew opening the cockpit and pulling me out of the plane. Dr Horowitz the Flight Surgeon of the 370FS (I think it was his name) was on the wing duty and helped in my removal to the field hospital. My leather flight jacket, glasses, RAF boots, saved me from severe burns but they were burned to a crisp and in fact burned through in places. I do not remember my ride in the ambulance to the hospital. I suffered first and second degree burns to my eyes, hands and arms, plus some black eyes when I hit the gun sight. I had my Sutton harness locked as was procedure on take off so the impact must have been severe to throw me into the gun sight. They later told me the guns kept firing as the ammo got hot. We were loaded with straight armour piercing incendiary so it must have been quite a sight for the ground crew as the plane came to a halt facing the Headquarters area.

To my knowledge this was the first time radio silence was broken as all thought I had been killed and Group was informed on Holland landfall that I was not killed. It naturally was a shock to some of the newer pilots to see a plane land in flames next to them while taking off on a Berlin mission, which was always tough anyhow.

Charles was released from hospital on 3 June, and was proud to fly a total of 10 hours 50 minutes, three days later during operations supporting the D-Day invasion. He flew a total of 126½ sorties and was awarded the jocular Dinghy Butt Hero Medal on 25 August 1944, as his spoof citation reads, alluding to hours sitting on dinghy pack with a Co2 bottle that 'got very hard'.

Under the provision of Army Regulation 00-00 17 July 1944 and pursuant to the authority contained in Section I, Circular 00, Headquarters 369th Fighter Squadron, 17

Charles Kruger (wearing the leather A2 jacket) with his ground crew. They named 'their' aircraft Tojo-Peach while Charles wanted Nancy for his daughter and June after his wife, hence the compromise 'Tojo-Peach Nancy June 3rd' – this being his third and final Mustang with the 359FG. (C. Kruger via Chris Gotts)

July 1944, the Distinguished Dinghy Butt Hero Medal is awarded to the following named officers . . . For gallantry in action while serving as flak magnets with the 369th Fighter Squadron on missions during the period from December 1943 to August 1944. Captains Kruger and Thacker . . . have with great devotion to duty and complete disregard for self successfully raised a crop of dinghy blisters. Measurement of the callous shows a rectangular 12' × 6" × 6". Upon this occasion we cannot be eulogistic enough . . . By order of Major Chauncey S. Irvine.

Despite his take-off troubles, Charles was lucky and noted that twenty of the original twenty-seven pilots in his 369FS were either missing or dead by the time he left East Wretham. He was posted to the Far East into the last P-51 Group to go to Iwo Jima, but sickness delayed his departure and probably saved his life. Leaving Charles to recuperate, his squadron landed on Iwo Jima after a long, tiring over-water flight. The battle was still underway, but the airfield was supposedly secure, and the pilots bedded down to be ready for action the next day. That night, a Japanese raiding party crept ashore and murdered many of his friends as they slept.

Charles retired from the Air Force on VJ Day having achieved the rank of Major. He moved to McAllen in Texas to establish an irrigation business, which, ironically, was almost next door to the old base at Moore Field from where he had gained his wings during April 1943, Class 43-D. His take-off troubles had then still been ahead of him, but the training received had helped him make the swiftest of decisions when things went wrong. That, and the blessing of good fortune, had seen him through.

CHAPTER THREE

Treachery

Amerian airmen were briefed on processes and procedures should they find themselves making an enforced arrival in enemy territory, and all commanding officers were ordered by Maj Gen Spaatz to ensure that a document entitled, 'Instructions for Officers and Men of the Eighth Air Force In the Event of Capture' was issued to 'every member of the 8th Air Force whose duties might take him over enemy territory'. Those that faced this predicament and successfully escaped or evaded capture were de-briefed on return, and intelligence gathered would be assimilated for the benefit of others. Some 'E and E' airmen even lectured on their experiences, but it was policy not to allow escapers or evaders to return to operational flying in the ETO, because, if recaptured and interrogated, they might reveal names of those who had provided assistance. Airmen appreciated that, if captured, they would face a prisoner-of-war camp, whereas any civilian found offering assistance risked execution, a punishment that often extended to their families. It was strongly emphasised during lectures and in the Instructions 'never, under any circumstances, [to] mention the name of any person who may have helped you to escape'.

Allied airmen might be lucky literally to drop into the hands of the Underground or be fortunate enough to have contact made and find themselves being passed down a 'line' to freedom. For obvious reasons, any civilian offering succour to a downed aviator needed to be extremely careful about the credentials of the supposed Allied airmen. German counter-measures included men masquerading as Allied aircrew successfully to infiltrate and then to destroy these escape lines, with horrendous consequences for those heroic civilians caught aiding genuine escapees. In some circumstances, the Germans might even run a line, for a period, if its continuing existence provided sufficient intelligence, with a reward deemed greater than allowing a few fliers to escape. All involved also faced the constant risk of betrayal by collaborators sympathetic to the enemy, who were also rewarded for their efforts. In short, for a man to escape or to evade was like weaving a blanket in the dark and praying that the pattern of events proved favourable.

1/Lt Osce R. Jones of the famous 4FG found himself reluctantly descending into this world of chance and potential capture on 7 June 1944. A diary he kept was sent to me by his widow, Thelma, and, with additional investigation by the noted French researcher, Rémy

Osce Jones watches for buddies not yet back. He noted that this picture was taken 'right after landing from an eight hour mission to Berlin'. *(Thelma Jones)*

Chuinard, it reveals one fighter pilot's experiences during a momentous period in twentieth-century history. Osce opened his account with a description of events on his base at Debden just before D-Day.

June 5th. . . . During the two weeks preceding the invasion, duties at the 4th Group were carried out in atmosphere of intense expectancy. Many types of training, including night flying, dive bombing and very precise exercises in navigation, were carried out. We knew the big show wasn't far off. On the morning of the 5th June we were called on a short escort show, but due to bad weather conditions the bombers were called back. This is the morning Hoffer [Lt Ralph Kidd Hofer] failed to return. After five hours we gave him up for lost, but at the end of the sixth hour he turns up saying that one box of bombers did not heed the recall, so he continued his escort. On the return trip he had shot up six more kites on the ground, which pushed his score of ships destroyed on the ground in one week up to 16. On this show he had seen a large convoy of Jerry trucks and tanks, which covered about ten miles of road. With this information the Col called wing and asked for permission to take a few ships over and raise a little hell with Jerry, so at about two o'clock eight kites, loaded with 1000lbs of bombs, took off to see what could be done to alter the situation. They obtained good results, but due to the size of the convoy eight ships hardly scratched the surface of this mass of equipment. Without wasting time they came back expecting to get the whole group, 48 ships, and to go back to do the job up, but good. This is where the big hint came of the nearness of invasion. Upon landing they found that all the ships in the group had been grounded and were in the hangers [sic] for something. This sort of thing was pretty rare in our group, so I decided to go take a look. My crew chief was the first man I saw there, so I asked him what was up. Taking me to the rear of the large building, he showed me my kite with its new war paint on. It was a very striking sight, five alternating stripes of black and white around the fuselage, each wing and the tail assembly. I then realised that something was definitely coming off. The painting job was to be finished by midnight at all costs, thus giving the mechanics a little over eight hours to paint 16 ships, but everything came off as scheduled, despite the short notice.

Similar activities occurred that night on dozens of airfields as the distinctive black and white bands were added to hundreds of aircraft involved in the invasion. The order to adorn the 4FG mustangs stipulated 18in stripes on all planes, five on each wing and five on the fuselage, so these high-visibility markings reduced the risk of confusing low flying Allied aircraft with those of the enemy. The Intelligence Office received a visit from the 4FG CO, Col Donald J.M. Blakeslee, just after 2000 that evening. He announced that the long-awaited invasion was underway, and the 4FG had a prominent role to play providing protection for the fleet and ground forces. Total air superiority was essential. An immediate security blanket was draped over all communications into and out of Debden. No one was allowed to leave or to make outgoing calls, and any incoming calls were diverted through the Group Intelligence Office. The normally busy atmosphere of mission preparation had an extra edge to it that night as information from 8 FC HQ was converted into detailed planning for the 4 FG's routes and patrol areas. Maps were marked up and the briefing room made ready.

Osce noted:

I was in the club Thursday night and as usual, hit the hay about nine thirty. At about eleven o'clock pm an orderly came in and told me that all pilots were to report to the briefing room immediately. 'This is it' was the first thing that entered my mind and upon reaching the intelligence shack this was confirmed. The usual map was covered with quite a few smaller maps, with boats, naval and army, and different sectors of the French coast laid out for each Fighter Group to cover and a few other maps that I can't recall at the present.

Col Blakeslee was there, dressed in his flying clothes, and when all was quiet came out with the thing we all expected. 'This is it boys.' Briefing went on for nearly an hour, covering everything in the minutest detail. We were to take off at three thirty am and go to the sector assigned us and patrol until nine thirty in the morning. We then saw that all of our training had not been in vain. The weather wasn't what you'd call ideal, as a matter of fact it was pretty sorry. Ceiling was about 3000 feet and an overcast of scud up to about 6000. I had expected to do a bit of night flying but not night cloud flying. The take off was uneventful, but the beauty of it struck me. The sky was lit up by flares that the bombers were to form on and the red, green and white lights of the fighters. Everywhere you looked moving lights could be seen. It was now that I realised the tremendous effort that was being put forth to protect the landing parties and protected they were.

June 6th. . . . We joined formation under the overcast and then started up through it. Not a hard task but things had to be done just right or someone would get hurt. We broke out at 6000 feet, and the group reformed. Above the clouds there was a full moon, and almost as bright as day. We then turned out our lights and headed for France. In the middle of the Channel I could plainly see the flashes of the big naval guns, but all else was covered and concealed by clouds. The clouds covered everything at dawn and continued to do so the rest of the day. It was a very uneventful day for me even though I did fly two shows and got in about ten hours of flying time over France. Half of our group was in our sector every hour of the day and those that did venture below the clouds found only a few trains to shoot up. That night, the sixth, I really did get in a bit of heavy sleep. I guess the tension of the day and ten hours in the cockpit had taken its share of my endurance.

Osce was lucky on that longest of days. Others were less fortunate, and the 4FG and its pilots made their contribution to history, but the cost was high, as is revealed in their records.

Field order 371 Part 1. Col Blakeslee led the first mission of the day, a Fighter Sweep by 334 and 335 of the Rouen, France area from 0320 to 0945 hours. Landfall was made over Dieppe at 0409 but dense cloud prevented pin-pointing and claimed Thomas Fraser who went down after 0642 east of Rouen to be captured. Changing winds caused the formation to drift east of Paris and come out at various points east of Calais. Hofer strafed a couple of

A mixture of marks and paint schemes as P-51B, C and D Mustangs of the 4FG, taxi out for take-off on one of their D-Day missions. *(Garry L. Fry)*

locos after blurting out over the r/t, 'Whoo, a train!' Lt Col Clark [Lt Col James A. Clark Jr] gathered 336 for a type 16 Control to the Rouen, France, area from 0635 to 1150 hours. Coming in behind the other two squadrons, 336 faced the same conditions.

The Field Order Report continued in Part 2.

Capt. Hively [Capt Howard D. 'Deacon' Hively] led 334 only in a fighter bombing show back to the Rouen, France, area from 1120 to 1400 hours. The squadron made landfall at 1206 over Dieppe and arrived in the Rouen area at 1215 to search for communications targets. A 15-car troop train was bombed with poor results but the boys ran into 10-plus FW 190s preparing to land at Evreux aerodrome. From 1230 to 1245 everybody took turns and four Focke Wulfs were shot down . . . Maj Happel [Maj James A. Happel] took 335 out for a dive bombing mission to Fleury marshalling yards, France, from 1220 to 1500 hours. After dropping their bombs, the boys came back without incident. Major Goodson [Maj James A. 'Goody' Goodson] took 336 out for a Fighter Bombing show and Free Lance to Rouen . . . again from 1335 to 1615 hours. Roaming the countryside was uneventful until flak hit Harold Fredericks near Evreaux at 1445. After crash landing he managed to evade capture and make it back to England. Oscar Lejeunesse was shot down by flak at the same time and bailed out . . . Col Blakeslee took 334 and 335 back out on a

Fighter Patrol to the Rouen–Dreux, France, area from 1820 to 2340 hours. Landfall was made at Dieppe at 1915. Near Rouen a 20-truck convoy was attacked by 335 Blue Section at 1840 but over fifteen 109s and 190s then bounced the Mustangs – all four pilots were shot down and killed [Capt Bernard J. McGratten; Lts Cecil E. Garbey; Harold L. Ross, Jr; Walter Smith]. At 2035 Edward Stepp was heard over the r/t talking to Mike Sobanski, 'Watch those behind you White Leader!' after Sobanski had requested a visual check of his aircraft after hitting some wires. Both men were killed. As if this wasn't enough, Mike McPharlin reported over the r/t at 2100 that his left magneto was out and he was aborting. On loan from the 339 FG in his 6N-Z, he had come back to Debden to fly the big one with his old 334. He was never heard from again. The boys came out at 2220.

Osce continues his diary.

June 7th. . . . On the morning of the 7th June, there was an early show. Not being on this one I slept until about ten o'clock. I knew I'd be on the one in the afternoon, so this was a good chance to catch up on my rest. Today we were engaged in ground strafing and dive bombing. The line up was put on the board and I was asked if I wanted to go on the show. Liking ground work better than aerial, I was eager to make this one so I was listed to fly on Col Blakeslee's wing. The group was going intact to Loudeac and then splitting up into the three individual squadrons and each taking a railroad north to the sea. Loudeac is in the centre of the Brest Penninsula and had three railroads leading north. The 335th's was going due north on the centre road. We flew around for a while and 366 squadron bombed a few small bridges with no opposition but with us it was a little different. The clouds, about eight tenths, were too low to allow dive bombing, so we resorted to glide bombing. The cloud base was about 3000 feet. As we approached Quintine, directly in front of us rose an umbrella of twenty millimetre flak that was thick as the devil. The Col had Dean Hill and me on his wings and when he saw this called and told us that this was our target . . . get the railroad station and tracks. He also told the rest of the squadron to fly clear of the flak area. Now glide bombing lacks the advantages of dive bombing in a big way. You can't obtain the speed of the approach or get away and you afford a better target for a longer time to the flak guns but this was the only avenue of approach left to us. I'll have to admit that when the Col started on his bomb run I was scared and plenty but there Hill and I stuck, right on his wing, as we went into target at about three fifty. I put my sight on the all important rail station and opened up with my four fifties. Just before I released my bombs I felt a sickening thud in the nose of my ship and saw my glycol come pouring out. As the target passed under my nose I released my bombs and in panic jettisoned my canopy. Pulling up I saw that the Col and Hill had gotten through alright but knew that I'd have to bail out soon. At this time glycol was streaming back into the cockpit and into my eyes. I unbuckled the safety belt, took off my helmet and prepared to leave my ship; but looking over the side I noticed the ground had been flooded by Germans and I figured escape from there was next to impossible so I settled down a bit. Had I flown south into southern France, chances are I'd have gotten out alright but I took up a heading to take me back home.

At this time I was flying about 700 feet from the ground and couldn't see any of the rest of the fellows anywhere around but I did notice that my ship was still running alright and was not beginning to get hot yet. A slight hope of getting home entered my mind so I put my safety belt back on, retrieved my helmet from the floor and started praying. Another ship from the 335th passed at this time and from the letters I recognised Brock. I called him and told that 'I'd had it' and asked him to escort me home and this he did; or should I say 'to the end of the line' for me. After about five minutes of flying, I noticed that my coolant was getting a little high and this didn't help my hopes of getting back. I was still flying a bit too low to bail out so I resigned myself to make a forced landing when it became necessary.

My coolant temperature continued to rise and finally passed the red line and then off the dial. I was about ten miles south of St Malo when the engine became pretty rough and started to steam. I saw a small cleared field below that couldn't have been more than a hundred yards wide and twice as long, so this is where I headed. I called Brock and told him I was going to set her down and told him to set her on fire as soon as I was clear. I guess God was at the controls with me then because when I had dropped flaps and was on my approach leg, my air speed had dropped to eighty and I was entirely too low. Throwing the throttle wide open and by the grace of God, I cleared the trees, or almost cleared the trees, at the edge of the field and settled down, wheels up, in the middle of the field. I didn't slide fifty feet and in this short field I was only fifty feet from the far end. The trees that I clipped had lost their uppermost branches to my prop and wings. I don't know what kept me from nosing over when I hit them, but I came out unscratched.

We had always been told that in a case like this, get away from the wreck as soon and as far as possible; so this I proceeded to do, but was no further then fifty yards when I heard

The beginning of a long trek. Resting in a French meadow between Crollon and St Senier-de-Beuvron, the burnt-out remains of P-51B 43-7042, WD-J, of 335 Fighter Squadron, flown by Osce R. Jones. *(Rémy Chuinard)*

Brock's guns barking and as I turned saw the ship on fire. On all shows we carried a parachute, dinghy and an escape kit. After about a hundred yards of running I realised that I still had on my parachute, dinghy and flying clothes so I sat down and removed these. I was in the country and figured that the Germans couldn't be far off but I had to get rid of this equipment. Finding a levee that resembled a ditch levee at home, I sat in a corner of a field and took off all this impediment but my jacket. Thinking that the levee was as good a place as any for my parachute and dinghy so over the hill I threw the stuff. Later in the afternoon I found that the levee was the side of a road and I had thrown my gear in the most obvious place possible. This left me in GI clothes, a worn flying jacket, my escape kit and a large hunting knife. Now according to the best authorities the best thing to do in a case like this is to find a good place to hide and stay put for two days until Jerry finished his search for you so this I intended to do. I ran for a mile or so going SE and spotted a large orchard covered with weeds about two feet tall. It was now about four o'clock and darkness didn't fall for another seven hours so I planned to hide in the middle of this field until I could take a good look around.

As far as I know I was the only man lost on that show other than the two that had collided in the clouds over England. I found out later that one had parachuted to safety but the other was killed in the crash that followed. In the morning show McGratten had taken a section of four out and none of them have been heard of since. Hill also is missing now; they think that he spun out in a cloud over France somewhere.

Group records state that Lt Kenneth D. Smith and Capt Donald J. Pierini collided a mile south of the airfield. Smith was killed. Pierini parachuted to safety. The file also incorrectly states that Osce was 'captured after running into the woods'.

The MACR (Missing Aircrew Combat Report) number 5723 for Osce in P-51B-7-NA, serial 43-7042, contradicts his account in that it was Major Happel escorting him, and a statement from Major Happel is included:

I was escorting 1/Lt Jones back from a bombing mission to Dol-de-Bretagne after he had been hit by light flak. He was flying WD-J. He was streaming smoke or glycol and losing power. He decided he would crash land because he was too low to bail out. He called in and said that he was crash landing and did so in the vicinity East of Pontorson. As soon as his aircraft stopped he was out and running across the field. I then shot up his aircraft on the ground. The time was approximately 16.25 hours.

Osce resumes his diary.

To get back to the story, I went to a place in this weed field and covered, as best as I could, the path I left in the grass and dug my self a semi fox hole. Using my hunting knife I made a hole about four feet long, a foot deep and a foot and a half wide. Here I took out my escape kit, took out a couple of compasses, the maps and my rubber water bag. Knowing my approximate position I started making my plans for a long walk to Spain. I was so close to the front that I could hear the big bombs and guns going off and laying in my hole I watched the P-47's patrolling their zones overhead. Until now I hadn't seen a single German soldier but had heard a few vehicles pass on the road that ran along the edge of the field I was in. As darkness fell I began to gain a little courage and scouted around a bit. I went to the edge of the town of St Malo looking for water but with no success, returned to my hole and waited. I had passed a house some distance back so I headed for this at about one o'clock. As I approached it I found that it was on the opposite side of the road, and that another road crossed right in front of the house. Being quite dark now, I proceeded to cross the road to the house, when I received one of the worse scares of my life. I had almost reached the far side when I heard, as it seemed, a terrific snore. Looking to my left I saw that the roads had been blockaded and that a Jerry guard was sleeping right in the middle of the obstruction. As quietly as possible I began making my way back and then broke into a run and really covered some territory. Still being thirsty, I decided to start on my journey and to look for water as I went. It was later in the night that I tried to milk a cow with little success. [Osce was born in New Orleans on 4 November 1920 and had been in Baton Rouge, Louisiana, since he was 12 so had no country upbringing.]

June 8th. . . . I knew that the Germans must be pretty thick around here so I stayed on the back roads and paths and when these ended I went cross-country. At about four o'clock am I came to a large clearing and found that it was a pasture. The moon had come out in the mean time and I could see quite plainly. In the middle of this field stood a large pump and watering trough so I made a dash for the thing. By this time I was really parched but had presence of mind enough to put the halizone tablets in my quart rubber bag to purify it. I rested here half an hour I guess and saw quite a few Ju 88s and Messerschmitt 110s headed for the front. According to my plans I was travelling in the south easterly direction and planned on entering unoccupied France just below Tours. I travelled all day long cross-country avoiding all roads and paths. I saw a few French farmers who eyed me curiously as I crossed their fields in the rarely seen US uniform. On the afternoon of the 8th, after covering about six miles since morning, I was on a path and stopped abruptly as I glanced ahead and saw that this path crossed a large highway some 200 yards ahead. Right across the highway where the path continued stood a small Jerry field piece staring me in the face. At the sight of this I realised that the Germans were still close at hand so I took to the fields again. My progress across country was very slow due to the fact that most of the fields held barley, waist high, and also every field had a mound of earth about six feet high all around it. I detoured about a mile to the right and then took up my SE heading again. I skirted a group of houses by about a hundred yards and again was astonished to see I was headed for a town and I didn't want this.

I was pretty tired now so I rested on the side of a wheat field up against the levee and went to sleep. I was quite sure that I couldn't be seen from the houses but this was a false assumption. No sooner had I closed my eyes then I was awakened by a French woman standing not ten feet from me. Of course I was startled but not scared. I pulled out the little French card that was in my escape kit and told her in my best French that I was an

Madam Guillet and her children pictured in 1944 by her home in Les Villettes. She risked her life to help Osce Jones. Paulette, centre, recalls how the children were very suspicious of the gum given to them and thought it was soap. (Rémy Chuinard)

American pilot and was thirsty and hungry. The woman took me to her home and sat me down in a big chair in front of a roaring fire. I had been wet the past couple of days because the fields in the morning were full of dew and in walking through them I became thoroughly soaked each day. She had three children to whom I gave a stick of gum each. They'd never seen gum before and didn't know what to do with it. I showed them but I guess they wanted to save it or were afraid of it, I don't know. I ate four eggs and a big bowl of meat and potatoes, pulled off my shoes and went to sleep in the chair in front of the fire. She woke me up and took me upstairs and offered me a big feather bed which I accepted immediately.

At nine o'clock she came in and woke me up. It was very dull outside and rain threatened. I had no idea how long I had slept so I asked her if it was morning or night. She told me that it was the latter so I looked forward to another night in the open and raining on top of that; however, she did feed me again with milk, coffee, boiled eggs, bread and meat and she told that the town was St James and was full of Germans. I asked her for civilian clothes but she refused me. I was most amazed when she gave me a chocolate bar as I left. I walked about two miles from her house and found a rather thick tree that I thought would give me a little shelter from the rain and laid on the wet ground and made an attempt to sleep.

Almost forty years later, while researching the diary, French aviation historian Rémy Chuinard retraced elements of the journey made by Osce. Finding the crash site, Rémy met an elderly local man who had proudly kept the dinghy Osce had thrown so conspicuously into the road. He also possessed the Mustang's tail wheel and an ammunition box retrieved from the wreckage. Osce's gloves and parachute had also been found at the time, but their continued existence was uncertain – perhaps the parachute had fulfilled a different duty as undergarments for local girls. Tracking the route taken by Osce, Rémy found the field with the large pump seen by the aviator that moonlit morning and then traced the route to discover the identity of that courageous woman who kindly offered sustenance and sleep to the weary pilot. Her name was Madame Guillet and Rémy located her daughter Paulette, now Mrs Chorin, who clearly remembered their American guest. Paulette was then 11½ and recalled it as a Thursday because the school was closed on Thursdays and she was at home. Her mother had gone to see a neighbour's cattle and stumbled across the downed flier, cold, wet and exhausted. The weather was chilly, and the Guillet family had a large open fire in front of which the young pilot had slumped into a chair. He took of his shoes, and soon both he and the shoes were dry and warm. Paulette remembered how conversation had occurred with the aid of a small phrase book he carried, with English on one side and the French translation on the other. 'I am hungry. I am sleepy' and so on. After a large breakfast, the young man had again dozed in front of the fire, and then Madame Guillet had gently disturbed him to offer him the luxury of a real bed, which he had occupied all that day. Questioned by Rémy about the gum, Paulette resolved the puzzle of their refusing it, because, never having seen it before, she and her younger sister at first thought it was soap. This all sounds very cosy and comforting, but it has to be remembered that such simple hospitality risked the lives of the entire Guillet family. While Osce recuperated, Madame Guillet had slipped into the village to try and locate someone more capable of aiding her visitor to escape. Some in the community greeted her news with alarm, adding dire warnings about the consequences. Unable to link with the Underground and undoubtedly concerned by comments from within the community, Madame Guillet hurried home.

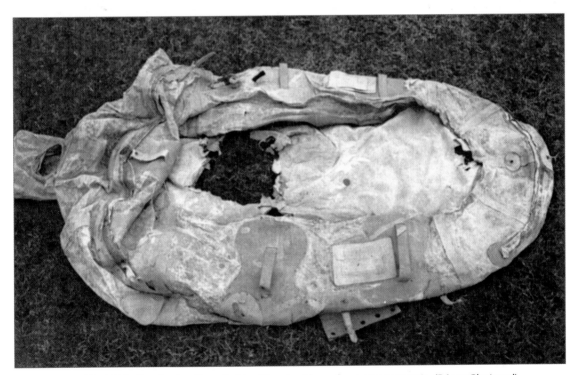

Pictured in 1990, the dinghy discarded by Osce had been kept as a souvenir. (Rémy Chuinard)

Osce was awoken after dark, and blackout conditions were closely observed as oil lamps were lit and a hesitant discussion ensued with the aid of the phrase book. By now, Paulette's father had returned from duties on a nearby farm and the subject arose about meeting his request for clothing. What to Osce seemed a refusal was simply the fact that, with a significant difference in stature between Osce and her father, the family realized they had nothing to fit him, and ridiculously short attire might attract attention, not act as a disguise. As the pilot prepared to leave, Paulette remembered him topping up his water bottles then adding some tablets, which she surmised were for extra energy. After questioning her parents to understand the direction and proximity of German forces, the airman departed into the darkness and a fate it would take forty years to uncover.

Osce resumes his diary.

June 9th. . . . The next morning, wet and cold, I started cross country again. I had given up the idea of the Jerry's catching me now and figured that with a little luck I'd get through to Spain in about eight weeks, without help from the French Underground. Later in the day I grew a little bolder and began travelling the back roads and the French eyebrows that lifted as they saw me were not few. I received another shock when I saw the first print of hob-nailed shoes in the dirt along the side of the road. I didn't realise at the time that the French peasants all wore hobnailed shoes. That night I reached a town called Fougeves and detoured around it and slept in a field again. This time I picked one that was quite near a farmer's house so in case of rain I might slip into his barn or shed. I covered about ten miles that day but figured if I could get civilian clothes I could cover twice that much.

June 10th. . . . My next goal was Ernoe, which was about twelve or fourteen miles farther down the road. Early in the morning just after I had detoured around another town and was going cross country I encountered a young boy, my age, in a field and approached him and told him that I was American etc. He took me to his home and showed me to his folks. They fed me well and gave me bread to last the rest of the day. I asked them for some civilian clothes and they talked it over a bit and brought out some blue coveralls, a vest and coat. I asked for a hat and they brought out a light green cap. I in turn left them my fur lined jacket, my hunting knife and a hundred francs. I had hidden in my jacket seams about four escape compasses and you should have seen the astonishment on their faces as I took them from their hiding places. I was really a sight now with almost a week's beard and in civvies. Guess I passed for French pretty well; for a while anyway. My feet were beginning to get a little sore now and I had even adopted a slight shuffle in my walk. I kept my uniform on under my disguise and proceeded on my way. I now didn't hesitate to walk down the main highways nor did I dread walking through French towns. It was fairly early in the morning and I was the only person walking the highway. I heard some motorcycles approaching but kept on walking on ahead. They past [*sic*] me and gave no signs of suspicion and the fact that my disguise was a success was proved a few minutes later. As I approached the crest of a hill I became aware that I had walked into the centre of a German bivouac area and there were Jerries all up and down the road. I had just past a side road when an officer stalked out and started walking opposite me on the other side of the road. We must have walked half a mile like this but no sign was given that he suspected anything.

Later in the day I heard the air raid sirens going on and saw eight '47's circling overhead. I was just north of a small town and stood and watched. They proceeded to dive bomb the town and after that they began to do a great deal of strafing. It looked like they were doing the French a great injustice but I found out later that this was not so. After they left, I entered the town and saw that they had bombed the railroad station and that was all, but just on the outskirts of town I found what had been the cause of all the commotion. The remains of a German convoy lay smouldering in ruin and quite a few men were wounded and laying in stretchers on the side of the road. I counted seventeen trucks and cars burned up and a number of trailers.

This day I exceeded all my expectations and walked forty-two kilometres, which is about twenty miles. This put me just north of Laval where I had quite an experience. Just outside of town I came to a railroad sunk about thirty feet into the earth. I had to cross this gully and was looking up and down when I noticed two soldiers, armed with automatic pistols. I ducked into a wheat field and let them pass. They had a Doberman Pincher on a lease [sic] with them, but I remained undetected. After they had passed, and were safely out of earshot, I managed to scramble up the other side to find myself in the grounds of a large factory that had been 'bombed at' but missed. This place was well guarded and I was pretty lucky to get away as I did. I later found out that I had gone through a large marshalling yard also.

All through the day I hadn't stopped to eat, so you can imagine I was famished. I took to the back roads just south of Laval and had walked about a mile when I came to quite a large house. I planned to get food and water here so I sat at the gate and waited. After about five minutes a boy came along on a bicycle and I stopped him, gave him the details and asked if he could feed me. He took me to the house where his folks gave me a quart of milk and a loaf of bread. I showed them my maps and told them my plans as best as I could. About this time a boy of 20 years came up and asked me in broken English if I was American. This started my first English conversation in almost a week. He told me that he had learned to speak English from a dictionary and we got along famously. I took out my maps and discussed my plans with him. He told me of the successes of the allies, pointed out the points of internal resistance and I found out that he truly hated the Germans. He had been a forced worker in Germany for two years and had escaped. He took my name and address and promised to write when the war was over. A funny thing along that line happened. I told him I planned to be in Spain in eight weeks. He answered that 'the Americans will be here in eight weeks' and surprisingly, he was right; almost to the day. He then urged me to come in and listen to the BBC but after learning that the Jerries searched every house at 10.30 pm I thought it best to leave and sleep before the Jerry patrol started out. This night I slept in a barley field but was full of milk and bread, so it wasn't bad at all.

11th June. . . . The next morning I started out before daybreak and walked due east, cross country to avoid a troop concentration that the French boy had told me about. In doing this I passed through the back yard of a large house and as I passed the back door I looked in and saw that the place was full of soldiers. I guess they had taken the place over, and were using it for barracks. However, they didn't see me, or if they did they didn't suspect me. A couple of hours later I again took the main highways and headed for La Fleche. About noon I passed through a small village that seemed to be deserted, but I did see signs of the Jerry around. A very large convoy had just passed through the town and the streets were all broken up. I don't think I saw more than five people in the whole place. Just on the outside of the town as I was leaving I saw two Germans seated on a small stone bridge that I had to cross, but the only thing I could do was to keep on walking. As I came abreast of them, one of them spoke to me in German, I think, and I answered with 'Nix, Nix' being the only German I knew and kept on walking. It must have been the right answer seeing that they didn't stop me or ask anything else. Just beyond this place I stopped and soaked my feet in a spring about a hundred yards from the road. My feet were plenty tired by now and it was beginning to get uncomfortably warm. It was here that I decided to cut off the tops of my English flying boots. It kept my legs a little cooler and made walking easier.

That evening, late, after covering about twenty miles I stopped at a house and crawled into the wood shed. I guess I stayed there two hours before a Jerry convoy started passing. After it had gone I figured that if I was caught here the occupants of the house would be held responsible so I took off again. About half a mile down the road I found a stream and on a hill about two hundred yards down the road stood a two story vacant house. It had started falling apart so I figured that this was a good place to spend the night. I approached the place and found that the owners had built just next to the place, so gathering a bit of hay from a nearby haystack, I had a half way decent place to sleep. Why I even had a roof over my head for a change. I think that I was as tired that night as I've ever been in my life, but this didn't keep me from imagining creeping Germans about the place all night.

12th June. . . . When I awoke the next morning I was fairly well rested but very hungry. I had noticed a large cherry tree right between the old dwelling and the new one. I proceeded to the tree and an enormous dog started barking. He was chained to the base of the trunk and was on hand for just situations as this, I imagine. I gave up my idea about eating cherries and started on my way again. I had stopped about four miles short of La Fleche. As I entered the town that morning, a funeral was in progress. Half way through the town the irony of the situation struck me, as an armoured division came charging right through the middle of the procession. The funeral march was broken up and as I passed the beautiful cathedral I noticed people going in singularly and in small groups. Moving past this large town I walked until noon and came upon a settlement that was composed of a large church and a few scattered houses. I was then nearly starved so I made up my mind to stop at all cost and get something to eat. This village was on a main road but the road wasn't on my map so I was slightly confused as to where I was. As I sat on a bridge crossing a small river, I stopped a man that was headed for town and told him I was hungry. He took me into town and to a small café. The woman that ran the place didn't want to feed me at first but after I showed her my maps and told them where I wanted to go she finally fed me some milk and bread. There were two young men in the place and they told me where I was and also told me how to get to the next town I was headed for.

I took my leave and headed down the road they had pointed out and a few miles on it turned into a footpath. The town I was going to was called Childess I think but am not sure. The country was rolling ground and very pretty. When I was about three miles out of town still on the footpath, up rode a boy of 14 years on a bicycle. He stopped in front of me and I told him I was American. 'Qui Qui', he said, as if he was expecting me and later I found out that he was. We smoked a cigarette and had a piece of gum and I showed him my dog tags, maps, etc. Now here was my big chance; he held out an envelope with a woman's name and address on it. Contrary to all the instructions I had received I reached out for it and he in turn withdrew it. I had muffed my chance. I should have just read the thing and committed it to memory but I was so excited at having contacted the Underground, I was thoughtless. We talked a little longer and he showed me his identity papers; and his address was the same as the one on the envelope but here again I failed. Not using my head I didn't memorise the thing. About this time a wagon load of women came down the road, so to keep from getting the boy involved, I told him I did not understand and continued on my journey.

I knew that there was help in this town, so when I got there about four o'clock in the afternoon, I decided to spend the night there and try and get contact with the offered help. I made an old garage on the edge of town my headquarters and at about two hour intervals I would make a pass through the town hoping to be picked up but to no avail. This town was definitely anti-Nazi and there were posters denouncing the Reich all over the place. I didn't see any signs of Jerries anywhere, and my chances seemed to be pretty good to be picked up, but no soap. I walked the streets, showing myself all over town and at about twelve o'clock midnight I went back to the garage and went to sleep.

13th June. . . .In the morning when I aroused myself, I noticed that there was a small strawberry patch just behind the building, so for breakfast I had a very fashionable meal, though not served in a like manner. I stayed around town until noon walking the streets, gazing into windows and stalling around in general. Now I realise that I should have stayed a week, if necessary, but at the time I was pretty impatient and anxious to get on my way so off I started again. The afternoon was uneventful and that night I found myself on the open road just one day northwest of Tours, the place that I wanted to cross into unoccupied France. That night I slept in another field and past a fairly pleasant night.

14th June. . . . On the morning of this eventful day I travelled down the highway between Tours and La Fleche and noticed quite a bit of movement of German Troops, headed for the front. Every town or village I passed through had a number of soldiers in it and also quite a few broken down vehicles of all kinds crowding the various repair shops. During the days on the road I had greeted many Frenchman with Bon Jour and Bon Soir, and nothing had ever come of it, but today it was different. As I left a small town, a tramp proceeded to join me and started talking French. I was reluctant to answer, but after a few Ouis and Nons, I told him I was American and he immediately dropped back behind me. This troubled me a bit, but I watched him as I passed a few German Officers on the road and he kept my identity secret. Finally I figured that he was all right so I pulled off into a field and slept about an hour.

When I resumed my journey, he has passed and wasn't even in sight, so I stopped thinking about him, thinking him loyal. About a mile from where I stopped I came to a road crossing the road I was travelling at 90 degrees, there was a small house on the left hand corner closest to me. Walking down the right hand side of the house, I noticed two officers talking about 50 yards this side of the house. I, of course, shuffled right on by them when I heard the men calling me in French. I paid no heed, and continued walking. They called again, this time sounding a little perturbed; still I didn't look around or stop. With his last call, six soldiers stalked out of the house with rifles and bayonets and at this I stopped and turned around. Directly behind me stood the officers, pistols drawn, and I knew I'd really had it. At this moment I noticed the French tramp leaving the house and knew then who had given me away. I found out after that the French are paid well to deliver an airman to the Jerries.

Anyway, I held up my hands at the command of the officer and the search began. They found compasses, maps, files, saws, my rubber water bag and a few other things, that made it a cinch, including my uniform beneath my clothes. They had me take off the civvies and I began to laugh. I was so tired that it didn't matter a lot what happened. The German officers weren't a bad lot. They gave me smokes and tried to talk a bit of English but failed. I found that one had been to Pensacola and New Orleans before the war started. He asked me if I was from Texas, which I of course said yes, and he seemed to be pretty proud of himself. From here they took me to a field headquarters back in a bit of woods that was well guarded, and here it was that I was first interrogated. I was surprised at the number of Germans that spoke good English, and in the course of the conversation found that I was one hundred and twenty five miles, in a straight line, from where I'd been shot down, so I don't know how far I actually walked but at the rate I was going the first week, I would have been in Spain by the end of four more weeks.

I stayed here at this mansion in the woods about two hours, and then they put me in a small jeep, German style, and took me to the city of Le Mans. Here I was taken to a building in the centre of the city that looked like a courthouse to me, surrounded by high thick walls and well guarded. There were lots of fortified rooms, built underground and well camouflaged, in the yard. My guard took me to an underground office where a German Colonel came in to ask me questions. I refused to tell him a thing and he told me that being as I was captured in civvies and wouldn't talk I could be shot for a spy. 'Are you sure you haven't anything to tell me?' he asked, and I said 'No'. He then told me that his only alternative was to turn me over to the Gestapo. As we left the office, two German

MP's were waiting for me outside so I figured it was a put up job. They put me into a '36 Chevy' and drove around the town a while at a wild rate, with no respect for the French pedestrians and finally wound up at a large two-storey house. They took me here and the car drove off. They called an English-speaking girl downstairs to question me but couldn't get anything out of me. They took me back outside and there stood the car again. This time they drove me to the city jail; my first experience with one of these things. There were twelve other airmen here, two Englishmen, seven Frenchmen and three Americans. We stayed here for five days and witnessed from our window a group of P-47's dive bomb a rail station not a mile away. We could see the flak pass just outside the jail yards, busy as a bunch of bees, but they did no damage to the ships.

On the night of the fifth day they rounded the bunch of us up at midnight and put us aboard a large bus and took us to Chartres. There we found about twenty more airmen, including some Aussies corralled in an old convent. Our guards were a bunch of kids about 14 years old. I was afraid that they would be a little trigger-happy but they proved to be OK. One night while we were there a big gun fight broke out in town but the Germans wouldn't tell us what had happened. The next day the kids were moved up to the front and were replaced by older men. It was here that I was first formally questioned. When I refused to answer their enquiries they gave me a pick and shovel and told me to start my grave. I wasn't worried, no, not much. I dug for a while then they called me back in. Found out later that I'd dug a latrine.

One afternoon they took six of us to the city jail and we passed the Chartres Cathedral, which is a beautiful piece of work. There's a book about it somewhere. I intend to read it someday. Prior to the time we got there, A-20's had bombed the water supply and while we were there, P-47's did a beautiful dive-bombing job on the electrical supply plant. We had a ringside seat for this show and it was carried out beautifully. The last night we were there, Mosquitoes bombing the city, and one bomb hit so close that we could hear the debris falling on the roof. At four o'clock am they took forty of us on a bus and sent us to Paris. Along the roads there were hundreds of shot up busses and trucks, and to add to our discomfort the bus had a flat tire, and we sat around in the open 'sweating out' the Mustangs and Thunderbolts.

We reached Paris without further trouble and went to the train station. While sitting on the train there were two air-raids and this didn't make us rest any easier. Finally we pulled out. The yards had thousands of burned out freight cars in them and we saw hundreds of exploded engines. As we passed through Verdun the siding there was full of flat cars with Tiger Tanks on them. No sooner had we left the station, than a group of P-38's began to strafe the tanks. We were really worried for a while, but they didn't shoot at us so we went on to Frankfurt. This is where the famous German interrogating centre, DuLag Luft [1], is located. The city itself had been flattened by bombing and the civilians were none too friendly. They took our fingerprints, photographs and characteristics here and then put us into 'solitary'. The first night there they called me into an office to question me. When I walked in they introduced themselves and one of them said: 'My but you've got a red nose, you must be one of the red nose boys.' All the ships in my group had red spinners. They then told me exactly who I was, who my roommate was, and a whole lot of stuff about our group that I didn't even know. They told me that they had an agent on our field that sent in a report every two weeks. They also told me that some of my friends were there, but I wouldn't admit a thing. They sent me back to solitary.

The next night after I had gone to bed, about eleven, they came after me again. When I walked out into the hall I saw Major James A. Goodsen the CO of 336th Squadron and also the last original member of the Eagle Squadron and they took us back to the office were we met three other 4th Group men. Here they questioned us again, fed us well for a change and gave us our first smoke in about two weeks. After talking for a while, the Major hinted that we should admit who we were as we couldn't tell them anything that they didn't already know so we 'fessed up'. The next day we were put on a train and taken to a Red Cross supply camp, Westlow somewhere between Frankfurt and Sagan where they gave us clothes, and toilet articles and our first American food in nearly a month. We were also given a chance to take a bath, the first one in three weeks. We stayed here three days then boarded the train again for Sagan. The trip was two and a half days long, but uneventful.

When we got to Sagan they searched us and gave us a slight physical check up, then assigned us to our block. Here I set till when?

In fact, Osce remained at Stalag Luft III, Sagan, until January 1945, when the camp was evacuated to avoid the advancing Russians, and Osce endured the notorious 'Death March' with a hundred more prisoners. Surviving this, he eventually returned to Baton Rouge and left the war behind. By 1989, he had retired as a successful insurance salesman and was enjoying his golf four times a week. An even greater pleasure was the blessing of his wife, Thelma, three children and eleven grandchildren all living within two miles of his home. He corresponded with Rémy in 1991: 'It is a good life and God has been so good to me to see me through the trials and tribulations of this life, and to grant me success in all of my endeavours.' His attempt at evading the enemy might not be regarded as a successful endeavour, but it was a magnificent effort to navigate his way through a foreign country and avoid capture for so long. The treachery of a tramp betrayed him, and others might have suffered had Osce not outwitted his captors by avoiding any revelation of the part they played.

On 11 February 1994 Osce Jones went to fly fighter escort for the angels and this story is his legacy.

CHAPTER FOUR

The Bengal Lancer

The elderly veteran mounted the school podium to a standing ovation from the morning assembly and, it seemed, felt more nervous than when entering combat all those years ago. His connection with this establishment was not one of former student and had been hidden, if not forgotten, for most of the intervening years. Today was Veterans' Day, 8 November 1994, in Bloomfield High School, New Jersey, and, as the applause diminished, the old man began to address his young audience. His words were given rapt attention as they unlocked the story of a challenge taken up by predecessors of the pupils present. The tale unfolded fifty years to a time when Bloomfield High had enthusiastically embraced the Schools At War Program and its efforts had helped win a war fought before the majority of those present had been born. He modestly revealed his own part in those dramatic events of days now distant but emerging with increasing clarity as he related the fears and conscience of a young man, then not much older than those listening so intently.

Frank M. Stillwell joined the US Army Air Force in February 1943 and, within the year, the young man raised on a farm near Monroe, New Jersey, had converted his ploughshare into a sword, only this sword had wings. Those wings were paid for by a New Jersey School and his tale restored to Bloomfield High School a lost legacy, that of 'The Bengal Lancer'.

On 5 December 1943, Frank Stillwell, a newly qualified pilot, prepared for overseas departure and eventually found himself winging a P-51 over England with the 496 Fighter Training Group based at Station 345 Goxhill, close to Barrow upon Humber. The 496FTG provided theatre indoctrination and allowed new pilots to assimilate local procedures before being assigned to combat units. Processed through a week after D-Day, Frank received orders moving him south to report to Station 378 at Fowlmere. Sitting on chalklands south of Cambridge, the airfield had originally been established during the First World War and had latterly been a satellite to the famous RAF Station at Duxford. Upgraded to accept a full USAAF fighter group, it became home to the 339FG for their brief but illustrious combat career from April 1944 until the end of hostilities. Frank found himself commencing operations with the 503FS and confronted the realities of combat when the squadron lost three pilots within the week, all to adverse weather conditions. This certainly made him aware that bad weather was their other enemy.

Clean-cut picture of the young pilot, Frank M. Stillwell, complete with classic white silk scarf. Sometimes considered flamboyant, the scarf was practical garb for the swivel-headed aviator for whom survival meant constantly searching the sky. A close-fitting collar would have been very uncomfortable. *(Frank M. Stillwell)*

This other enemy would directly affect Frank only a few weeks and some thirty combat missions later, with events that almost cost him his life.

August 5 1944 was a day that will be forever etched in the deep recesses of my memory. The weather was less than favourable at Fowlmere that morning. The sky was completely overcast and the ceiling was 700 feet. When such conditions prevailed, it was standard operating procedure for each flight of four to join in close formation underneath the cloud layer, and then to climb up through the overcast. I was leading the second element and Ed Flaherty was my wingman. The flight leader and his wingman cleared the runway as we began our take off run. We became airborne and immediately started a climbing turn to the left in order to join up with the flight leader as soon as possible. I crossed under the flight leader and moved into close formation on his right wing. Almost immediately the flight leader began to climb up through the cloud layer. We were in the overcast about one minute and I was concentrating on flying close formation on the dim outline of the flight leader's plane. Suddenly I felt a violent jar and saw a large portion of my left wing disappear. Beginning with the inboard end of the aileron, there was a jagged diagonal line across to the leading edge of the wing. At the same time I saw an aircraft disappearing under the flight leader's plane. The reality of the situation struck me like a bolt of lightning. I sensed being in deep trouble. Fortunately, my P-51 did not become uncontrollable. I lost sight of the flight leader and had to go on my own instruments. By holding quite a bit of right stick pressure, I was able to keep my aircraft level. A quick decision was made and I decided to descend down through the overcast to visual conditions. I broke out of the clouds at 700 feet and was happy to note that, with some extra power, the P-51 felt fairly stable. Now the next decision had to be made, which revolved about whether I should attempt a landing with my disabled plane. I remembered there was an airfield at Manston that had a real long runway. Perhaps a fast approach and attempt to drop the landing gear at the last moment before touchdown might be a possibility. I just did not relish the thought of bailing out of a fighter aircraft under those conditions. Before I had a chance to call for a steer to Manston, my engine stopped running. It is really quite amazing how well your mind functions when you are faced with a life or death situation. I can still remember with distinct clarity that I disconnected the radio jack and the G-suit hose. I reached for and pulled the emergency lever for jettisoning the cockpit canopy. To my dismay, nothing happened. I unfastened my seat belt, raised my body up and gave a good push on the canopy. Finally, it flew off and I felt a sudden rush of air all about me. By this time the plane was beginning to lose altitude and there really was not that much space left between me and the ground. I forced myself out the right side of the P-51. I suspect that when I released the right pressure on the control stick, the plane snapped into a sharp diving turn to the left. I believe for this reason I cleared the tail section as I hurtled back into the slipstream. There was no time to achieve terminal velocity before pulling the ripcord on the parachute. I remember looking at the handhold at the end of the ripcord, grabbing it, and giving a giant pull. Momentarily, I blacked out when the parachute opened. I was probably moving at 200 miles per hour. I learned later that one of the parachute panels split. When my eyes came back into focus, I was shocked to see the burning wreckage of my plane was directly under me. I was about 400 feet above the ground. At that point I took time out to offer a verbal thanks to God for sparing my life. By then it was obvious I was not going to land on the burning remains of my plane. The next few seconds were really quite pleasant. I could see I was coming down in a grain field about 100 feet from the inferno. There was not enough time to face the drift so I hit the ground moving sideways. Needless to say, the grain field was very hard and I impacted it like a sack of potatoes. I had barely gotten to my feet when a jeep came tearing across the field. I was picked up and transported to an airbase that was located nearby. They took me to the base hospital where I was examined by a flight surgeon. There did not seem to be anything wrong with my physical being so they took me back to my base at Fowlmere. By the time we got there my right ankle was beginning to swell slightly. Doc Stuhlman had some X-rays taken and decided I needed a leg cast for a hairline fracture in the anklebone. This put me on the disability list for six weeks. I hope I never have to use crutches again. . . . I have often wondered why the engine of my aircraft quit after the collision. As I see it, the propeller of Ed's

Station 378 at Fowlmere, home to the 339FG. The P-51B in the foreground is believed to be 43-7180, which was salvaged on 15 December 1944. The P-51D 44-13392 in the background has a motif and the name 'Fabasca V'. Note bombs resting between the two Mustangs. Each aircraft is tethered to the soil of Cambridgeshire.

P-51 chopped through the lower section of my plane's fuselage. Most likely it damaged the cooling system and the engine overheated. Things were happening far too quickly for me to look at the temperature gauge. The really scary part is when I stop to ponder just how close that four bladed propeller was to the seat of my pants . . .

Frank's aircraft as number three was a P-51B-15-NA, serial 42-106934 coded D7-Z. The other aircraft involved were a P-51D-NA, 44-14012, D7-B flown by the Flight Leader, Maj John R. Reynolds, and a P-51C-10-NT, 42-103567 D7-H piloted by 2/Lt Edward C. Flaherty as number four.

It seems that Flaherty became disorientated in the clouds and drifted into Frank's aircraft. Flaherty had been flying too loose a formation and lagging astern, so possibly over-corrected to catch up. After chomping into Frank's aircraft, the unfortunate Flaherty slid still further to starboard and clipped the fighter flown by Reynolds. Sliding beneath the Major's Mustang, Flaherty narrowly missed Reynold's wingman, 1/Lt Ray W. Amerman, in the number two slot and disappeared from view. Maj Reynolds, struggling to control his damaged aircraft, now ascended on Amerman's wing until the two of them broke clear and the extent of the damage could be more readily assessed. The left elevator and rudder were damaged, but Reynolds could now compensate for better control and decided to risk descending and returning to base. He landed safely, but Flaherty had entered a spin after the collision and crashed. At low altitude, he jettisoned his canopy and jumped just before his P-51 smashed into farm buildings at Thriplow, Cambridgeshire, and burst into flames. Some of the farm buildings were destroyed and livestock killed. Poor Flaherty was found dead about fifty feet from the wreckage, his ripcord D-ring was still in its pocket, although the main canopy was one-third out of its pack.

Fifty years later, the Aviation Research Group headed by enthusiast and 339FG historian John Harris, investigated the story of the collision. If there were any remains of Flaherty's machine, they were presently beyond reach beneath a concrete base and the reconstructed farm buildings. However, interviewing Frank during the 339FG reunion at Fowlmere in April 1994, John realised that Frank's crash site had to be closer to the airfield than originally envisaged. Studying the incident, John deduced that, for the jeep to find Frank so promptly, the site had to have been close to one of the nearby bases at Duxford or Little Walden. He drew a radius of 15 miles from Fowlmere and, a few days later, was discussing his theory with a colleague, Julian Evenheart. Reflecting on John's idea, Julian found it triggered the memory of hearing about a Mustang crash near Saffron Walden. Armed with hope, enthusiasm, but only scant information, they nonetheless undertook some fieldwork and set off to ask questions in the vicinity. Their investigations soon introduced them to a Mr Dale, who remembered receiving a fright when he and his brother were cycling along the road from Saffron Walden to Ashton. As schoolboys, they were accustomed to the sound of aircraft, but the one they saw that morning sounded as if it was in trouble. Looking up, they saw a Mustang with its motor seeming to 'cough and splutter' and then it flicked on its side and the pilot was thrown out. It was now so close that the two boys became afraid it might crash on them and frantically pedalled to get out of the way. Their furious and frightened efforts had barely taken them 100yd when there was a tremendous bang in a field close by and one of the lads was so distracted that he also crashed, headlong into the roadside ditch. However, being resilient, the two boys had soon retraced their tracks, eagerly seeking some souvenirs. Reaching the edge of the field, they realised that they might get more of a souvenir than they had bargained for, because bullets were now exploding in the wreckage and some were too close for comfort. Sensibly, they allowed the danger to diminish their enthusiasm, but souvenir aspirations were rejuvenated when they saw the pilot's parachute lying in the opposite field. Silk or the more modern nylon would make a fine trophy, but the youngsters were now anxious in case the pilot had jumped too low and might be nearby, injured or dead. They would wait many years to find out and acquire a souvenir, for they had barely moved towards the parachute when an American jeep raced into view and they were soon ushered away.

From Mr Dale's description, John felt he had located the crash, and this theory was supported when a copy of the USAAF Form 14 Report of Aircraft Accident arrived a few days later. Moreover, Mr Dale was now the landowner and granted consent for a search. With him as a guide, an initial metal detector search was made by the ARG but to no avail – the field was devoid of any hint, not even the tiniest fragment. Their already dampened enthusiasm all but disappeared in a downpour and their only witness now left them to it. Undeterred, John pulled out the very grainy xerox pictures from the microfilm, and, the rain having ceased, he patiently set off attempting to match the background. John later recalled:

It was then that I realized that you could match the features in the photos from two fields as, in the original photos, [it] showed a small wood in the distance and two small trees in between the crash site and the wood. Now, after fifty years, the wood had grown larger and another wood had grown at the top of the field, two woods. I crossed over the ditch by two large trees and started walking backwards across the field. I had not gone more than 75 yards when I found my first piece of wreckage, another 10 yards and a .50 calibre bullet. Our witness had shown us the wrong field! A search with metal detectors soon found the impact point and a good reading was shown with a deep seeking Gemini. I rechecked the photos and apart from extra growth in the wood and the larger trees, it was a positive ID.

On returning home I contacted the landowner and requested his permission to carry out a recovery with a JCB; he gave his permission, so I applied to the MOD for a licence to recover the remains, which was granted some weeks later. . . . Five of my colleagues met me at the site one Saturday morning to carry out the recovery, and after marking out the site, the JCB proceeded to remove the topsoil for about twelve feet around the impact area. This revealed several small pieces of skinning and a few .50 calibre bullets. As the excavation depth increased to approximately six feet, more wreckage was found in the spoil heap and in the hole but we soon realized there would not be the large amount of wreckage we had originally thought would be there. It was now obvious the large metal detector readings we had were from the large amount of exploded .50 calibre bullets left in the crater. The artefacts found were however interesting and included 300–400 .50 calibre bullets; 3 seat harness buckles; oxygen flow gauge complete with label; fragments of engine and supercharger casing; fragments of engine cowling retaining the red and white group markings; corroded and burnt airframe; two engine bearers; supercharger gear wheels; canopy Perspex; fragments of armoured glass; hydraulic tubing; cylinder head and barrel from a small air/vacuum compressor . . . remains of three instruments; fragments of propeller cuff and one large piece of fuselage skinning in excellent condition from behind the cockpit area.

Not a great amount compared to some recoveries but it was from Frank's P-51 and we had found a part of Frank's life which he lost, which to me was more rewarding. A few weeks later after I had cleaned and preserved the finds, I sent Frank two kilos of his P-51 . . . He in turn has used these to carry out his own presentation about the time he was a fighter pilot . . .

Frank's presentation to the assembly in Bloomfield High now continued with the school's role in his story. He had recovered from his broken ankle but, with his P-51 now in pieces, he

John Harris sent Frank two kilos of his lost fighter, and the former pilot made up this superb display of parts. The fragment top left still bears evidence of the red-and-white checkerboard around the cowling. Frank's seat harness buckles are centre right. *(Frank M. Stillwell)*

needed a replacement aircraft. Recognising that Frank hailed from New Jersey, his commanding officer now assigned to him a very special Mustang. The shiny new fighter, serial 44-15134, looked at first just like any other, but inside the cockpit was affixed a citation from the US Treasury Department stating that this aircraft had been purchased through the united efforts of the Bloomfield schools. In addition, there was a letter addressed to the pilot asking that he communicate with the Bloomfield schools so that his exploits and the career of the aircraft could be followed. There had clearly been a lot of effort in getting this machine to Fowlmere.

The story could have slipped through history's floorboards entirely but for the persistence of Peter Wilson, a retired Vice Principal of Bloomfield High School. Pete was himself a USAAF veteran, having served as an armourer with the famous 354FG, the 9AF unit that pioneered the P-51 into combat. An avid reader on aviation matters, Pete had been perusing a copy of *Aces and Wingmen II* by Danny Morris when he noticed an interesting caption beneath the picture of a 339FG Mustang. The aircraft bore the name 'The Bengal Lancer' and Pete was surprised to read in the caption: 'This particular aircraft was presented by the children of Bloomfield High School, New Jersey, who sold War Bonds.' Pete was puzzled, the history teacher in him intrigued. During his entire thirty-two-year tenure at Bloomfield High, he had never heard of this story.

Questioning both the faculty and former students, he initially elicited only perplexed responses, but this just spurred Pete on. 'I determined to research the story not only because of my curiosity, but also to be able to in some way complete the Bengal Lancer story for those who had worked so hard back in the 1942–45 era.' Pete's investigations revealed how the young people of Bloomfield had patriotically answered the call from their nation during a time of national crisis. A Schools At War Program had drawn a tremendous response from the wartime school community, but this was not taught in the current curriculum. Pete's efforts now culminated in the assembly hall on Veterans' Day as he resurrected the story for his young audience.

During the United States' participation in World War II 1942–45, Bloomfield students supported the war effort with incredible dedication, as was demonstrated by their joining pre-flight aeronautic classes, commando classes, farming courses; being junior Red Cross volunteers and making victory gardens. In addition, there was a New Jersey Victory Corps, which helped students prepare for service, as well as other means of helping the community war effort, such as the collection of strategic war materials and books for the servicemen. Bloomfield students of all age groups in the public and private schools participated in one of the most productive and successful local activities, the Schools At War Program. The Schools At War Program enabled everyone in school to join in a united effort, to sell war bonds and stamps. So successful was their sales of these bonds and stamps that they were responsible for the presentation of . . . now listen , . . . a B-17 bomber, some dozen jeeps, twenty-five field ambulances, three evacuation hospitals and six P-51 Mustang fighters. What an incredulous example for future generations were these tremendous student efforts . . .

Instigated by Secretary to the Treasury, Henry Morgenthau Jr, the US treasury issued Defense Bonds – later called War Bonds – which the Schools At War Program supported to fund the procurement of equipment needed by the nation's armed forces. Two of the original Bloomfield students involved, Monica Williams Shirvanian and Carol Pilloni Lockhead, had been traced by Pete and, to the delight of all, attended the Veterans Day assembly honouring Frank Stillwell. Carol later told the author:

In those days there was a national campaign to 'Buy Bonds' to 'Bring our Boys home'. Every school had a program in which each week we bought savings stamps – usually one or two – for 25 cents each and glued them into a booklet. When full, the booklet, worth $18.75, was turned into a war bond, redeemable at war's end . . . if your classroom had 100 per cent participation for the week, we hung a small flag on our door denoting our effort. Our town challenged the school children of neighboring Montclair to see which could buy the most bonds within a specified time. Bloomfield won. When our fighter plane was

One of the pictures from the Bloomfield, New Jersey Independent Press, dated 6 October 1944 taken when Mr H.T. Hollingsworth, Superintendent of Schools, presented six Mustangs to Maj Lonergan, Public Relations Officer at Newark Army Air Base. Left to right: Barney Recinello; William E. Reid; Merrill A. Bigelow; Maj Lonergan; Mr Hollingsworth; Revd Dr T.F. Burke; Walt Simpson; Margaret Dower; Cynthia Pomeroy and Trilby Boerner. William E. Reid managed the local Schools At War Program. The aircraft, Army Air Force number 44-15134, taped and sealed for overseas shipment, became 'The Bengal Lancer'. *(Frank M. Stillwell)*

presented to the US Army at Newark Airport, a representative from each of the seven elementary schools, the junior high and the high schools was selected to attend the ceremony. My father, a prominent physician, was one of the first men in our community to enlist in the war. Perhaps this was the reason I was chosen to represent Center School, for it surely wasn't because of scholarship on my part, since I had not yet learned the joy of academic achievement. . . . It was a great thrill for me to meet Frank Stillwell, a handsome, modest gentleman who captured the hearts of the young people in the high school audience. . . . Peter Wilson is a hero also, because without his diligence this story would never have had an ending.

Carol was pictured with other students during the official ceremony when Mr H.T. Hollingworth, Superintendent of Schools, presented the Mustangs to Maj Lonergan, public relations officer at the base. Carol was fascinated to learn how the aircraft had been flown to New Jersey from the manufacturing plant by women pilots who were part of the organization called the WASPS (Women's Air Force Service Pilots). The machines now had their propellers removed, and all seams were now sealed with a heavy, weatherproof cloth tape for the seaborne part of their journey into combat.

On arrival in the UK, the fighters were reassembled, sometimes modified to meet local requirements, then test flown before being ferried to combat units, often by women pilots of the Air Transport Auxiliary, performing a similar service to the WASPS. In the summer of

Dated Saturday 25 November 1944, Frank poses by 'The Bengal Lancer'. A lack of exhaust stain indicates the youth of his new mount. No spurs but flying helmet, oxygen mask, goggles, parachute, Mae West, even a first aid pouch. *(Frank M. Stillwell)*

Pictured later, exhaust staining smears the fuselage of D7-D. Rudder colouring for the 503FS was red. *(Frank M. Stillwell)*

1944, the young fighter pilot contemplating the efforts of so many youngsters felt that putting a P-51 into combat contributed to the preservation of academic rights for them and for countless others now being liberated from a regime that strangled academic freedom. Reflecting on the background to his new mount, Frank discussed its origins with Capt Eldred Carrow, the 503FS Intelligence Officer, who also hailed from New Jersey. Carrow told Frank that Bloomfield High School called their athletics teams 'Bengals' and Frank remembered the 1935 movie entitled *The Lives of a Bengal Lancer* starring Gary Cooper. He did not see himself as the swashbuckling Hollywood hero, but felt the film caught the spirit of the school's intentions, so 44-15134, D-7D, became 'The Bengal Lancer'. The white–red–white banded spinner with the red-and-white checkerboard banding around the cowling were the Lancer's battle plumage. Bloomfield schools could be proud of the P-51's appearance, with its name in nicely curved lettering beneath the starboard exhaust stack, but, fine as it was, their P-51 had been bought for battle and Frank's first opportunity to give a return on their investment occurred on 18 November 1944.

It was a strafing attack against oil targets in the Neuburg area. Before reaching the target, we were attacked by several groups of Me 109s. I singled out a Me 109 that was slightly ahead, and turning to my right. As I turned on the gun switch, I experienced an eerie feeling. Perhaps it was the sudden rush of adrenalin into my veins, or maybe it was the fact I was unavoidably locked in mortal combat. I pushed the throttle to the firewall and began to bring the Me 109 into my K-14 gun sight. The trigger for the six guns was located on the control stick. My right index finger rested on the trigger, and the six machine guns began to fire. The tracer bullets sparkled on the right side of the engine as direct hits were made. Smoke streamed from the Me 109 as it went down. I will not know until judgement day whether that German pilot lost his life by my hand. It is at such times, when the welfare of your family, and nation is at risk, that your duty to protect them is high on the list of moral obligations.

These were Frank's thoughts some fifty years later and they contrast with the morale-boosting public-relations radio broadcast he made only a few days after that combat in a feature entitled 'Combat Thrills', hosted by a well-known wartime celebrity, Ben Lyon. A pilot himself, Lyon had starred in the famous aviation war movie *Hell's Angels* and then tasted the real thing by flying on operations with the RAF. Ben had an affinity with the airmen he interviewed, even though the scripts were couched in propaganda-type prose, and this example was 'Passed for Publication' by the Supreme Headquarters Allied Expeditionary Force (SHAEF) Field Press Censor.

LYON. This is Lieutenant Colonel Ben Lyon speaking to you from London and presenting another edition of Combat Thrills . . . exciting experiences of the airmen of the United States Eighth Air Force. Though the thrills and chills of these fighting men of the sky are many and varied . . . there is always one which tops the rest . . . one which they will forever remember as their biggest Combat Thrill against the enemy. Today we have the story of 23-year-old First Lieutenant Frank M. Stillwell, Jr., of Prospect Plains, New Jersey . . . a P-51 Mustang pilot of the well-known 339th Fighter Group. Lieutenant Stillwell's story is the story of his fighter plane . . . known as 'The Bengal Lancer' . . . and of what it means to some kids back home in New Jersey. When did it happen, Frank?

STILLWELL. It was that day recently when 'The Bengal Lancer' and I shot down our first enemy aircraft. Such a day is usually the biggest event a fighter pilot can have over here.

LYON. How did 'The Bengal Lancer' get its name?

STILLWELL. Well, Lieutenant . . . to begin with . . . I was flying a new airplane. It wasn't just an ordinary P-51 Mustang . . . though it looked like one. This Mustang was one which had been purchased by the boys and girls of Bloomfield, New Jersey. They had made a $475,000 subscription to the Fifth War Loan Drive . . . and my plane was one of six those school kids bought . . . and the only one to be assigned to our group.

LYON. You're from New Jersey, too, aren't you, Frank?

STILLWELL. Yes . . . which made my appreciation even greater. I decided that the most fitting name for that Mustang would be 'The Bengal Lancer' . . . after the Bloomfield High School football team known as the Bengals. Those students had sent along a letter with the plane . . . wishing me luck . . . so you can really understand Lieutenant, how much I was hoping that I could bag something the first time out in it. We were somewhere near Mannheim . . . about twenty minutes from our target area . . . when we saw three Jerries. I was flying at 17,000 feet and the Nazi planes were above us. I pushed everything forward and started grabbing altitude to get within striking distance. I lined up on a Messerschmitt 109 . . . but my first burst seemed to have no effect, so I stayed on his tail and closed in to about 450 yards. This time I gave him a long burst and saw hits around the cockpit and cowling. I was on top of him when he went into a spin . . . obviously shot to pieces. My wingman confirmed the plane's destruction.

LYON. You really came through for them back in Bloomfield High . . . with the assistance of the 'Lancer' of course. It must have made you plenty happy to be able to return their present with the gift of an enemy airplane destroyed.

STILLWELL. I'll admit that I felt pretty good about it, Lieutenant. Everything was fine . . . only . . . that is, except for . . .

LYON. Except for what, Frank?

STILLWELL. Well . . . When I returned to my station . . . I learned that my film had jammed . . . the stuff which records the action in the air . . . and that meant I would have no pictures. You see . . . I had sort of hoped to show them in the Bloomfield public schools someday.

LYON. That was a tough break, Frank. Anyhow . . . pictures or not . . . you and 'The Bengal Lancer' did a real achievement that day which those New Jersey students won't ever forget. This was the unusual Combat Thrill of First Lieutenant Frank M. Stillwell, Jr., of Prospect Plains, New Jersey. Thanks and best of luck to you both. This is Colonel Ben Lyon saying goodbye from London.

Not mentioned in the broadcast for security reasons was some new equipment worn by Frank in trials to improve the performance of US fighter pilots. The 339FG had been selected by 8FC to test some unusual flying apparel, nicknamed the G-suit by pilots. Stemming from pre-war experiments, both the RAF and USAAF developed pressure suits to prevent pilot blackout – blood draining from the brain – in sharp, high-speed manoeuvres. If successful, this suit would enable pilots to make tighter turns, either in defence or for offensive advantage. The American Berger Company had improved on earlier examples. Initially 9FC units had been equipped, but more suits became available as manufacturing output increased. Frank was chosen to test the latest version, the G-3 suit. Tight fitting, the suit was equipped inside with five rubber bladders covering the abdomen, thighs and calves. By inflating beneath the garment, the bladders compressed the veins, significantly reducing any draining of blood from the brain to the lower extremities. The suit functioned by a hose and special valve connecting it to the Mustang's vacuum pump. During high-g turns, the bladders inflated in direct proportion to the amount of centrifugal reaction exerted on the pilot. Frank would shortly come to appreciate the suit's benefits when he was attacked and needed to turn sharply away from a dangerous situation, as he later recalled.

On November 26, 1944, the 339FG sent 56 aircraft on a mission to Hanover, Germany. At approximately 1300 hours, the 2nd Bomber Division of B-24s radioed they were under heavy attack south-east of Dummer Lake. When we arrived there were about 200 FW 190s attacking the bombers. We dropped our external gasoline tanks. A huge battle developed, ranging from 26,000 feet down to a lower cloud level. I closed on a FW 190, and began firing at it. I saw several hits and it caught on fire. At that instant my P-51 was struck in the left wing by gunfire. The panel over the guns was blown off and a belt of .50 calibre bullets lay on top of the wing. I went into a steep diving spiral towards the lower cloud level. Just before entering the clouds I managed to stop the steep spiral and levelled off. My gyros on the instrument panel had tumbled, so I quickly reset the artificial horizon instrument before going into the clouds. About ten minutes later I climbed up on top the clouds, and not a plane was in sight. My magnetic compass was not operating, as the sending wires from the master compass in the left wingtip had been damaged. At that time, I had no idea where I was heading. A quick thought entered my mind. If I rested my head back on the crash pad, and manoeuvred the plane so the canopy edge was in line with the sun, perhaps I could reach someone by radio, and have him do the same manoeuvre. Then I could ask him to read his magnetic compass, give me the heading he was on, and I could set my gyro compass. I managed to contact another pilot by radio, explained my problem, and how he could help. In a minute he gave me the heading and I set my gyro compass. Now, at least, I was able to head in the general direction towards England. After flying for about an hour, the cloud layer below me disappeared and I could see the ground. A few minutes later I spotted an airfield. I lost some altitude, and was finally able to identify the airplanes on the airfield as B-26s. It occurred to me that the prudent thing would be to land on the B-26 base, have my P-51 checked, refuel and reset the gyro compass.

The Bengal Lancer handled just fine on the landing, even though it had a sizeable hole in the left wing. A crew chief examined the damaged wing and removed the belt of .50 calibre bullets. He did not detect any major structural damage. After refuelling, I reset the gyro compass and headed for England. The B-26 airbase was located in France. By the time I landed at Fowlmere it was nearing nightfall. Operations had already written me off as missing in action. I forgot to mention why I did not spend the night at the B-26 base. You see, I was scheduled to go on rest and recuperation leave in the southern part of England the very next day. At that point I needed it.

While Frank was enjoying his R&R, 'The Bengal Lancer' was repaired and used by other pilots. Having your own aircraft was preferable, but it was not policy for junior officers to have an aircraft designated for their use alone. On return, Frank continued accumulating missions, mostly in the 'Lancer', and, while further aerial combat eluded him, he and his school-sponsored P-51 earned their keep flying valuable escort duties to protect the 'big friends'. There were also strafing sorties attacking airfields and disrupting enemy communications and transport systems. As Frank had realised early in his combat career, that 'other enemy', the British weather had to be challenged on many occasions. When he was nearing the end of his operational tour, the 'other enemy' had another attempt on his life.

On January 31, 1945, we were scheduled to escort bombers to Bremen, Germany. The weather conditions were very bad, but we did take off. About thirty minutes after take off,

A bitterly cold scene in January 1945, possibly at Bassingbourne, when the 339FG staged from the 91BG base while Pierced Steel Planking was being laid to improve conditions on the runways at Fowlmere. *(Frank M. Stillwell)*

the mission was scrubbed and we were recalled. As we turned around and headed for Fowlmere, it began to rain very hard. It was impossible for the flights to stay together in formation and it became every man for himself. I radioed for a steer to our home base, and then dropped low enough to see the ground. Because of the heavy rain, the visibility straight ahead was zero. However, I could maintain level flight by peering over the leading edge of the wings. There were a lot of planes trying to return to their bases at the same time and the risk of collision was high. I was flying about 300 feet above the ground when I spotted flares being shot up from an airfield below. Keeping the airfield in sight, I made a 360-degree turn, dropped my gear and landed. Thank goodness someone had the foresight to keep shooting flares at the end of the landing runway. After I parked my plane, I noticed that some other pilots from the 339th had also landed there. We walked over to the control tower and went upstairs. Much to our surprise, we were greeted by General Carl Spaatz and General Jimmy Doolittle. They noticed that we were wearing the new g-suits and they wanted to know how well they worked. It was a great moment in my life to be in the presence of two famous aviators. The field where we had landed was Duxford.

Under new management. 1/Lt Dennis B. Rawls had to fly a full tour on B-17s before achieving the cherished ambition of becoming a fighter pilot and being assigned to 'The Bengal Lancer'. *(Richard C. Penrose)*

In February 1945, Frank flew for the last time in 'The Bengal Lancer'. He was an integral part of its story, but the now-veteran aircraft would continue its 339FG career in new hands while Frank embarked for Prospect Plains, his wife Doris and their young daughter, Sandra. He had flown sixty-five combat missions, and, after a furlough with his family, he went to the Central Instructors' School in Waco, Texas. Having graduated, he was transferred to Aloe Field, also in Texas, where he taught only one class of Advanced Aviation Cadets before the war ended. He continued on reserve status until recalled during the Korean War, but found himself posted to Iceland on non-flying duties as an Aircraft Controller. Seeking a discharge some months later, he dabbled in aviation work as a civilian instructor and crop duster, but, recognising the limitations of this existence, he studied so that he could start a successful business career, from which he retired in 1985, his days with the Lancer now only memories.

The next pilot to clamber proudly into the cockpit of 'The Bengal Lancer' was especially pleased to have the 'office' to himself. 1/Lt Dennis B. Rawls was no novice and is distinguished amid an elite band of pilots who flew both bombers and fighters in combat, although his fighter pilot's record with the 339FG saw him involved in the destruction of two aircraft – both Mustangs! One of these was 'The Bengal Lancer', but it is only fair to this self-effacing former fighter jockey to allow a description of his B-17 experience with the 569BS, 390BG, based at Framlingham before relating his less auspicious career in Mustangs.

Dennis had enlisted as an aviation cadet on 27 November 1942 and entered the training process the following February, ambitiously hoping to achieve the coveted status of fighter pilot. It was not to be – not yet. He graduated from the cadets in February 1944 and found himself ordered to Plant Park in Tampa, Florida, for bomber crew assignment and then to MacDill Field, training on B-17s. Reaching England during the spring of 1944, he flew the first of thirty missions in July but still felt that

to be assigned to a lumbering B-17 was very disappointing. At every turn I requested a transfer, only to be told, 'when you reach your next station they can probably transfer you'. The same story was offered at every station, even at the 390th Group. They said, 'maybe when you have completed half of your missions'. I had an opportunity to meet my Group commander, Col. Frederick Ott, and later Col. Joseph Moller.

Sympathetic to the young pilot's pleas, Moller would eventually be the motivating force behind his transfer, because he was a friend of Col John B. Henry, the 339FG commander. Before then, Dennis had his duty to perform in B-17s and might well have had 'The Bengal Lancer' among the many welcome 'little friends' who preserved him from German fighters. Against flak, the fighter escort could only assist after the event, as Dennis relates.

The mission was to Merseberg, Germany . . . they were heavily protected with anti-aircraft guns. The operators of those guns were very accurate with their tracking flak. Sometimes it would sound as [if] you were driving on a flat tire, a continuous plop, plop, causing the aircraft to bounce and making you wish you could withdraw your head further under your helmet and behind your flak vest. We were flying the Lead of the slot element, right under the squadron leader. If you flew too far astern, you took a chance of having the ball turret gunner's casings from the lead plane falling and hitting your aircraft. If you flew up tight you got a neck ache looking almost straight up to the lead plane. The bomb run from the Initial Point to the target always seemed too long, particularly when they are using a tracking flak. Our bombardier would drop his bombs when the smoke from the lead plane dropped out. Just after bombs away we took some terrible hits from flak. By this time we had just started our evasive manoeuvre. Our No. 1 engine was hit and the propeller was running away and uncontrollable – it had gone into flat pitch, causing the aircraft to yaw left. The No. 4 engine's warning lights were alerting us that they had been hit. We were able to feather it. No. 3 appeared to be failing. We now shifted our attention back to No. 1. By now, being in flat pitch and running away, we were unable to feather it. It became very hot and started a fire. Fortunately the propeller tore itself off before the fire could invade the engine and wing. Once the No. 1 prop had fallen off, things began to settle down. We began to assess our situation.

With our No. 2 engine running fine and our No. 3 engine just drawing about 20 inches of Hg. Manifold pressure, we were losing altitude. Our thoughts turned to jettisoning equipment to sustain flight. At that point we were alone in the sky, now below the bomber's altitude. Alerting our crew . . . for enemy fighters, we continued our slow descent. Shortly thereafter, a flight of beautiful P-51s approached us and said, 'Don't worry, big friend, we will escort you out of this area and see that you get to a safe area'. After all this excitement, we settled down and realized that our No. 3 engine was functioning OK. It just wasn't drawing more than about 20 Hg. Our engineer said he would check and see if some of the control cables might have been severed. Sure enough, just inside the fuselage, the control cables for the throttle had been cut. On interphone, he manually pulled the cable to adjust the engine to normal. Now we had two good engines! At morning briefing, we were told that Brussels, Belgium, had been liberated and could be used for emergency landings. Our navigator plotted our course and we proceeded to limp in. Other than being faster on final approach than normal and having to really get on the brakes after touch down, the landing was effected with welcome relief from all crew members . . .

With discretion, Dennis avoided the details of two days spent in the Metropole Hotel in Brussels, only saying it was 'better than any flak leave we had experienced'. He also participated in the second 'Shuttle' raid during August 1944, when he took his B-17

across the North Sea and the Danish Peninsula; down the Baltic Sea to bomb at Rahmel, an aircraft depot near Gdynia, Poland. We flew on to Mirgorod, Russia, having to land in a rainstorm . . . The next day we flew a mission out of Russia to Trzebinia, Poland, returning to Mirgorod. On the 8th we flew to Foggia, Italy. While en route we bombed Zilista, Rumania. On 12th of August we returned to England. While en route we bombed Toulouse, France. It was truly a memorable experience . . .

Another memorable experience was in store for Dennis. Completing his thirty bomber missions, he got his transfer to fighters with two other ex-bomber boys from the 493BG.

We were assigned to the 503FS. Our training consisted of take off and landings from the rear seat of an AT-6. Truly a good representation of what you will see, or not see, when you are flying the P-51. We spent about 5 hours acclimating [sic] to a single engine and one throttle. During this time we were given cockpit checks in the P-51 and eventually the blindfold check, prior to our first ride. I feel they weren't going to take a chance with our first flight in the P-51; they put [us] in the oldest aircraft on the field. The hangar queen was a P-51B model, with many hours, and I'm sure if it could speak, could tell many tales. Finally, the date for our check out came. The older fighter pilots in our squadron came out to watch the bomber pilots do their thing. It is difficult to describe the thrill when I first pushed the throttle forward on that old but beautiful little friend. The torque of that Merlin, the thrill of guiding that plane down the runway, lifting off and feeling the acceleration. After a few stalls and a little more familiarization, I returned to the base for my 'fighter approach and pitch out'. The pitch out was great but my habit in bombers seemed to innately return and I squared off the circling approach like a B-17. Needless to say, I heard about that approach when I landed. Of course, flying the missions, sitting in that small cockpit – I am 6'1" and at that time weighed 185 pounds – unable to get up and move around as we did in the B-17 – presented the necessity to acquire new habits and self-discipline.

One of the responsibilities they impressed on me during my initial fighter training was, 'the element leader who you were with was the gunner and you were to guard his tail and allow him to concentrate on shooting down the enemy'. On my first mission, I was assigned to fly the wing of my squadron commander, Major Dale Shafer. Dale had many hours of fighter experience . . . having begun with the Royal Air Force. He flew Spitfires in North Africa and, after the US became involved, he was commissioned into the Air Corps. We were escorting B-17s on a raid when a gaggle of German fighters were sighted. Before I could realize what was happening, the command 'drop tanks' came over the radio, and we were spiralling down to attack the Germans. The first pass was made with Shafer firing and getting some hits as we pulled up in a steep left turn to return for another pass. By then the gaggle was beginning to break up, but Shafer attacked another and [was] pulling up steeply to the left. While we were in the left turn, I slid out to his right and could see an Me 109 coming in on Shafer's tail. I tried to call him to break left but, by then, the airways were full of conversation from different pilots engaged in the heat of battle. When Shafer rolled out, the Me 109 rolled out on his tail. This put my aircraft and the 109 almost wingtip to wingtip. I was looking over at him looking over at me. I knew I had to act now and I turned into him. He, in turn, turned into me and, when I completed my turn, looking for him, he was diving into the clouds below. What a first trip in fighters.

Dennis continued flying his beloved fighters, including 'The Bengal Lancer', until 4 March 1945. That day the Eighth Air Force intended to mount major operations against airfields and other objectives relating to the use of the Me 262 jet fighter but found their scheme thwarted by adverse weather conditions and, instead, struck numerous targets of opportunity. Dennis delved into his memory and files for events that saw the demise of 'The Bengal Lancer'.

From the records I have, the Nurnburg mission . . . was routine. I do recall that there had been a rather heavy snowfall and we had to use the perimeter taxiway to runway 29 for takeoff. With our high-octane fuel we taxied at a rather high RPM to keep from fouling the plugs. There was a considerable distance to taxi, requiring excessive brake use to keep slowed. After takeoff I depressed the brake pedals to stop vibration of the wheels. I feel [sic] at this time the brakes were overheated and locked. Upon return from the mission, while over England en route to Fowlmere, our flight commander executed some formation acrobatics. I was feeling great as we broke for landing. Having flown as wingman to the flight leader, I was second landing and touched down on the left side of the runway. With a

The demise of 'The Bengal Lancer', 4 March 1945. Personnel discuss the process of recovering the aircraft. The USAAF Cumulative Loss Listing shows the aircraft as salvaged owing to battle damage by 4 Mobile Recovery and Repair Squadron. *(Dennis B. Rawls)*

Note how the propeller blades were bent and scuffed as the P-51 slid along on its nose before flipping onto its back. *(Dennis B. Rawls)*

Rescuers bravely burrowed beneath the canopy to free Dennis, but the singing of 'Nearer My God To Thee' was less than comforting. *(Dennis B. Rawls)*

left crosswind, my left wing was slightly low. When Bengal Lancer's left gear touched the ground, the plane lurched to the left and the right wheel touched the ground as the plane went up on its nose. I don't know how far I slid, but I was turning off switches, pulling back on the stick and praying for divine guidance. As the plane was slowing I tried to eject the canopy to no avail. Then the spinner dug into the turf and the plane flipped over with the canopy still in place. Completely trapped, I lay on the back of my head as fear of fire ran through my mind. I soon heard vehicles approaching and voices as help arrived. They quickly analysed my predicament and decided to extricate me by digging a hole under the canopy to let me egress through the broken canopy. Whoever the heroic individual was digging me out, he tried to keep my spirits up by singing 'Nearer My God to Thee'. I was feeling very close to God, but I wasn't sure why he was humming that particular hymn. When the hole was completed, they told me to disconnect my oxygen and headset. When I released my seat belt and had started tumbling out, my hips suddenly jerked upward as my G-suit hose connection held me. Someone quickly cut it with a knife. My gratitude and respect for those men who came to my assistance at a time that could have been life threatening to them, remains uppermost in my mind. 'The Bengal Lancer' was demolished, but fortunately only my pride was hurt.

Dennis successfully resisted the charge of Dereliction of Duty, because it was felt that the brakes on 'The Bengal Lancer' had overheated and seized after take-off. Meanwhile, he had to 'borrow' other P-51s and suffered another mishap on 15 March 1945, the day when another, seemingly routine, fighter escort mission was required. As Dennis relates:

We were using British 108 gallon external tanks which were elongated and cigar shaped. I think we were taking off to the northeast and the runway had many washouts along its bed. I was wingman to the flight leader and flying Bill Bryan's D7-J 'Big Noise', 44-15074. My leader gave the head motion to advance throttles and we moved down the runway. Shortly after the tail came up, we came to the undulating portion of the runway. The P-51 would bounce off the ground without flying speed and then return to the ground. Prior to take off speed, my right wing started to rise. My first thought was prop wash from the preceding element. I tried to control the wing down to no avail. By this time I was turning into my element leader. I had no choice but to pull back on the stick and try to go over him. Adding full power, I was able to pass over him left wing low and was slicing back to the ground. Needless to say I was exerting all my strength to level the wings. When I touched down my left wingtip hit the ground, but my wheels maintained

Dennis borrowed Bill Bryan's 'Big Noise' and bent it! At least he was the right way up on this occasion. Note damage to left wing. The aircraft, D7-J, 44-15074, became another candidate for the attention of 4 Mobile Recovery and Repair Squadron and is shown as salvaged owing to battle damage because the mishap occurred during an operational take-off. *(Dennis B. Rawls)*

integrity to keep rolling. I looked out and the left wingtip was bent up about 45 degrees and I knew I couldn't possibly get airborne. Ahead to my left was a line of P-51s; a blister hangar to the right and a big stack of crated wing tanks straight ahead. I elected to continue into the stack of tanks, chopped the power and cut off all the switches. I struck those tanks with tail still in the air. Upon emerging from the tanks with my landing gear sheared off, I ended up just off the perimeter track. Again, the ground personnel were at my side and trying to remove me from the cockpit. Their concern for my safety was above their normal call of duty, and I am deeply indebted for it. Again, by the grace of God, I was spared injury.

These mishaps might prompt thoughts of ineptitude rather than misfortune. Nothing could be further from the truth. Dennis actually flew 160 combat hours on escort and strafing missions until the end of the war. To his intense disappointment, the opportunity to offset the debit of two P-51s never arose. After the war, he stayed in the reserves and went to college, obtaining a degree in Mortuary Science and Business. He passed the state board exams and became a licensed funeral director and embalmer in Florida. He maintained his flying proficiency in the reserves and worked as a Funeral Director until 1956, when he returned to aviation as a pilot with Eastern Airlines at the 'too old to fly commercial age' of 32. His Mustang misadventures can be put into perspective against his full tour on B-17s and more than twenty-eight years flying a variety of airliners from the DC-3 and its piston-engined brethren to the A-300 and Lockheed L-1011. During this time, Dennis never forgot how 'The Bengal Lancer' had ended its days. The US Cumulative Loss Listing might proffer some comfort, because P-51D 44-15134 is at least listed as salvaged by 4 Mobile Recovery and Repair Squadron because of *battle* damage. Thus, it might be claimed that the proud old Lancer died in combat.

Pete Wilson's investigations drew together the programme for the Veterans' Day assembly in Bloomfield High School. Together, he and Frank enthralled their listeners, and the subsequent plaudits were deservedly plentiful. Frank felt it had been one of the great days of his life and, as the man who deserved the honours, he felt privileged to be there and to thank the school for its past contribution to present freedom. His own legacy is now a more prominent matter of pride for Bloomfield High. Frank died of a massive stroke in October 1998. From his estate, he willed a large and magnificent painting of 'The Bengal Lancer' to the school so that it could be displayed to remind succeeding generations of the part their forebears played in the war effort. It is also a tribute to a young man from New Jersey who left his role as storekeeper with the Hardware and Supply Company to bring another piece of hardware to life defending freedom as 'The Bengal Lancer'.

CHAPTER FIVE

Ace in a Day

The term 'ace' – indicating a pilot with five aerial victories or more – was coveted and sought by some. Others, not deliberately aspiring to the status, attained it in the 'normal' performance of their duties, while many pilots did the same duties but rarely saw the Luftwaffe. Their skills could have been the equal of an ace but the opportunity never prevailed. A few suddenly found themselves achieving acedom because circumstances and skills gave them the chance, and a few pilots even found themselves awarded the 'ace-in-a-day' accolade.

Enthusiastic public-relations personnel and the press often seized upon this title, and one pilot so dubbed did not desire the publicity for simply doing his duty but still found his exploits selected for such treatment. William R. Beyer became an 'ace in a day' and his 361FG newsletter *The Escorter* provides a contemporary capsule biography, polished by PR, dated 7 October 1944.

A picture for PR purposes – Bill Beyer (left) being interrogated about the combat by Capt Roy Webb. Note that Bill has his name stencilled on his 'Mae West' – so named because pilots, always imaginative on this topic, felt the inflated life jacket resembled the ample bust of the famous actress. *(Steve Gotts)*

The man of the hour here is a little five foot four and a half inch guy who hardly looks the type the movies would cast as a pilot but 'Little Bill Beyer' 1/Lt Air Corps is proof that all is not gold that is Hollywood. The Danville, Pa., 'Hot-Rock' recently carved for himself a notable slice of Luftwaffe, setting a mark unequalled in a single mission by any other Group pilot. He also has a previous victory in the air. The 125lbs of flier graduated from Danville High School and worked as a tool grinder in a hometown factory before enlisting in the Army on January 20 1942. He was an armorer and then a S/Sgt glider pilot until deciding that it'd be more interesting to fly something with an engine and guns attached. Taking flight instruction at Florida and Alabama airfields he won wings on November 3 1943. Silver bars recently replaced gold.

Good naturedly dubbed 'Bright Eyes' by his squadron mates, Lt Beyer's favorite pastime is playing accordion which is pretty big for him. He really gives out with the music and 'sends' himself, too. In civilian life his avocation was taxidermy. The well-liked by everybody airman is the 21 year old son of Mrs Lorraine Beyer of Danville. His sister Betty is a Sgt in the WAC, serving in the US.

There were genuine granules of truth in the PR release but they lacked depth and omitted several fascinating stories on Bill's journey to becoming a fighter pilot.

Born on 5 July 1923 in Danville, Pa., Bill came from a poor but honourable and hard-working family unfortunately lacking the resources necessary to support his further education. These were the years of the Depression and desperate efforts to hold national political stability under Roosevelt's New Deal as the country struggled for economical recovery. Attending a free vocational school in Williamsport, Bill soon demonstrated an innate talent for matters mechanical. However, continuing financial pressures forced him to decline the opportunity of a die-making apprenticeship with the potential of a lucrative career in manufacturing high-precision tooling. The need to support his mother meant finding a job, and young Bill was soon contributing a tool-grinder's wages to the family funds. Then Pearl Harbor deepened the world's turmoil and changed millions of lives, including Bill's.

In January 1942, two of Bill's buddies dropped by and asked him to join up with them. Bill left his job that day and thronged with hordes of young men crowding the US Army Air Corps recruiting centre. There were so many applicants that Bill slept on the floor while awaiting his turn. Processed through the preliminaries, he was soon on a bus to boot camp in Biloxi, Mississippi. Here Bill went through

what they called basic training – more like torture or see how much you can take. Up early every day – callisthenics . . . breakfast – more drill and exercises . . . We were pretty tough kids, having to rough it all our lives – no cars or bicycles and always walking to go ice skating or swimming in the river but, after a week in boot camp, our muscles were so sore we could hardly move.

After two months, things eased when Bill signed up for armament school and went to Denver, Colorado, where hospitality was heaped by local folks on the recruits in their midst.

For three months Bill was educated on the intricacies of the machine gun and his aptitude for mechanics saw him do well during the tests and achieve selection for a school in Brooklyn, New York. Here he studied the Sperry Gyroscope and the refinements of the Sperry gun sight plus turret installations on modern bombers. He passed 'with flying colours' and was then assigned to a B-24 group working up at Spokane. While there, Bill realised his diminutive stature and particular expertise on ball turrets portended a posting involving long, uncomfortable and dangerous hours in the small sphere.

Not being too enthused about that, I was walking around the post and noticed a billboard with some job openings. One was radio school and another was glider pilot training. Not really caring which one to try for, I had a penny in my pocket and heads I go to radio and tails to glider pilots. It turned up tails on the first toss . . .

Bill soon found himself sent to the staging centre for glider pilot training at Santa Anna, California, and thence to Clovis, New Mexico, for basic glider training which encompassed weather, aviation rules and regulations, then, more importantly, an introduction to flying in the delightful little Piper Cub. Bill took to this docile, single-engined high-wing monoplane like 'a duck to water' and soon went solo. By October 1942 he was at Wickenberg, Arizona, and airborne on silent wings for advanced glider pilot training. 'They had a few Switzer sailplanes so we had to take turns . . . The other times they had engine type Aeroncas without the engines. They had almost zero gliding characteristics that they seemed to drop like a rock.'

Having witnessed the successful use of gliders by German forces, the Allies were pressing forward with their own glider deployment plans, and Bill was soon swishing through the darkness seeking to descend on dimly lit smudge pot landing zones. He proved adept at this and proudly received his wings and Staff Sergeant rating on 18 December 1942. He then graduated to the 83ft 8in wing-spanned Waco CG-4A with a 48ft 3in fuselage capable of carrying fifteen troops. After four weeks of handling this challenge at Stuttgart, Arkansas, Bill learned that the army apparently had sufficient pilots and his class was to be discontinued and dispersed. He was given the option of navigator-bombardier training or becoming an aviation cadet for pilot tuition. His enthusiasm for being a pilot made the choice an obvious one, and he soon moved to Arcadia in Florida and the thrill of an open cockpit in the Boeing PT-17 biplane. Only later did he learn that the cessation of the glider pilot programme was rescinded, but by then, he was well advanced on his journey to be a fighter pilot.

Bill noted his thoughts on Arcadia:

The instructors were mostly civilian. The recruits stood in line and the instructors took turns walking and choosing the ones they would like to have. I was chosen by a Barnstormer by the name Tic Tyler. He was a short muscular person and an excellent pilot . . . the one person I can honestly say prepared me for aerial combat. He was so good with the plane and able to do any manoeuvres with ease. I think he took a liking to me because he taught

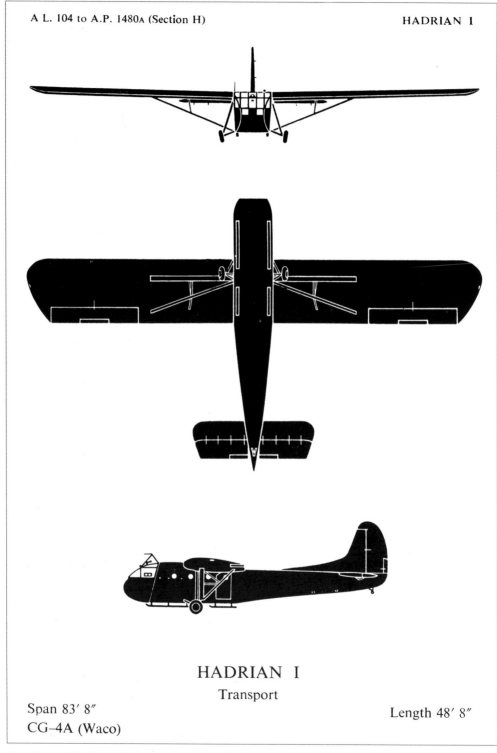

HADRIAN I

HADRIAN I

Transport

Span 83' 8"

CG–4A (Waco)

Length 48' 8"

The Waco CG-4A, or Hadrian in British parlance. Bill's experience piloting this large glider added to an accumulation of skills required in combat.

me more manoeuvres than anyone else and made me to feel at one with the plane. We had a contest to see who could land the closest the other side of a rope stretched between two trees in a field. Most everyone came close and when my turn came, I came in on the rope and saw I was going to be short but I kept on coming and [at] the last second gave it full throttle, pulled back on the stick and plopped down right on the other side of the rope. I won the contest and was awarded a small cigar clipper . . .

After being thoroughly taught by Tic Tyler, Bill had 'a good feel for flying' and moved on to the BT-13 at Gunter Field, Alabama, where he 'did well and learned a lot more technical material' before graduating from basic training and progressing to the advanced school at Napier Field, Dothan, Alabama, where he was

introduced to the AT-6. It was a good aerobatic plane and a lot nicer to fly . . . We also had a lot of link trainer experience. That was a small enclosed replica of a cockpit and you had to fly by instruments. It was really tricky until you learned how. They scheduled us for a night flight to several towns in Alabama. We had to fly by radio beams sent out from the towns. It was a dark night and we flew from a grassy field they had set up a control tower on. These were solo flights and being the first time it was a little apprehensive. I got to the third checkpoint and my radio went out. My adrenaline hit its peak and I had to figure out where the landing field was. I collected my thoughts and chose a heading I thought would take me back. Luckily it was the right heading because it wasn't too long until I saw the smudge pots and control tower. I made a pass by the tower and wagged my wings, indicating I had no communication and wanted to land. The next time I came around the tower gave me a green light indicating ok to land. I was at a landing attitude and mode so I cut the throttle and the plane very gently settled on the grassy ground like a whisper. O' my – the landing gear did not come down because of the power outage and I made the smoothest belly landing I ever made. The plane had no damage except a bent propeller and I wasn't reprimanded at all. That was one time when the glider training came in handy, having flown and landed them at night.

The training was thorough and good enough to have us graduate as single fighter pilots and send us on to be checked out in a fighter aircraft. I graduated Nov. 3 1943 and arrived Nov. 29 1943 at Page Field, Ft Meyer, Florida, to train in P-47 fighters. The P-47 was a big tough looking plane. No extra seat for an instructor in there . . . Lots of ground school before take off in this plane and we had to sit blind folded in the cockpit and point to each control and instrument before being allowed to take it off the ground.

On 5 February 1944 Bill was transferred to Dale Maby Field, also in Florida, where P-47 tutorage continued along with the opportunity for experience expansion on other types. Bill continues, 'By this time I had a lot of confidence and felt pretty cocky.' He would soon find this self-assurance challenged by the Curtiss P-40. Having checked on the basics of this famous fighter, Bill launched enthusiastically into the wild blue yonder and was soon cavorting among the clouds enjoying this new type. The next thing he knew, 'the plane had gotten into what they called a spin around the prop. Actually, the torque of the engine caused the plane to rotate and I had no control of it and we were headed straight toward the ground.' One day, in the not-too-distant future, this vertical descent would be deliberately replicated in combat, and then, as now, Bill did not panic. Drawing on the depth of training, he recalled the recovery procedure for such an alarming occurrence. Contrary to instinct, the solution was more power in order to regain control. Steeling his nerves, Bill advanced throttle and the P-40 howled out of the heavens, straight down. With the Floridian landscape fast approaching, a vestige of control returned and grew. With impact only seconds away, Bill regained enough control and, after curving dangerously close to the countryside, he levelled the P-40 out, an older, wiser airman. 'It was a good experience and let you know you are sitting on the edge at all times.'

On 14 February 1944, Bill was sent for embarkation and soon found himself in the darkness of a New York pier, shuffling up the gangplank of a troopship. 'Carrying all the gear we needed, we were sent to a small room filled with hammocks hung in rows. The ship was filled with these rooms and people.' Security and anti-submarine precautions saw them pulling out of port in total darkness. Conditions on board were primitive, and poor food – if eaten – tended not to stay eaten, with many sufferers from sea-sickness using their helmets as vomit buckets. Zig-zagging to avoid torpedoes added to the motion and extended their unhappy transit, but, on 25 March, Bill arrived in the UK, 'at night and everything was blacked out – you couldn't see your hand in front of you'. Bill found the British 'spoke with an accent and they had their own customs. Most got around on a bicycle with a tin cup hanging on back of the seat, because at tea time they stopped wherever and had tea.' A fond memory would be retained of their fish and chips, but he felt their culinary efforts with chicken made it taste bad. Overall, 'they were nice people and would give us fresh eggs and milk and provide entertainment for us'.

As with many newly arrived pilots, Bill was inducted into the intolerant wartime skies over the UK via the 495 Fighter Training Group at Atcham, far to the west of the main operational zone used by the Eighth Air Force. Early in April he journeyed eastwards to join the 376FS, 361FG at Bottisham on the outskirts of the university town of Cambridge. There were no cosy cloisters for these students in aerial warfare.

The enlisted men had Quonset huts to sleep in and the officers were given quarter in big old houses donated by the English. It was pretty crowded, we slept on cots and close enough to touch anyone. At one bed location, two pilots did not come back in a row so we put that bed off limits. Not much to do many days between missions so I went to London and bought an accordion I didn't know how to play and it's a wonder they didn't throw me out of the house. We had a few things of value to us and would designate them to go to [a] certain person if we got shot down . . . it seemed like every move I made I left behind any friends I had. Always new people to meet and get along with except when I started cadets, a person I got to know was Vic Bocquin and we stayed together and even ended up in the same fighter squadron, probably because of the closeness of our last names.

Bill joined the 361FG in April 1944 to fly the Thunderbolt. This example, E9-D 42-25969, was a P-47D-22-RE assigned to Capt. John D. Duncan and was one of very few NMF (Natural Metal Finish) examples used by the group before they converted to the Mustang. The nose banding was bright yellow. Drop tank is 108 US gallon of metal manufacture. *(Steve Gotts)*

Bill's initial tenure at Bottisham was brief because, in early May, he was sent to RAF Station Bircham Newton in Norfolk for 'the purpose of pursuing a one week course of Instruction in Air Sea Rescue Procedure'. One incident during this assignment still haunted him sixty years later. He was in his P-47 putting into practice some of these procedures close to the Dutch coast when he observed a tiny, yellow speck against the North Sea's dismal grey hue and descended to investigate. There, in isolation, the solitary figure of an airman could be seen sitting bolt upright in his dinghy but, strangely, offering no excited wave of recognition when Bill swept low overhead, not even a hint of relief at being found. Perturbed, Bill buzzed several times over this lonely, seemingly desolate individual without any gesture of recognition, not even an indication of awareness. Bill now assumed even more responsibility for this hapless soul, and, gaining altitude, he repeatedly called for support but was unable to raise anyone. He now considered the somewhat impetuous gesture of bailing out and swimming to rescue the downed flier. Climbing to a higher altitude, he readied himself to abandon the P-47 while continuing his radio appeals for assistance. Finally, and thankfully before a young man's foolhardiness overcame common sense, the ASR services acknowledged his call, and he gave them the position of his curious casualty. Perhaps the man was a German who felt that playing possum might be safer to avoid the risk of a strafing run by the US fighter. Years later, Bill wondered whether the outcome of this gesture by a 'young inexperienced fighter pilot' convinced he was 'invincible' might simply have resulted in him being shot by an ardent Nazi, or whether the casualty was simply another young boy fearful of being captured. His sojourn on ASR operations concluded without further excitement, and he returned to Station 374. His experiences on ASR 'spotter' sorties assisted in the development of what later became the 5th Emergency Rescue Squadron, a specialist USAAF unit equipped with specially adapted P-47s carrying smoke marker bombs and under wing dinghy packs. Research by the 5 ERS historian, Sid Harvey, indicates that the man in the dinghy was, as Bill suspected, a German survivor from a Messerschmitt 110 that had itself been shot down during the destruction of a B-17.

Now re-established with the 376FS, Bill had

one almost fatal experience in the P-47. On one escort mission, just as we reached enemy territory, my radio went dead. I had to indicate to the leader that I had no communication and had to return to base. I left the group and headed back to England by myself. The first airfield I saw was an English base and I decided to land there. I made my approach and before touch down I saw I might run out of runway so gave it full throttle and started to go around. My flying speed was almost gone and the prop pitch did not drop back to a take off pitch and I started to sink toward the ground. Out of runway and ahead of me was woods. It just happened there was like a gulley that dropped down between the hills. The P-47 was mushing out and I kept sinking but just able to keep from stalling out. Gradually I picked up enough speed to pull out of the gulley and gain enough altitude to make a landing pass, which I did and made this a good landing. Another close one but not the last.

We started going on bomber escort mission [then] strafing miscellaneous ground targets – trains, water towers, airfields, etc. I can remember waking up early in the morning to hear the sound of bombers taking off. They had to get in the air and in formation long before the fighters. We would then be woken up, taken to breakfast then off to the briefing room to be shown the mission for the day. Then off to the flight line and take off and assemble, to finally catch up with our wing of bombers before they got near enemy territory. The bombers were a sight to behold. They always flew high enough to draw vapour trails and with the large number of bombers on a mission it looked like they were laying down highways in the sky. What a brave and courageous bunch of guys when they had to fly through the dense flak blanket the Germans put up. A lot of them got many holes in them and many got shot down. We as a fighter escort would be able to move away from the flak and watch in awe of the bombers.

During June 1944, the 361FG were re-equipped with the P-51, and Bill later noted:

It was a more manoeuvrable plane and had a longer range to escort bombers deep into Germany and still be able to fight and return home. We checked out in the P-51 the same

June 1944 saw the P-47s depart and P-51s arrive. This is 44-13894, and the extended yellow nose became the hallmark of 361FG Mustangs. *(Steve Gotts)*

as the other fighters. Reading up on their characteristics and locating all controls and instruments. Blindfolded. The first flight up was a thrill. A fast spunky plane that shook like an old Model A Ford when on the ground.

A lot of close calls on this plane too. On an escort mission with wing tanks on we went with the bombers to their target and brought them almost home then took off on our own. There was low visibility so we opted to fly on our own. I called the radar station for a heading, which seemed OK. I flew quite a while and called in again and got the same heading. I flew and flew depending on their advice. Sometime later I barely heard a voice saying, 'Titus 3' – which was me – 'Turn around. Turn around, I gave you the wrong heading!' I was apparently out over the Atlantic ocean heading south west and would have run out of gas over the ocean. I turned around and flew back, emptying my wing tanks, dropping them and reaching my base before I ran out of gas . . . On a more favourable note, I was returning from a mission and over the English Channel when I saw an object in the water. I dropped down only to see some guy in the water surrounded by his parachute. I buzzed him several times and he almost leaped out of the water to show me his position I climbed directly above him and called air sea rescue and they got an immediate fix on him About a week later a call came to my base from this person I had located. He was so thankful and wanted to know what he could do for me. I didn't want anything but then thought of his 'chute so I said just send me a piece of your parachute which he did and I sent it home to my mother and she made something for my young sister Patty out of it.

We were sent out to dive bomb some German troop ships in a Dutch harbour. When we arrived there were about a dozen ships . . . Our squadron of 16 P-51s loaded with a 1000lb bomb each positioned ourselves about 15,000 feet for a bombing run. As each one went down to release their bombs, the entire decks of all the ships seemed to light up with some sort of gunfire, the muzzle flashes looked like little lights. As I watched, I thought, 'Hey – it's going to be your turn next.' As I went down it was like flying into a hornet's next. I dropped my bomb and with full throttle headed back up all the time seeing the tracers go by my wings . . .

Such background information and activities did not inspire the press – even Bill's first 'slice of Luftwaffe' failed to gain the status and PR propaganda of his later achievement. However, its impact was significant – a fact only established decades later by the American author and historian Donald L. Caldwell. The action occurred on Sunday, 17 September, when Bill's experience on gliders undoubtedly came to mind as the skies of Eastern England reverberated to the sound of aero engines. A vast armada of aircraft rumbled majestically east. No – not bombers; many of the aircraft made no contribution to the noise. The whisper of their presence was lost as they floated over the churches and fields on cables behind the fleet of troop carriers. Hundreds of gliders signified that Operation Market Garden – the audacious plan to capture three bridges, put a spear into the side of the enemy and shorten the war – was underway. The over-ambition, heroism and misfortunes surrounding that assault are superbly documented elsewhere. Fate might have placed Bill in one of these gliders, but his role was now their protection. For them to succeed, it was essential that the Luftwaffe was prevented from reaching the vulnerable transports and gliders, so fighters of the RAF, 8FC and 9FC were deployed in their defence.

At 1345 hours Beyer as Titus Blue Leader was leading a patrol from Hasselt in Holland over the German border to Wesel on the Rhine. Some 16,000ft below, the countryside looked peaceful, the details of battle and disputed borders partially hidden beneath a scattering of clouds whose gentle progress graced the death and carnage. Overhead, experienced pilots recognised a more sinister cloudscape, one ideal for an ambush. A layer of high altitude cirrus and surrounding haze above the Mustangs created conditions ideal for an ambush – a fact not lost on another pilot nearby, one with a black *Balkenkreuz* on his fuselage.

Receiving news of the massive Allied glider and paratroop operations, *Luftflotte* 3 headquarters mustered their forces to retaliate, but bad weather precluded full use of available resources. Only the famed *Jagdgeschwader* 26 got airborne from aerodromes nearer the landing zones, but they were determined to break through the cordon of Allied fighters.

Klaus Mietusch was the senior pilot with III/JG26, and with a formidable tally of victories already, he would today add to some seventy claims made in five years of combat over England, Malta and Russia and now in defence of the Reich. Mietusch had been hesitant earlier in his career, and his personality was not the confident cliché for the role; he was a more studious self-doubter who overcame his perceived failures and became a determined aerial killer. His technique was one of savage simplicity – get as close as you can and blast the enemy to pieces. His aircraft, the Me 109 with a Daimler Benz 605 engine plus a cannon and two machine guns, was very capable of doing so, and he was adept at handling it. This compensated for the generally superior performance of his adversaries, often the P-51 Mustang. No wise P-51 pilot ever took an Me 109 for granted, although the dilution of skills caused by the steady attrition of their enemy's core experience was now evident. Still only 25, Mietusch, with over 450 combat sorties, was now an 'old man' – one of the experts and a career officer in the Luftwaffe since 1938. He had seen the German Air Force through its glory days but recognised now that replacement pilots could not compensate for inadequate training and depleted fuel resources forced even further cutbacks. The legend of JG26, the yellow-nosed Me 109s of 'The Abbeville Kids' fame, would last in aviation history, but many of those boys were now dead, their expertise lost. His formation now comprised only fifteen machines, which he guided through a layer of cloud at 15,000ft, leading them like the ageing hunter of a doomed tribe. It was the old man who spotted their quarry, a squadron of Mustangs cruising with serene nonchalance just beneath the cloud. Mietusch could scarcely

Maj Klaus Mietusch – centre – Kommandeur of 3 Gruppe, Jagdgeschwader 26, was a hardened combat veteran with over 450 combat sorties to his credit. *(Steve Gotts)*

believe his luck, and, with cunning use of cloud cover, he stalked the enemy. Then, clicking on to transmit, he signalled his tribe, 'Otter Mietusch, I am attacking.'

Bill Beyer's Blue Flight was at the tail end of the 376FS and their patrol had already lasted some two hours, swinging back and forth between checkpoints with no hint of the Luftwaffe seeking to interfere with the airborne forces. The wingmen whose task it was to protect their tails had possibly been lulled by the Merlin's somnambulistic thrum. All that was about to change in a flash of violence. Beyer attributed divine intervention for causing him to glance astern at that precise moment, otherwise his entire flight could have been cut from the heavens.

Curving in behind the yellow-trimmed Mustangs, Mietusch might have registered their common colour code as he selected the rearmost American and opened fire. At that instant, the P-51s scattered like startled starlings, but it was too late for one, as cannon and machine-gun bullets from the German ripped it apart. The aircraft flown by Lt Woodrow W. Glover exploded in flames and went twisting earthwards in an agony from which there was no

Ambushed by JG26, the aircraft flown by Lt Woodrow W. Glover spun earthwards in flames. *(Steve Gotts)*

escape. Beyer's wingman also spun away as the US fighters reacted or died. Several suffered battle damage but returned somewhat chastened to Bottisham.

Whipping his P-51 through a violent 180-degree turn, Beyer swung head on into the enemy formation, and, even though they closed with a combined airspeed exceeding 800 mph, his mind registered some detail, as if in slow motion. Mere feet separated him from his would-be assassins and his brain registered the image of one German fighter pilot to his lower right. The man wore a long brown scarf and Bill felt instinctively that this was a 'very well dressed hot pilot'. Emerging unscathed behind the enemy, he hauled his Mustang aggressively through another 180-degree turn. Stung by being bounced so effectively, Bill wanted revenge and had his throttle to the wall in pursuit, but most of the Messerschmitts simply zoomed back up into the haze and vanished, leaving only one seemingly eager to fight. This, for Bill, was the culmination of all that training – from the Switzer to the Stearman; Tic's admonishments and imparted expertise; the P-40 incident and beyond. Bill now needed every vestige of his experience as he contorted the Mustang through a series of high-speed manoeuvres, as both he and the Me 109 pilot each sought a weakness, an opportunity to fire. This German was good. Bill Beyer, with not one victory, now faced a man with seventy-two.

Mietusch sensed talent in that Mustang and knew he, himself, was not invincible. His victories had been hard earned and, on ten occasions already, he had survived being shot down (see Chapter 1), returning a scarred and wiser man. He also knew his machine well and had a deep knowledge of its strengths and weaknesses against the more modern American design. He could outclimb the P-51 – it would outdive him; well handled, their rate of roll was comparable. Even though there was only four years' difference in age, this fight set self-confidence and youth against wily experience, as each now sought to outmatch, outguess and outgun the other. Circling like sharks, neither could get that decisively clear, zero-deflection shot. Mietusch tried several split-ess manoeuvres, diving and feinting a turn in one direction but splitting it part way through to roll out in the other, but the P-51 curved through, seemingly unperturbed, every time. On some occasions, the ace came tantalizingly close to an opportunity, but the American forced him to evade as this high-speed duel continued. Mietusch now tried a trick risky to himself but one that might put the American in front of his cannon.

Beyer felt sure he had his opponent. He closed in, fired, and then, suddenly, caught the deception, the danger to himself. Without any sign of airbrakes, flaps or wheels, the German had virtually stopped in mid-air. In moments, Bill would overshoot and present himself close in front of that vicious cannon – it could be a 20 or 30mm and would tear him apart. The German had chopped throttle deliberately, giving his opponent the briefest of opportunities to shoot but chancing the P-51 would miss, fail to realise in time, and skid past him. Mietusch almost had the Mustang – a few moments more – his finger poised over the trigger.

To Bill, it was like skidding on ice into an accident you could not avoid. He had caught on to the deception, but was it in time? Should he 'shoot and run' or try to stay behind his enemy? Deciding, his hands danced around the cockpit: throttle chopped, flaps down – he even dropped his undercarriage – anything to slow that remorseless slide into danger. If he overshot, he would most likely be killed in a storm of cannon fire. Kicking hard on the rudder pedals – a left–right shimmy – Bill skewed the P-51 from side to side, flat weaving and fishtailing; anything to avoid passing his opponent. The German's trick had given Bill no real time to aim, but neither did he slide past. Then, smoke surging from its engine, the Me 109 spurted away with Bill now hurriedly reversing every action to give chase and prevent the German seizing the initiative by curving fast around on to his tail. Three times this happened, intermingled with split-ess manoeuvres and other tricks using scattered cloud cover. On one occasion, the Mustang's propeller almost sawed into the Messerschmitt's tail. A series of dives mixed with these stop–start tactics, punishing g-force and a twisting horizon had wrestled them from 15,000ft to 1,000ft. Both were running out of sky; neither had caught an advantage. Now came a deadly form of Russian roulette.

Shoving the control column firmly forward and dropping flap, Mietusch put his fighter into a vertical dive, intending to cut it so fine that the American would realise too late and be unable to recover.

Bill saw the 109 dive away, and he nosed steeply down in pursuit; there was no horizon now, just solid earth. He lowered his flaps to hold the dive but avoid excessive speed and sensed this was the finale – a deadly, nerve-wracking dance, with death partnering both pilots. He recognised that losing his nerve and pulling up would give the German a chance. He would be slow, the German faster, able to get behind. Choosing to stay, he followed, as the ground grew relentlessly nearer, ready to absorb one or both – two brave young men duelling to destruction.

Judging his moment, Mietusch pulled out, aileroning through another split-ess and hoping the American would fail to recover or not guess the feinting turn of his own recovery.

Beyer was still diving but calculated the moment the Me 109 had to pull out and saw it rolling into a split-ess. He pulled back on the control column, and his Mustang swept so low over the landscape that Bill felt his wheels would have touched had they been down. He was less than 5ft up, but the P-51 responded sweetly, and he suddenly had a fleeting moment to catch the Me 109 if he could guess which way it would twist out of its split-ess as he followed through. It was now only 200yd at 40 degrees deflection, but worth a squirt. His Encounter Report shows 1,544 rounds fired. Some of these struck around the cockpit of the still turning Messerschmitt. Had it faltered? It continued turning, but the life force within seemed to have vanished. The nose of the 109 tilted earthwards for the last time and it struck the ground in a splash of dust and debris as it disintegrated.

Assuming the pilot to be dead but seeing no fire from the broken carcass below, Beyer was determined that this particular Messerschmitt would be of no further use to the fatherland, even as spares. Lining up on the wreckage, he strafed it until it caught fire. Only then did he climb and set course for home.

Klaus Mietusch was the posthumous recipient of Oak Leaves to a Knight's Cross, one of the highest awards for a German fighter pilot. In the grimly brutal statistics of air combat, his death had undoubtedly saved the lives of other Allied airmen. Bill Beyer would soon contribute further to the erosion of the Luftwaffe, but the impression of his opponent's skill and courage that day stayed with the American. Himself of German descent, Bill felt 'full honors and respect for Major Klaus Mietusch' when he learned of his opponent's identity.

The aircraft flown by Beyer that day was a P-51D, serial 44-13872, and carried the 376FS squadron fuselage code E9-J. Two days later this machine was assigned to 2/Lt Robert C. Clement for another operation supporting the increasingly beleaguered troops at Arnhem. As the 376FS returned during the early evening of 19 September, they encountered adverse weather conditions after crossing in over the English coast. Clement was flying number three in a five-ship element when his leader ordered an instrument letdown from 6,000ft through the overcast beneath which Bottisham was now hidden. As the formation descended, Clement was evidently in trouble and struggling to hold his slot in the formation. With E9-J wobbling erratically, Clement's wingman became increasingly perturbed and finally pulled away from to descend on his own. The squadron emerged at 700ft over Newmarket, and the leader radioed for the missing Clement but received no reply. Observers saw a single Mustang appear out of the clouds diving at 45 degrees, but, strangely, the fighter made no attempt at

The unfortunate Bob Clement. The interior of his A-14 green rubber mask can be clearly seen. Oxygen was essential for survival at high altitude and the mask was worn for long periods. An expiratory flapper valve shut on inhalation of oxygen and opened on exhalation. The whistle attached to his collar was for attracting attention after ditching or being injured and immobilised after a parachute descent. The AM and crown denote British Air Ministry issue. *(Steve Gotts)*

recovery and continued its steep descent until it exploded on impact some two miles east of Newmarket. Clement's body was found amid the wreckage.

Fifty-four years later, members of the EAARG investigated the site. Wartime pictures provided by the 361FG historian Steve Gotts showed a broken Merlin resting upright in a shallow crater with two bent machines guns and a propeller blade on the surface nearby. A 1998 detector survey of the site indicated wreckage still extant, and preliminary excavations revealed the propeller boss only 14in down. A full team effort was arranged for 19 September 1998, exactly fifty-four years to the day.

Digging through the light, sandy soil proved relatively easy, although soil acidity had adversely affected the aluminium, resulting in a lot of blue corrosion. Digging deeper rewarded the team with some components in better condition, including the top of the control column and other pieces from the cockpit. Further down they uncovered the remains of the engine seen in the wartime pictures and deduced that those in charge of the original recovery had simply pushed the broken Merlin on to its side, to keep it below plough depth, and had then thrown in other pieces, including the guns, before filling in the crater. The EAARG found some personal reminders of the pilot, including one of his dog-tags, the remains of his goggles and his oxygen mask. Not only would items displayed from this recovery record the fate of the unfortunate Clement, but the guns in particular recalled the combat between the veteran Klaus Mietusch and the beginner, Little Bill Beyer.

A rusting machine gun recovered on 19 September 1998 amid wreckage found near Cheveley from Clement's 376FS P-51D 44-13872, E9-J. *(Steve Gotts)*

Bright Eyes' next engagement with the Luftwaffe was in Mustang E9-Y, serial 44-14042, a machine normally assigned to Lt J.D. Smith, but Bill put his borrowed mount to very effective use, as his Encounter Report reveals:

Combat. 27 September 1944. 376 Fighter Squadron. 1015. Vicinity Eisenach. 5/10 cumulus to 5000 feet. [visibility] Air to air good. Air to ground good. FW 190's. Five FW 190's destroyed.

I was leading Titus Red Flight on an escort mission to Kassel. We were sweeping back and forth under the bombers when they were attacked. I saw about 40 enemy aircraft as they broke through the bombers and headed for the deck, so I told my flight to drop their tanks. I picked a gaggle of about 8 FW 190s and attacked them from above and to the rear. I lined up with the last one and opened fire at about 400 yards closing to about 100 yards. I got hits all over the fuselage and wings knocking pieces off and he started smoking then he ducked into the cloud layer. I throttled back to see what he was going to do and he came back up so I opened fire again getting more hits. He jettisoned his canopy and disappeared into cloud in a spiral to the right. I made a 360-degree turn to the right above clouds and told my flight I was going through the cloud layer. As I broke through I saw his parachute off to my right. I then flew up to a little town where I saw another FW 190. By then I only had my wingman [Lt Robert W. Myers] with me. I got on the 190's tail and he did his best to lose me, doing split esses and tight turns. I had the K-14 gun sight so I could see I shouldn't shoot while we were turning because the reticule disappeared with too tight a turn. I followed him through all his manoeuvres until he started to climb. I opened fire on him [from] about 100 yards getting hits. He jettisoned his canopy and bailed out. I made a turn to the right and took pictures of the crash and also watched the pilot float to the ground. I pulled up to 1,000 feet and spotted another one and made a pass at him giving him a short burst and he immediately jettisoned his canopy and bailed out. I followed him down and took a picture of the crash. While I was chasing this one, my wingman, Titus Red Two, saw one that passed underneath him and he followed it getting hits on it. I then saw another FW 190 and gave chase. I got on his tail and he gave me a good ride for a while. This one chopped his throttle and threw down flaps to make me overshoot, but I saw what he had done and I did the same. I had to fish tail to keep from over-running him. He pulled up in a gentle turn to the left and I opened fire, getting hits on fuselage and wings. He also jettisoned his canopy and bailed out while I was still firing. I followed his plane down and got pictures of the crash. While I was chasing this plane Titus White Four had joined me. When another 190 made a pass at me, Titus White Four, Lt Robert R. Volkman, got on his tail and before he could open fire this pilot bailed out. I was flying south after I shot the fourth one down and saw another 190 approaching me from the south. I immediately pulled up into a steep climb and did a wing over coming down on his tail. He went into a turn to the left pulling heavy streamers. I had to put flaps down to keep inside of him. The reticule had disappeared, but I gave him a couple of bursts to scare him. He broke for the deck and really chewed the grass with his prop. I took several shots at him but I got in his prop wash and he was skidding from side to side.

We almost hit a tree, then he lead [sic] me towards some power lines. I saw the pole sticking up so I pulled up over them in a crab so I could keep him in sight and he went under the wire. I came down behind him again right on the deck and opened fire at about 75 yards. I saw hits around [the] engine and it was on fire. He went on into the ground and crashed into a house and blew up. I didn't think I got a picture of him blowing up because I could see he was going to hit the house and I was too close behind him to follow any further. I was then out of ammunition so I flew cover for Titus White Four. The enemy wasn't any too eager when he found out that his attacker could stay on his tail so most of them bailed out. I claim 5 FW 190s destroyed. The fight took place around Eisenach about 1015 to 1045. 1,713 rounds expended. Aircraft E9Y 44-14042. William R Beyer. 1st Lt Air Corps.

It is clear that Bill had learnt from his encounter with Mietusch and employed the lessons to his advantage, but the background to his most recent battle was far from favourable to the Eighth Air Force. That day, the 361FG were part of a relay of fighters covering over 300 Liberators of the Second Air Division attacking the Henschel engine and vehicle factory at Kassel in central Germany. Maj Roswell Freedman commanded forty-five Mustangs from Bottisham and they rendezvoused with the bombers as planned, but thereafter things went awry. The mission was led by the 445BG, and a navigational error by the Tibenham-based bombers after the Initial Point was compounded by another error that took them further from the main force, stretching the resources of the fighter escort and exposing the 445BG formation to attack.

Taking advantage of the situation, *Sturmgruppen* JG3, with their heavily armoured FW 190s, virtually annihilated the Liberators when they caught them adrift from the main bomber force. Effectively employing tactics developed for a Sturmgruppen assault, the FW 190s closed in on the bombers and used their standard armament plus two additional wing-mounted 30mm cannon. Their role was to charge the bombers, trust to the protection of their armour as they closed in, and then fire in unison on the bomber formation like a battery of field artillery. It typically took only three strikes from the Rheinmetall-Borsig MK108 30mm cannon to destroy a heavy bomber, and, provided the *Begleitgruppen*, their lighter, more manoeuvrable fighter escort, kept the US fighters at bay, the *Sturmgruppen* assault would be devastating. This proved so for the hapless 445BG who suffered the highest loss for any individual group on a single mission when twenty-five of their aircraft were shot down. Had it not been for the 361FG hearing their frantic appeals for help, the entire 445BG might have been massacred. As well as Bill's contribution, his squadron commander, Lt Victor E. Bocquin, accounted for three, and other 376FS members took the total to eighteen, then a record on a single mission. The 361FG lost one of their number: Lt Leo H. Lamb died when his Mustang was rammed by an enemy fighter and crashed near Gotha. As mentioned by Bill, he was assisted by the K-14, a precision-made, gyro-computing gun sight that undertook the calculations required for deflection shooting. This technology helped US fighter superiority as the K-14 became increasingly available. However, opportunities became scarce and more sporadic as the depleted Luftwaffe sought to husband resources; fighting only when it felt it had the advantage as it sought to stem the inevitable implosion of Hitler's Third Reich.

Another killer for combat aircrew operating in unpressurised aircraft at such high altitude was anoxia – oxygen starvation. This could be fatal, because the pilot would simply fall asleep and either he never woke up or his aircraft fell out of control and it was too late when the pilot came round at a lower altitude. Bill had a close encounter with this demon.

I was in the top flight at 30,000 feet covering the bombers at around 20,000 feet. We were above and behind the bombers. The next thing I knew I was thirty feet under a bomber and he was on his bombing run with the bomb doors open. Unknown to me, the oxygen hose popped out of its fitting leaving me with no oxygen. Now these planes don't fly by themselves, it was difficult to even use trim tabs over any length of time, my plane had to descend and catch up with the bombers without any action on my part. It should have turned over and spun into the ground. I have to Thank my Angel for this one for sure . . .

Bill's next victory occurred over a month later on 2 November, when he claimed another FW 190 while leading Yorkshire squadron on a mission to Merseburg. Responding to a radio appeal for help further back, Bill reversed direction and went after enemy fighters attacking the last box of bombers. Too late to prevent the attack, the 361FG pursued the enemy to the deck. Skilful use of cloud cover by the fleeing Germans handicapped the hunt, and Bill lost his first target, but caught another as it emerged from concealment. This FW 190 tried to entrap his pursuer by leading Bill low over a large town where German anti-aircraft guns had target practice. Still clinging to the wake of his opponent, Bill then found himself drawn over

Triumphant trio. After shooting down an FW 190 on 2 November 1944, Bill Beyer is pictured with the men who helped him achieve victory. Left, S/Sgt James H. Williams, crew chief and Sgt Henry S. Wiechers, assistant crew chief. Aircraft 44-14144, E9-N. *(Steve Gotts)*

an airfield he identified as 'Erfurt Bindersleben'. At 1,000ft, he again presented the defences with a prime target but refused to give up the chase. To the dismay of his enemy, the P-51 swept through unscathed and closed in on the FW 190 near the aerodrome's edge. Opening fire at 400yd, Bill registered numerous hits and continued doing so until forced to break away with only 25ft of altitude left. As he pulled up, the Focke Wulf crashed and exploded.

His encounter was mirrored many times that day during the strongest response from the Luftwaffe since September. In bitter combat, forty bombers were lost, although US claims totalled 102 aerial kills with a further 26 aircraft destroyed during strafing attacks. American action and air superiority continued to abrade their adversaries, and it was almost a month before Little Bill's last encounter during what would be his group's highest-ever tally.

26 November saw the 361FG again providing escort to Second Air Division Liberators, and Bill was leading Red Flight just above and in advance of the bombers as they droned steadily towards their Initial Point. At 1210, the Mustangs met a gaggle of some 150 Me 109s and FW 190s coming straight at them. This was simply the first of three such waves, and efforts by the 361FG to turn and take advantage up-sun were too late. The first wave broke on the climbing Mustangs. Realising the situation, Bill swung defiantly to meet the enemy. He could see the flash of their cannon, but, as they swept past, all the Mustangs emerged unharmed. Allowing the last of the wave to roll over them, the Mustangs swung about in pursuit, with Bill selecting the nearest FW 190. The German curved through a neat split-ess but Bill followed cleanly through, then, inexplicably, the German pulled up into a loop. This is a fine manoeuvre for an air display or even an afternoon's fun, but its soaring, upwardly slow predictability invited unpleasantness in a combat scenario and Bill promptly obliged. Relying on his wingman to protect him through the process, Bill followed suit, firing accurately all the way up – over – and down. Instead of concluding his performance by pulling out, the FW 190, streaming smoke, continued straight down and exploded on impact. Had they not been so busy, Bill's Red Flight might have applauded, but their leader had seen a lonely Me 109 and leapt away to engage it. Within only two turns, Little Bill was on its tail and firing. A sparkle of strikes flashed around the cockpit and the Messerschmitt rolled over, its cockpit canopy detached, and Bill expected the pilot to follow, but the German surprised him by seeking to dive away, hoping his ruse would gain time to escape. Another accurate stab from Bill's guns forced one final, almost lazy, split-ess but no further effort at evasion as the Me 109 dove into the ground and exploded. Red Flight witnessed both Bill's victories, and, climbing back towards the bombers, they were bounced by another FW 190, who paid dearly for his audacity when Red Three, Lt Claude Hanley Jr, clobbered him. This added to victories by other Red Flight members, Lts Delmar R. Ford and Kenneth J. Scott – a contribution of five towards the 361FG total of twenty-three, including two gained in an amazing feat of flying from Lt George R. Vanden Heuvel. With his guns malfunctioning and under attack from FW 190s, 'Van' found himself sandwiched between two German fighters bearing in from opposite sides. Judging his moment, he flicked his Mustang aside and was astounded to see the enemy aircraft collide head-on and explode.

Bill Beyer landed at Little Walden, the group's new home, with nine victories to his credit, making him the second highest scorer in the 361FG but their only 'ace-in-a-day'. His last mission on 2 December 1944 was to lead fifty-two Mustangs on an escort to Bingen marshalling yards. Later that month, 'Bright Eyes' bade farewell to the 361FG and went home. After a period of leave, he flew heavily armoured P-39s acting as targets for bombers who fired rubber projectiles that registered hits on the Airacobras. He visited an old girlfriend in Arkansas and was married two weeks later – three children and six grandchildren followed. After leaving the USAAF, Bill attended university, then went into business for the next forty years. He eschews the glamour often associated with fighter pilots. 'I am just an ordinary person who lives for his family, loves the Lord and tries to live accordingly.'

This modest hero played his part on a stage set amid the heavens where an epic drama saw some players brutally written out in vicious combat between young men struggling to do their duty. Bill was one of the lucky ones – he earned his return to Danville and the things in life denied to so many. He also helped gift freedom to the nations over whose terrain his Mustang once flashed silver.

CHAPTER SIX

Sweating it out

'Sweating it out' was aviation parlance for simply waiting, an anxious spectator, or for working through a situation yourself – often one laced with fear and trepidation. A fighter pilot, perhaps with his engine running rough, would 'sweat it out' as he chugged the lonely, long and desperate distance over an icy sea, his heart skipping a beat every time his motor did likewise. On his home base, worried ground crew also 'sweated it out' – waiting for their aircraft and pilot to return. On bomber airfields, there was the same experience as a hardstand stood empty, the last straggler not yet home. 'Sweating it out' might turn into a joyous reunion, a funeral pyre or the chilling reality of Missing In Action – you just never knew.

Eugene F. Britton in his P-51B-10-NA 42-106611, CV-K, with crew chief Charles Bosken. *(E.F. Britton)*

```
St. Engines  0746 Take Off 0756 Insignia _____ __
SET COURSE    0821              ALTITUDE  10,000
```

TO	MILES	CC	ETA	ALTITUDE
Enc Coast	38	124	0830	12,700
I/P	95	124	0851	19,000
R/V	65	128	0903	22,000
Escort			1109	A-Apeldoorn
Enc Coast	83	318	1131	B-Munster
Base	42	319	1142	C-Kassel
				D-Giessen
				E-Maastricht
				F-Dusseldorf
				G-Koln
				P-Frankfurt

Typical mission information given to fighter pilots. *(E.F. Britton)*

One P-51 pilot found himself 'sweating it out' twice in one dramatic day during the most emotional mission he ever experienced. That day, 10 November 1944, 1st Lt Eugene F. Britton was airborne supporting a 'maximum effort' required from his 359FG. This meant everything capable of an escort combat mission was aloft from East Wretham. Gene found himself leading a somewhat irregular Black Flight comprising three Mustangs acting as high cover for the high cover group. Unfortunately, a Mustang in one of the regular flights reported a loss in oil pressure and aborted. Complying with standard operational procedure, Gene dispatched one of his flight to fill the slot. Within minutes, a similar occurrence found Gene as Black Flight leader with no flight to lead and his role as top cover put him alone, high over Germany – an 'extraordinary situation' that gave the lone aviator an unparalleled view. With his Merlin 'breathing hard' in the rarified atmosphere, Gene observed the vast panorama of sky and the long phalanx of bombers with fighters weaving in escort. It was like 'watching a movie of World War II'.

Not only was Gene the highest in the 359FG; he was also the last man over the target and witnessed events below as bombers wounded by flak slid inexorably from formation. A heavy overcast silhouetted the B-17s as they concentrated on radar, controlling the release of their ordnance on Butzweilerhof and Ostheim airfields near Cologne. The cloud lay like a giant quilt across which crawled small, dark silhouetted shapes of heavy bombers surrounded by black bursts of flak – brief, ugly flowers on the silken white brilliance, expanding and evaporating as they drifted astern of the formation. Unless a direct hit tore a bomber from formation in a smear of grotesque crimson and an even larger black stain in the heavens, these flowers seemed innocuous; the death and chaos from countless shards of shrapnel were evident only when one of the majestic Fortresses faltered and fell away from the protection of its

'A heavy overcast silhouetted the B-17s . . .'. A scene typical in the skies over Germany during 1944.

peers. Gene saw several, clearly struggling as the main battle force moved inexorably away, unable to help unless there were sufficient spare fighters.

Gene was still holding his lofty vantage point to the rear of the 359FG when they were released from escort and flew home to record an 'uneventful escort'. Gene would soon think differently as he turned back to see how the stragglers were coping. The sky, so recently congested, now seemed strangely empty, but then Gene spotted a lone B-17, a vulnerable straggler alone and 'sweating out' a slow journey home. The Fortress had 'taken a lot of flak', but, like any wounded animal, could be dangerous to approach. Gene knew the B-17 crew would be ready for a fight, and any fighter that approached would be treated with suspicion. All guns that could be brought to bear were pointing right at him as he closed in. One false move on his part could have been disastrous, so he angled his P-51 for the least hostile, maximum recognition line of approach. He could almost feel the relief on board as the approaching fighter proved friendly.

Gene looked over at the B-17, the proverbial airborne sieve. Two engines on the starboard side were out, with possibly one on the port side pulling inadequate power. As he nudged nearer, he clearly saw the first of several notes appearing in the window behind the pilot, 'NO RADIO . . . NO INSTRUMENTS . . .WHICH WAY?' A crewman appeared, tapping his headset and shaking his head slowly from side to side. Gene's heart went out for the souls on that stricken B-17. He was their only hope, their guide and guardian angel. He had no alternative but to sweat it out with them. They obviously had no idea which way to fly for home, and the steady deterioration in altitude made doubtful any chance of success, but the crew were clearly determined to get as close as possible and at least reach friendly territory.

Gene radioed for a heading to the nearest Allied airfield and signalled for the crippled bomber to follow as he reduced power and slid alongside. To his amazement, the pilot of that big bomber now flew like a P-51 wingman. At 19 Gene felt like any other 'hot' P-51 pilot, but his counterpart in that battle-torn bomber now performed a superb feat of airmanship as he suckled nearer Gene's Mustang. Further messages were relayed from the cockpit and waist windows giving Gene a clearer image of their predicament: radio out, instruments useless and barely one good motor.

Lacking power, the bomber could not maintain altitude, and the layer of overcast looming closer spelled trouble. Gene would have to risk a collision and keep it visual or the bomber crew would emerge with no idea where to go. Without vital instruments, the B-17 needed him as a stable, visual reference point, and Gene concentrated as never before on holding formation. Nearer the cloud tops now, they were tripping on patches of turbulence causing the giant wingtip to undulate between his own starboard wing and tail plane. Gene's fear and admiration grew almost in proportion. The man controlling the badly injured Boeing 'must

Taken by Eugene using a small Brownie camera he carried on a mission over Mersberg, 368FS aircraft in finger four formation. 'Betty Louise', 44-14652 CV-L, is nearest camera. 44-14500 'Griffin' (?) is next. Rudder markings were yellow, the anti-glare panels in front of the cockpit black and the cowlings bright green. *(E.F. Britton)*

have been one hell of a pilot'. Gene was accustomed to holding close formation when they ascended or descended through cloud but not with a 103ft-wingspanned cripple. The B-17 was running with maybe only one third of its power, and its pilot kept stability with a combination of consummate skill, brute strength and sheer, courageous will power.

The tendrils of cloud scudded beneath the aircraft as they surfed for as long as possible, but then the blue disappeared and the two aircraft sank into the darkening overcast. Gene held steadier than ever before, his wing stretching a metaphorical hand to comfort the bomber. Concentrating on his instruments, he resisted the temptation to look at that vast silver aerofoil 'flopping up and down' between his own wing and tail. If he succumbed to vertigo, they would all most likely perish. He would never be able to forgive himself if he spun clear: he might recover, but the bomber would stand no chance. Down, down, deeper and deeper into an unending grey void. Gene was exhausted. Then the hue of grey altered, the tone changed and, at last, mother earth appeared, fine and level as the final feathery tentacles released the companions.

They were clear, but the 'grim news' was their rate of descent. The bomber clearly had little time left. He now made radio contact with 'Banana Control', and requested landing instructions. Far from the soft-toned sympathy Gene had expected, the voice at the airbase told him 'in no uncertain terms' that under no circumstances would that 'wreck flying off my wing' be allowed to crash-land on *his* field. Gene later discovered that it was a 'primary supply field' with C-47s landing and taking off continuously. With only one runway open, they understandably did not dare to jeopardize supplies for the advancing army and risk closing the field with a 'beat-up' B-17 on its belly blocking the runway.

Gene was angry and frustrated, but, by means of hand signals, he conveyed the bad news to his companion. He signalled that he could do no more. The airfield had 'no room at the inn', and the ailing Fortress was now too weak to go elsewhere. The landscape offered no suitable sanctuary, and Gene watched helplessly as a crash seemed inevitable. How tragic to have helped them live this long only now for the plane to explode and burn.

Then Gene spotted a field, larger than the others, more suitable if only the B-17 could drag its weary self that extra distance. He pointed, but the B-17 was already on to it, slewing its nose to align with the open land. No doubt his crew were at crash stations. The B-17 pilot gave Gene a final salute and turned to concentrate on the task of belly landing his bomber.

Gene had done all he could. Even now he would not leave his 'big friend'. It was only moral support, but Gene held the P-51 alongside, right down to the ground. In fact, damn nearly into the ground. So intent was Gene on the B-17 that he almost scraped his Mustang in alongside. The Fortress hit and vanished in a slithering cloud of dust and debris as Gene pulled his P-51 up and banked steeply round to survey the wreck. At first he saw only a plume of dust. Thankfully, no fire. Curving round again, he could see the broken bomber more clearly as the dust settled. Had anyone survived? Then figures emerged. One... two . . . three . . . then more – waving at him! Gene was jubilant. Soon nine dishevelled airmen stood waving their thanks to this little friend.

So excited by their survival was Gene that he almost forgot his own predicament. Fuel. Sweating in the B-17 had taken so much gasoline, he himself could not reach home. The

B-17 had crash-landed close to the airfield at Le Coutet, and Gene now headed for it to land and refuel. Things were very busy, and it was some time before the wandering Mustang was refuelled and ready, so Gene was late returning to England and now began 'sweating it out' for himself. He was in a single-engined aircraft over an inky black sea with nightfall approaching. Nearing the coastline of Suffolk, he faced additional worries and grew increasingly apprehensive about the welcome reception he would receive from British anti-aircraft defences. 'They were known to be quite jumpy about any aircraft coming into their area.' Gene had his IFF (identification friend or foe) on, but even this had failed to prevent incidents of mistaken identity, sometimes with tragic consequences. Judging from the dark landmass and the curve of the Rivers Stour and Orwell below, he was south of Ipswich.

Suddenly a searchlight stabbed skywards. Gene flinched, but, instead of the accompanying blast of an AA barrage, the single column rotated as if beckoning, then laid itself on a heading for East Wretham. How did they know? His IFF would say 'friend' but not say which friend. As he appreciatively followed the friendly beam, he was amazed when another one picked him up and then laid almost horizontally, continuing to mark his course. In this manner, Gene found that, far from sweating out that last few miles, there seemed to be a remarkable level of coordination that shepherded him homewards until he was within range of East Wretham. At this point, the searchlights were extinguished, allowing him to discern

The unconventional control tower at East Wretham, Station 133. Eugene was very pleased to get home after sweating out the return from his fifty-fifth mission. The checkerboard truck – right – was a runway control vehicle and has the perspex nose piece from a B-17 as its observation dome. (C. Baldridge)

the airfield's outer circle of lights, which curved towards the runway, guiding him to the lead-in lights and thence to the outer funnel. Once in the funnel, he eased steadily earthwards until he could see the illuminated totem poles positioned either side of the runway. As he settled on his final approach, a flare went up that burst with such brilliance that the entire field was illuminated. A touch on the controls, and his Mustang was almost there. Unfortunately, the flare now went out and the all-enveloping darkness was unnerving because his night vision had been lost. Gene now had to grope blindly through the last 50ft. Any misjudgement could see his Mustang crunch in at more than 100 mph, shearing off the wheels and making his arrival an undignified slide on the fighter's belly. If he dropped a wing, it would be worse – much worse, and thoughts of a cart-wheel and explosion ensured Gene literally 'sweated out' that last 50ft for himself. The cold clammy sweat of fear gripped him as he felt for the runway; the world seemed to have vanished – where was it? Then the wheels thudded solidly onto terra firma and, while it might not have been the prettiest landing of his career, the touch-down from his fifty-fifth mission was one of the most reassuring.

He never identified the crew of that B-17, although a chance meeting with former Fortress waist gunner some years later led to them swapping war stories, and the man told his own tales of a P-51 that 'sweated it out' with them as they crash-landed on the Continent.

CHAPTER SEVEN

A New Experience

Slightly embarrassed with the VIP status accorded to him by these British enthusiasts, the elderly veteran picked a careful progress along the edge of the ditch. To record this new experience on Bedingfield Hall Farm, Suffolk, England, a portrait-format Yashica guaranteed quality of detail in whatever images took his fancy. Fit for his age, he had nevertheless to concede that his camera rested on a somewhat portlier frame than that of the young man whose arrival here had been so dramatically different over four decades earlier. A strange idea occurred, perhaps the basis of a novel? What if he had not parachuted clear, and this was his spectre observing the recovery of his own mortal remains from the long-buried

Cyril T. 'Tom' Bendorf, 84
Fighter Squadron, 78 Fighter
Group, Duxford, 1944–5.
(Tom Bendorf)

fighter. What if his life had actually ended here? His work as a lawyer, his children – some older now than he had been then; his home in Turton, South Dakota: what if none of that existed and his name was inscribed on the Wall of the Missing, like so many of his lost comrades? There were over 5,000 names on that wall in the US Military Cemetery near Cambridge, and Cyril T. Bendorf, 84th Fighter Squadron, 78th Fighter Group, could so easily have been one of them.

In 1944–5, 'Tom' Bendorf had been part of an elite band of men flying fighters from their base at Duxford, nowadays home to the Imperial War Museum. Tom had already donated to the IWM his leather A-2 jacket and white silk scarf so symbolic of a fighter pilot's derring-do. In reality, those scarves were not for glamour but provided comfort and avoided the chafing from a tightly fitting collar. Duelling in the heavens was not derring-do but an assassin's dance demanding vigilance for survival. Constantly alert, swivelling his head, a fighter pilot needed to scan all sectors of the sky every few moments, given that an aircraft and its pilot could be destroyed in less than a second.

Tom hoped events today, 26 August 1989, would see additional exhibits emerge from the aircraft he had abandoned forty-four years earlier. He was fascinated by the fervour shown by these young aviation archaeologists, none of whom had been born when his plane went down. I, like the others involved, was delighted Tom had made the journey and shared the same anxiety regarding the existence of enough wreckage to make his travels worthwhile. David Wade of the East Anglian Aviation Research Group had first located evidence of the lost machine and obtained strong readings on his Fisher detector. Having traced Tom, David encouraged the former fighter pilot to attend the anticipated recovery for what we hoped would be an exciting new experience, but David's apprehension was palpable as the bright yellow JCB backhoe snorted and rattled into position. Away from the noise, I pressed Tom to describe how his fighter had fallen and so nearly reclassified him into grimmer wartime statistics.

On 4 January 1945, Tom was transitioning from his fondly regarded P-47 Thunderbolt to its sleeker alternative, the North American P-51 Mustang – in his case, a brand-new D-20 variant, serial number 44-68206, made by North American in their Inglewood, California, factory. Following its arrival at Duxford, the aircraft had been examined technically by ground personnel then allocated to Tom for a 'shakedown' flight including an altitude test and gun check. It had already been identified by the 84th Fighter Squadron code, WZ-P, as well as acquiring the distinctive black-and-white chequerboard on its cowling, a bold advertisement for its 78th FG credentials. Despite conceding the new fighter's graceful appearance, Tom still preferred the portly P-47 and had flown over 200 hours in Republic's robust machine. However, 8th AF High Command decreed standardisation on the P-51, and the personal preferences of a junior birdman counted for nought, so Tom's sortie today would be to break in his new mount. His P-51 debut the previous day had given him a 90-minute taster in another machine, but today Tom would evaluate this new aircraft. He began with a careful visual inspection following the guidelines set out in the pilot's handbook he had been studying. This began with a cockpit check confirming the ignition and battery switches were off, trim tabs were neutrally positioned and his flap settings corresponded visually. A few

Mustangs undergoing maintenance in one of the First World War hangars at Duxford. The 'Endurance' message refers to pre-war occupancy by Gloster Gauntlet biplane fighters of 19 Squadron RAF. Like their British predecessors, the 78FG adopted bold markings using a black-and-white checkerboard scheme.

further points were noted before Tom dropped from the port wing to walk around his machine checking security of all access panels, tyres for wear or creep, undercarriage strut pressures, that the pitot cover was removed and so on, until he returned to the starting point and climbed into the still unfamiliar cockpit.

Settling into his seat, Tom further regretted the loss of his roomier P-47 as the Mustang's cockpit rim squeezed closer to his shoulders, but, having no choice, he continued to try to transfer his loyalty, as had many other Eighth Air Force fighter pilots. The 78th was the last but one to hold on to the Thunderbolt, and its conversion left only the famous 56th Fighter Group still clinging doggedly to its beloved P-47s. Tom had to concede that the Mustang's speed and manoeuvrability had seen P-51s dominate the skies, and its remarkable range had arguably saved the daylight bomber offensive. Unleashed from close escort, Mustangs had also taken the fight into Goering's back yard, where young Americans challenged their

German counterparts in a machine the equal of Germany's best piston-engined fighters. Today, Tom would wring a bit more from this thoroughbred and see how it had earned its reputation. Flicking on the battery switch, he instilled the first indications of life into the inert airframe. The 24-volt electrical system operated instruments, interior and exterior lighting, his radio, guns and gunsight, plus supporting aspects of the engine management system. It had been the introduction of the British-designed Merlin engine to the North American fighter that had produced, according to some, a marriage made in heaven for fighter technology. Utilisation of American manufacturing resources to produce the Packard-built variant ensured capacity matched demand. Satisfied, Tom turned off the battery to rely on the ground starter unit that was plugged in to avoid draining battery power when the Merlin fired up. Selecting the fuel tanks, he then set the engine controls. First nudging the throttle open an inch, he chose, 'idle cut off' and adjusted the propeller speed control for the big, paddle-bladed Hamilton Hydromatic constant speed airscrew to fully forward. Yesterday's initiation had introduced some familiarity, as he confirmed settings for the radiator shutter, oil cooler carburettor and supercharger before ensuring the ignition was off. This was essential to avoid accidental firing, as his ground crew pulled the propeller through by hand, manually drawing oil from the sump to protect the engine on start-up. This done, Tom switched the master booster pump to normal and primed the engine to offset the January chill during a cold start. A quick check with the crew chief confirmed clearance, and Tom turned on the ignition then pressed the starter switch. The propeller blades juddered into hesitant motion, then the Merlin snorted out a flash of exhaust flame as the engine caught, and they blurred into a single disc, virtually invisible. The Merlin's rhythm settled as Tom once more confirmed his flying controls – ailerons, elevators, rudder: fine. Instrument readings: also fine. The temperature gauge edged upwards as the engine warmed into a satisfied crackle, and Tom turned on the master battery switch before having the umbilical from the ground battery disconnected. Tom continued his pre-flight procedure: hydraulic pressure, flaps functioning, magnetos, generator, and on through a list confirming all aspects of the aircraft met with his approval – his life depended on it. Satisfied, he signalled, and a crewman slid below the mainplane to haul clear the chocks, as Tom checked with Duxford's control tower. Clearance given, 'Shampoo 46' taxied out, Tom snaking his fighter over the turf. This was the only way to view forward, because the angle of the protruding engine cowling blocked direct visibility, and contact with a ground obstruction would lead to an embarrassing, one-sided conversation with the squadron commander.

Reaching the end of the grass strip, Tom gunned the engine and swung the Mustang into wind. Everything had been second nature in the P-47, but being in a new aircraft required his pre-flight checks to be methodically conducted until they achieved familiarity – though never complacency. Ice-cold air created from his propeller surged past the open canopy as Tom ran through settings for trim tabs, propeller, fuel tanks, flaps, supercharger, carburettor, radiator and oil cooler. All was OK. He pushed the joystick forward to unlock the tail wheel and dabbed a burst of power to run forward a few feet and ensure its alignment. WM-P seemed sweet enough and ready to roll. Even when it was idling, the engine noise dominated his senses, and, as he steadily advanced the throttle, the Merlin's clamour reverberated over the open Cambridgeshire countryside. The Mustang was a lively steed, and Tom knew it required careful handling, as power galloped from all twelve cylinders. Gently holding the tail down, he felt the accumulation of power and energy, easing on enough rudder to counter the fighter's tendency to drift right. This was caused by inherent directional instability, a known weakness of the 'D' model and another reason for Tom's distrust of the type, even though the addition of a dorsal fin alleviated the problem. The rumble from his undercarriage lightened as the wings acquired lift, and Tom greased the P-51 from terra firma into its element. Nothing showy, just a steady ascent through 150 mph, then a climb eastwards over Suffolk towards the North Sea to practise handling this steed and to test fire his guns in relatively unoccupied airspace.

At over 20,000ft, Tom tested the performance and handling characteristics of his new mount. His very survival demanded an intimacy with this machine that meant exploring every nuance of its behaviour. When there was an Fw 190 on your tail, reactions had to be fast, and many Mustangs were thrown about at speeds, attitudes and altitudes that tested every sinew of their pilots and every rivet in their aircraft. The book might tell you that 'spinning is *not* permitted when drop tanks or fuel in the fuselage tank are carried', but Me 109 pilots did not go by the same book. Another piece of advice in the manual was to 'watch oil pressure carefully during aerobatics and avoid more than a momentary drop'. This was fine until you were caught in the mêlée of a dogfight. Modern electronic engine management systems take care of many issues faced by Second World War fighter pilots. Like his companions, Tom had to watch not just oil pressure but fuel consumption and balance, oxygen, hydraulics and coolant controls, as well as navigate long distances while rubber-necking to protect himself, his comrades and the bombers under escort. During this exercise, Tom deepened his acquaintanceship with the P-51 and his last task before turning homewards was to test fire the six 0.5in machines guns at high altitude. Now above 27,000ft, he knew the outside air temperature would be over minus 40 and some P-51s, particularly the earlier models, had been troubled with gun stoppages when the guns froze at altitude. The entire *raison d'être* for a fighter was to use its guns effectively, and it was virtually valueless if it could not do this. Other problems had arisen with loading ammunition into the linkage feed mechanism, and today's evaluation was not just about piloting the machine but also to ensure that the weapons had been satisfactorily loaded by ground crew who were also converting to a machine that was more difficult to arm, service and maintain than its predecessor.

Such tests occurred in a predetermined area over the North Sea, and, confirming the heavens were empty, Tom checked his instruments, moved the guns from safety and prepared to fire. On operations, the ammunition carried could vary between 270 and 400 rounds per gun, depending on load and range factors. The rate of fire per gun also fluctuated but averaged some 650 rounds per minute, and continuous fire was cautioned not to exceed two seconds to avoid burning out the gun barrels. Tom squeezed the trigger, snapping off several bursts. Lines of tracer laced with their invisible armour-piercing brethren converged on an imaginary target some 250yd away then curved seawards in the distance. The guns ceased, apparently empty. Routinely, he scanned his instruments. Startled, he checked again, almost in disbelief, staring at his oil pressure gauge. This should have registered 70–80 psi but now read zero! Fuel may be food for an engine, but oil is its lifeblood. If oil circulation failed, it was a coronary failure for the engine, with only one outcome: the motor would die and Tom was still nearly 100 miles out over the North Sea. His demise would be as certain as that of his engine unless he could make landfall.

One thing clearly registered from the pilot's manual: a strict avoidance of ditching. The under-fuselage air scoop would be like diving from the top board with your mouth open. Water scooped in would cause the P-51 to head straight for the seabed. Tom shuddered at the image as he curved the crippled P-51 through 180 degrees and cut back to 15in of mercury on his pressure gauges to nurse the motor while transmitting his first distress call on Channel 'B'. Starved of lubrication, the engine temperature began a steady climb to overheated self-destruction, but Tom needed every mile the doomed Merlin could offer as it brewed up, hotter and hotter. Tom conserved what he could from the dying engine as he let down towards the coast.

At 14,000ft, the ailing fighter crossed the coast, so at least he would keep his feet dry, whether he jumped or rode the stricken machine all the way down. During his descent, Tom diagnosed his actions, trying to see if an error on his part had created his present predicament. Nothing registered; his inexperience in the P-51 had, if anything, added caution to his actions. He had now opened the coolant radiator and oil cooler shutters, but it seemed as if the oil pump itself had failed, so this action only delayed the inevitable. Without a pump, the 10 gallons of oil carried was useless. The Merlin was now reduced from an orchestration of sweetly tuned mechanics to the chaos of a lost conductor and it finally failed catastrophically, with all twelve connecting rods slamming out through the crankcase, although Tom would not know this until our excavations. The propeller froze and the wrecked engine vomited oil and coolant, covering Tom's windscreen and robbing him of forward vision, vital if he had to crash-land.

Even without the details, Tom knew there was no point in attempting to restart the Merlin, no chance of making base and no airfield immediately available. The P-51 was also no glider, but Tom trimmed his flaps to get the best performance, while he swiftly assessed the unpleasant options – crash-land or jump? Robbed of forward vision, he dare not risk a crash-landing. Deciding to jump, he radioed Duxford and told them he was bailing out. Calmly, Capt Al Cowart acknowledged and requested of Tom to 'give us a call when you get to a phone'. Disconnecting his oxygen hose, his g-suit and headphones, Tom unclipped his seat harness and prepared to jettison the hood. For this, it was advisable to lower your seat and keep your head down to avoid being struck by the departing canopy. This done, Tom tugged the emergency release and the world suddenly grew louder as the canopy vanished, exposing him to the cold cut of air at 7,000ft. The thin Perspex bubble had shielded him; now it felt as though he was sitting on the edge of a precipice and the earth was a long way down. The textbook bailout procedure now called for him to climb from the right hand rim of his cockpit, crouching behind the windshield, then dive towards the starboard wingtip. The manual cheerfully advised: 'right side is recommended because the slipstream will help you clear the airplane. The wing will then pass your body or it will be possible to slide off the wing without striking the tail.'

Peering over the cockpit rim, Tom felt this process was 'a crock of shit' and he did not like the idea one bit. Changing his mind, he determined to attempt a belly landing and dropped back into his seat. Powerless, the P-51 had shed altitude, so he needed to move swiftly to re-harness himself and choose a suitable spot on which to scrape his miscreant Mustang in on its belly. He might be able to side-slip until the last moment so he had some idea of the terrain. New problems arose as he fumbled for the discarded seat straps and locking mechanism for his harness. He now found he could not re-hook the webbing and the chances of death or serious injury were too great to risk a crash-landing. A sudden stop might catapult him from the aircraft, or, at a minimum, impact with the K-14 gun sight would hardly benefit his features. As he rapidly juggled these issues, the P-51 sank ever nearer a now less-than-inviting landscape of small fields with all too many trees. Speedily impacting a sturdy English elm would be sure-fire execution. If he did not act soon, he would have no choice – he decided to jump while he still had time.

Another disenchanting feature of the P-51 was a known difficulty to part with it on bailout. Air pressure was known to pin pilots in their seats, and experience had educated Mustang jockeys into emulating a departure tactic employed by many Me 109 and Fw 190 pilots – roll the ship over and drop clear. Preparing himself, Tom snapped the stick right and the horizon obediently rotated. Tom felt gravity take over as he started to fall. Dropping only a foot, his departure was abruptly arrested. Stuck half in, half out, he dangled 2,000ft high, with a panoply of fields and trees passing absurdly overhead. This vista was now rolling by with an alarming amount of detail becoming apparent. Tom's feet had caught between the gun sight and the cowl, leaving him pinned across his armour-plated seat back and held fast by the slipstream. His P-51 seemed determined to take him to a gory end, his unrecognisable remains buried in a smoking hole with a fighter he did not like. If machines had a conscience, his must have taken pity on its pilot's predicament. More likely, a quirk of aerodynamics, perhaps disrupted by his body in the slipstream, suddenly flipped the P-51 upright and Tom tumbled back into the cockpit.

He was now nearing the minimum height to survive a bailout. Below 600ft, his parachute had no time to deploy. The altimeter reading was already at 700ft. His only hope would be to try the 'pop-stick' trick. Smoothly rolling the fighter until it was again inverted, but this time bracing himself in the cockpit, Tom popped the stick sharply forward and let go. The Mustang's nose reared towards the sky and its rider was thrown sharply from the cockpit, popping out 'like a champagne cork'. His only problem this time was a glancing blow from the tail of the aircraft on his left shoe as he shot clear. Now falling fast, Tom realised his trajectory gave him only seconds before he slammed into the earth. Clasping the ripcord, Tom tugged hard. He was head downward, and the ground now seemed to be hurtling up to meet him. The parachute pack snapped open; the drogue 'chute and a stream of white silk whipped by over his left shoulder. Impact was moments away. The main canopy cracked open and shroud lines smacked painfully across his left jaw. In the next instant, his descent was arrested so sharply that he felt as if his head 'had been tugged clean off'. Swinging in a violent pendulum, he completed one wild arc, then, halfway through the return, he crashed heavily into a ploughed field.

Spilling his parachute, Tom sat a moment to collect his wits, but the next moment the strong northerly wind suddenly reinvigorated the crumpled silk and it ballooned into life. Caught off guard, Tom was jolted over and dragged across the landscape. Scraping painfully along, Tom now fought the folds that had just saved him, but his desperate efforts had no effect on the impromptu sail and he was pulled helplessly for some 100yd. Then, during a brief lull, Tom almost deflated his tormentor but was beaten and again snatched off his feet to be hauled another 50yd. Finally, tugging the lines, he collapsed the canopy, and, getting to his feet, he staggered quickly forward to capture his erstwhile rescuer turned tormentor. Gathering armfuls of silk and shroud lines, he bundled it together then sat victoriously on the now inert material. Triumphant, he flattened the silk until it was compliant, then set about getting some revenge as well as acquiring a souvenir of the occasion. What better than a new silk scarf or a bargaining tool for some young lady – parachute silk or the recently introduced nylon made some very delicate underwear! This was possible only if the parachute had sustained damage, but, nursing his bruises, Tom felt he was the more harmed of the two, and this stubbornly unscathed piece of Army Air Force property was in better shape than the very expensive Mustang now burning fiercely a short distance away. Tom had narrowly avoided having his anatomy shredded across a barbed wire fence; now he put the barbs to purpose and deliberately ripped two panels of the parachute to get it declared unserviceable, so that he could claim his souvenir silk. In the event, 'some bastard' in Supply refused to let him have his trophy, and Tom would wait over forty years for his memento of the day.

Taking in his surroundings, Tom spotted what looked like a military observation post nearby. It was a 'wooden hut', mounted on stilts and manned by personnel Tom assumed were British Army but who were probably from the Royal Observer Corps. As Tom was reporting to them and requesting use of a telephone, a Police Constable cycled up and queried whether there was any ammunition on board. A pall of smoke issued from the wreckage, but Tom, confident he had expended his ammunition, assured the Bobby that there was no danger. At that moment, the crackle of exploding ammunition was heard and bullets went zinging across the hedgerows. Tom never forgot the dirty look he received from the now disbelieving PC. The East Suffolk Police report submitted to Superintendent Rumsey by PC122 Albert Read stated factually and unemotionally: 'Thursday 4th January 1945. Broadway Farm, Monk Soham. MR 656 846. Burnt out American Mustang number unknown model P-51. 11.30 hours. Pilot 2/Lt Cyril Bendorf No. 0829621 baled out and received injury to jaw. Engine trouble. Home station Duxford.' Telephoning Duxford, Tom was told a P-51 had been found with its pilot dead and they had feared the worst, but Tom soon reassured them that he was still numbered among the living. Transport was arranged from the nearby 493rd BG base at Debach and Tom was taken swiftly back to his home station.

At Duxford, Tom completed the inevitable paperwork and was unamused when questioned about the possibility of a ricochet striking his coolant system. Tom doubted the sanity of the question: a ricochet at 27,000ft – not unless bullets bounced off clouds!

Where's it gone? An officer from the recovery crew peers into the crater containing the remains of 44-63206 and determines to declare the lost machine as salvage. *(Tom Bendorf/David Wade)*

Tom had flown forty-six missions prior to the crash and, after the 78th FG had converted to the P-51, he accumulated some thirty more without further incident, but, personally, he never felt entirely comfortable with the Mustang. He later recalled:

Why do I not like the P-51? I had a real love affair with the P-47. It was a pilot's airplane. It took you where you wanted to go and it brought you back. It accepted severe damage if it was necessary to ensure your return. The P-51 was the WW2 airplane most easy to bring down. I flew 14 missions in the P-47 and 32 in the P-51. The '51 tried to kill me about once a week – I believe I was on my sixth '51 when the war ended. I never saw an instrument out of green in my 250 hours or so in a P-47. In the '51, I had engine failures, coolant shutter failures, oxygen failures, heater failures, gas selectors impossible to move, overflow returns to different tanks depending on who built the airplane. Every mission became a roll of the dice. Not so in a P-47. Which was faster? Depends on the altitude. Which could turn tighter? Depends on the altitude and who was flying. In which would I wish to be? No question. The noble P-47. The P-47 had no coolant lines from nose to tail. It was not necessary to blow out the carbon every half hour. If you overshot the field, landed long and nosed up, the '47 did not break in half as the '51 did. The '47 had a living room cockpit and you could reach everything. The '51 had a tiny cockpit and you couldn't reach anything. In a forced landing, the '47 protected the pilot at all costs. The '51, however, left the pilot's brains smeared all over the gun sight. The '47 was built like a tank, the '51 was tinny, rattled and came apart in the air. After the war, the '51 was limited to 350 mph because of its proclivity to dropping a gear and discarding a wing when excessive g forces were met. No '47 ever came apart in the air. The only way in which the '51 was better than the '47 was in gas consumption. In no other way.

Apart from his Mustang mishaps, Tom's war was otherwise mostly uneventful, and his forty-six sorties were primarily fighter escort with some strafing of enemy airfields and transportation. Tom alludes to the vulnerability of the P-51 to ground fire. A single strike in the coolant system could see the demise of the aircraft in minutes, whereas the rugged Pratt and Whitney R2800 radial in his preferred P-47 kept on rotating. One airborne adversary that threatened the Mustang's supremacy was the Me 262. Tom's only encounter with the twin-engined jet fighter saw him fire, but, unfortunately, he missed. A close encounter with another example of the Luftwaffe's latent technology occurred over Germany when he and an Arado 234 jet bomber almost collided. As Tom later recalled, it 'scared the shit' out of him. Fortunately for the Allies, neither example entered Luftwaffe service soon enough or in sufficient quantity to have a material impact on Allied air superiority. Jet technology would ultimately see piston-engined aircraft relegated to secondary roles and then vanish entirely from front-line duties. The P-51 remained in service longer than most of its contemporaries, continuing with smaller air forces into the 1960s, with one development even considered for tasks in Vietnam during the 1970s. By the 1980s, even the mighty Mustang was an archaic form of fighter and had taken an honoured place in the annals of aerial warfare. So too had the airmen who had flown them, and the younger aviation archaeologists now beavering away hoping to retrieve Tom's troublesome example wanted to add representative items for museum display as a tribute to its pilot. But was it still there?

Local resident Geoff Jay, then a lad of 15, heard the Mustang crash and remembered how the water-logged winter landscape handicapped vehicular access. A truck had parked nearby and servicemen collected scattered surface debris. He recalled seeing a propeller in the crater and remembered local youngsters finding souvenirs in the ditch for several years after the war. In time, evidence of the fighter vanished, so how much remained extant was now a matter of luck.

David Wade directed the JCB to score two strips of soil about 40ft long and 15ft into the harvest stubble on either side of the ditch. This would be replaced to ensure any earth polluted by oil or aviation fuel remained underneath, avoiding crop contamination. The land revealed consisted of heavy, clay loam, making location of small finds quite difficult, because they were easily encased in lumps of clay. The P-51 had impacted in the side of the ditch, and David instructed the JCB driver to remove earth and clay gently from the area where detector readings were strongest. Within minutes, Tom was presented with a piece of black-and-white checkerboard from the engine cowling – things looked promising. However, our enthusiasm was dampened by the discovery in the topsoil of fragments from the Merlin's engine casing, indicating the motor had broken up – but how badly?

At 1045 our hopes were rejuvenated by the exposure of a propeller blade with its yellow tip paintwork in fine condition. Tom's long-ago assertion to the Police Constable suffered

26 August 1989. A comparative picture to that on page 99 taken forty-four years earlier. David Wade directed the digger to score and set aside two strips of top soil so there was no risk of contaminating crops.

further embarrassment with the discovery of some ammunition, but, to be fair, very little compared with other excavations. Within fifteen minutes of exposing the propeller tip, a combination of using the machine carefully and hand digging more delicate areas had revealed a section of wing with a black void beneath. Deciding the remnants of the wing could easily be detached, Geoff Barker attached chains, and the broken section was hoisted clear, exposing further wreckage still in excellent condition. Now working on the fuselage, we were delighted to reveal the P-51's specification details still clearly stencilled on the starboard side: P-51D-20-NA 44-63206. The fact that this was upright surprised Tom, who thought his aircraft had crashed inverted, but the Mustang had again rolled upright and gone in at 30 degrees. The cockpit had been torn open, with parts and remains of the instrumentation smeared along both sides of the broken Merlin. Discovery of his seat harness delighted Tom, and, handling the buckle, he observed that it felt 'different – kinda personal', compared to the many mechanical parts now emerging. After forty-four years, his memory had dimmed and some finds were a mystery, but the red knob from the mixture control was clearly recognisable. A lot had happened in his life since he had last touched these controls.

The discovery of his seat harness delighted Tom – it was more personal than other items emerging from the crater and he took pleasure in cleaning up the keepsake for himself.

After lunch, we had revealed enough of the clay-encased engine to attempt a lift, so it was shackled to the bucket and, after something of a tussle, became airborne again for the first time in over four decades. Pondering the broken carcass, Tom ruminated on his narrow escape. Any lingering doubts about his own culpability for the crash were removed when later examination confirmed that all twelve con rods were protruding through the crank case, and subsequent examination of the oil pump revealed some foreign metal, thus explaining the cause of the crash. He was disappointed for the enthusiasts that the Merlin was so badly

David Wade ruminates on the best route for recovering the Packard V-1650. The angle of impact can be seen from the rocker cover in the left foreground. The tip of a propeller blade protruding illustrates that the surviving blades from the Hamilton Standard Hydromatic airscrew had folded back along the length of the engine.

broken and felt they deserved something more pristine, but we were delighted with it and further pleased to find the four-bladed propeller still had three blades attached. These had folded back alongside the engine, rather like the grip of an octopus. Once the propeller had been hoisted clear, the digging team replaced a broken land drain, tidied up the site and took the opportunity for a photo shoot before a fine summer's day concluded in a typically British downpour. Reflecting on the day's events, Tom recalled his career as a fighter pilot and how he could so easily have been a wartime casualty. A modest man, he shied away from

Pondering on his problems forty-four years earlier, Tom finally learned the cause of the trouble once the Packard Merlin had been stripped down for investigation and restoration.

considering himself as heroic. Pressed by the enthusiasts, he shrugged and said very simply, 'we did the job we had to do'. Today had been a new experience, reminding him of those days now distant and other, grimmer experiences. He had been blessed with time to acknowledge and live a full life; many had not. Tom was pleased that items from the tangled pile of debris were destined as museum exhibits in tribute not just to his own contribution but, more importantly, to that of many fallen comrades who also did the job they had to do but who were robbed by fate of the many rich experiences life can bestow.

Supervising a successful recovery, David monitors retrieval of the propeller.

CHAPTER EIGHT

An Implacable Enemy

Fighter pilots operating from the UK during the Second World War faced an additional, implacable, unforgiving and remorseless enemy. Contrary in all seasons but particularly bitter in winter, the British weather claimed countless airmen, and its notorious vicissitudes ranged from calm but deadly freezing fog to the towers of cumulonimbus, beautiful but, laden with turbulence, just as treacherous.

Often trained in relatively clear, reliable climates, American fighter pilots in Europe were constantly challenged by harsh, unforgiving weather conditions. Courageously they sought to combat the elements when their 'big friends', also struggling aloft, needed protection from that more tangible enemy, the German interceptor. Two highly skilled pilots manned the bomber cockpit, but their fighter compatriots flew alone, and fighter groups devised methods of climbing safely through the 'soup'. The technique most commonly employed was for the more experienced leader in a finger four – so called because the aircraft flew slots akin to the fingertips on an outstretched hand – to climb on instruments. Developed by the Luftwaffe's Condor Legion during the Spanish Civil War, this formation offered the best flexibility for mutual protection. It did not prove as demanding on pilots as previous 'parade ground' patterns harking back to pre-radio days. Then, manoeuvres were signalled by hand from an open cockpit, necessitating close formation for visual contact. This demanded more focus on the leader and potentially less awareness of impending attack. Such formations had cost the RAF dear during the early days of the Battle of Britain, but, rapidly adopted by both British and American fighter pilots, the finger four formation continues in use today.

However, during the Second World War, when climbing through dense clouds, American fighters had to revert and close up like chicks to their mother for visual contact as the most experienced pilot concentrated on his instruments. The nearest – his No. 2 – tucked into starboard, and No. 3 flew to port with No. 4 tucked in on No. 3. The man at the extremity might be unable to see the leader, just the shape of his closest companion and frequently no more than a few feet of seemingly disembodied wing. Such pilotage demanded skill, yet even the most experienced could lose control as the sinister confines of cloud closed in and another malicious miscreant climbed into the cockpit. Vertigo. When the senses become disoriented, the sensations of attitude are deceiving. Doubts about the instrument readings creep in and can grow. The senses say you are diving or turning; surely the instruments must be lying? Premature reaction to correct the imaginary problem only creates the situation you thought you were in. You can be climbing, with your leader's wingtip in your lap; then a momentary loss of concentration and that guiding reference point vanishes. Alone, unsure, even the most skilled of pilots can fall victim and many did. The result might be a terrifying tumble from a cloud base with the ground hurtling to meet you. Given time, recovery would simply result in sweaty palms and injured pride. If the cloud base was too low, a pilot's last moments would be the horrifying reality of too low, too late and a blinding flash as he crossed the threshold into eternity. The only blessing being that it was quick.

During the winter of 1944–5 weather conditions were foul, but the European conflict continued unabated. By 13 January, the Nazi war machine had just conducted and been defeated during its last serious land offensive in the West, the Battle of the Bulge. Dealing with this threat had delayed the Allied advance, but it had now recovered, while, to the east, the Soviet army opened a new offensive on 12 January to help relieve the pressure. Saturday 13th saw south-eastern England covered in dense low-lying cloud. As daylight filtered feebly through an almost impenetrable gloom, bombers of the Eighth Air Force ascended, seeking the crystal clarity above. Once they were assembled, their endeavours were directed against the railway infrastructure, further to disrupt the flow of enemy war material towards the front line and support ground forces still regaining the initiative.

As the heavies set course, the process of relaying fighter protection was under way. Groups of fighters were planned to rendezvous with their big friends in a manner that saw the baton of protection handed from one group to another. The concept was a seamless shield protecting the bombers, and every fighter pilot knew he made a difference. Outmoded by an increasing threat from the new Me 262 jet fighter, Allied piston-engined aircraft sought to saturate the skies in maintaining air superiority. Lives depended on the timely arrival of fighter protection and lives had to be risked providing it.

At Duxford, Tom Bendorf, now fully recovered from his Mustang mishap on 4 January (see Chapter 7), was today flying wingman for 1/Lt Herbert W. Elin, an experienced officer with over 589 hours to his credit but, like Tom, still inexperienced on the P-51, having had only three hours on type. Both men had enjoyed playing poker the previous night, but Tom's luck had been out. Elin, on the contrary, had his silver billfold reassuringly laden with winnings from a lucky streak. Confronting clouds drizzling down to 200ft, both hoped that good fortune would favour their flying today. The dismal skyscape shrouding the airfield made a depressing perspective for thirty-six other pilots also facing the anxieties of simply getting airborne. Under Major Downing, the 78 FG were responding valiantly to Field Order 1513, and the rasp of Merlins crackled across the countryside of Cambridgeshire as the fighters waddled over the turf into their take-off positions on the PSP (Pierced Steel Planking) runway laid only a few weeks earlier to combat water-logging. Their role was the provision of freelance support for the Third Air Division's Flying Fortresses.

Taxiing out, Tom knew he would have to glue himself to Elin as soon as their wheels left the wet grass. He would concentrate on his leader, while Herb focused on his instruments to

1/Lt Herbert W. Elin had 589.30 flying hours to his credit primarily on the P-47 as pictured. His experience with the P-51 amounted to only 3.30 hours and his instrument time 6.45 hours during the previous six months. *(David Wade)*

guide them both into that other high, bright world they knew would be glistening above the gloom. This was Elin's first combat sortie in the Mustang and he studied even harder to compensate for the unfamiliar cockpit layout. No sooner had they lifted off than the horizon vanished and the world became a seemingly solid grey. As the P-51s curved into a climbing left turn, Tom tucked in close to Elin, but, as they continued their ascent, he found holding formation increasingly arduous. Focusing intently on the other P-51, he struggled with visibility so poor that he could see only the outer section of Elin's port wing, like a spiritual hand through the mist. Tom knew that taking his eyes off the other aircraft would risk losing his leader and increase the chances of a collision if he then tried to close up on where he thought Elin should be. Unable to check his own instruments, Tom clung perilously close to Elin's aircraft, but his anxiety and doubt increased; something was wrong. Rising blindly within that grey shroud confounded his senses, creating inner conflict and uncertainty. The wing of Elin's machine was precisely in place, yet Tom's sensation was of descending, not climbing. Was he deceiving himself? Was he suffering vertigo and would breaking contact with Elin cause him to lose stability and send him spinning out of cloud too late to recover? Or, was Elin being deluded?

Tom knew that the gap between mist and mother earth would allow only a fleeting glimpse before impact. Now that inner voice was shrieking at him. He flashed a glance at his own instruments. Dear God! The altimeter was unwinding, his artificial horizon and turn and bank indicator confirmed his feelings. They were diving in a tight starboard spiral!

Taking immediate recovery action, Tom yelled a rapid warning to Elin to pull out. His leader's aircraft had vanished the instant Tom had taken his eyes away from that wingtip, and Tom now feared the searing oblivion of a mid-air collision. Pulling out, he craned his neck round, seeking his companion. Over his shoulder, he caught a flash of red, like someone firing a red warning flare diffused in the mist. Badly shaken, he levelled out a few feet over the landscape and gathered his wits before daring to climb again into the murk. Tom hoped Elin had heard his warning or seen the red flare alarm.

On completion of the mission, Tom learned the terrible truth. The flash he assumed to be a warning flare had been the last instant in Elin's life. A shallow angle of impact indicated Tom's frantic warning had apparently been heard and Elin was desperately trying to pull out in those final moments. There was not time, and his P-51 slammed into farmland and exploded near Wimpole Hall, some 7 miles north of the 91BG base at Bassingbourne in Cambridgeshire. Elin, an experienced pilot with nearly 600 hours to his credit, had seemingly succumbed to vertigo. The Accident Report stated simply, 'Crashed while on instruments', and later commented: 'Instrument flying immediately after take off is always a dangerous undertaking in a fighter type aircraft. Lt Elin had no alternative other than to attempt the take off as the accident occurred on an ordered combat flight . . .'

The rest of the 78FG carried out this order and arrived at 26,000ft over Luxembourg at 1045 hours. Rendezvousing with Third Air Division B-17s, they took station to protect their charges. There was nothing untoward until a warning from 'Nuthouse' control sent them to investigate suspected bandits, but their enthusiasm for combat was frustrated when the 'enemy' were identified as P-47s. After two hours they were ordered home, not a shot fired in anger. Impervious to their weaponry, the enemy that day had taken a comrade just as surely as an Me 109. Elin was only the first.

Later that morning, Police Sergeant Leslie Dunnett studied a torn, olive-coloured fragment from an airman's shirt. This had been taken from the debris of an American fighter, now a smear of disintegrated, smouldering pieces strewn across the landscape. Peering at this grim piece of evidence, Dunnett discerned a name and some numerals, part of the flier's official number. It looked like 'Schlisker' with ??3????99.

Serial number 0830095, 2/Lt Robert L. Schlieker, was a pilot with the 362FS, 357FG, based at Leiston, Army Air Force Station F373. Straddling the Suffolk countryside between Leiston and Saxmundham, the 357FG acquired its nickname from another town nearby. On their arrival at Station F373, a German propaganda radio broadcast startled the group in greeting their presence and calling them 'The Yoxford Boys' – the name they carried into legend. As the first fighter unit in 8FC to be equipped with the P-51, they could thank one of those idiosyncracies peculiar to large organisations. Strangely, the USAAF had designated its first, strategic, long-range Mustangs to the more tactically oriented Ninth Air Force. The 354FG of 9 Fighter Command had the distinction of being the first USAAF Merlin-engined Mustang unit to enter combat. This caused consternation to 8FC, which desperately needed long-range escorts, and the situation was exacerbated when the 357FG was also assigned to 9FC. Luckily, relationships at local level were good, so a deal was struck between the two Fighter Commands to swap the P-47 equipped 358FG from 8FC in exchange for the 357FG.

That had been a year previously, and the 357FG had shown the value of the deal by becoming one of 8FC's top-scoring fighter groups with many aces listed in its ranks. One of these, 1/Lt Otto D. Jenkins, usually flew a P-51, serial 44-14245, named 'Floogie II', which had only recently returned from repairs following a belly landing on 23 December. Today, Schlieker, a comparative tyro, would be taking 'Floogie II' into combat alongside thirty-nine other Mustangs. Maj Bud Anderson would be leading to escort Fortresses attacking railway yards and bridges at Mainz. First, however, would be a hazardous climb through five-tenths cloud from 800ft, thickening to a dense, turbulent mass from 2,000ft. This soon swallowed the ascending fighters. Flying No. 4 position in his flight, Schlieker held his position as the leading Mustang vanished and he strained to keep station. His total of 193 fighter hours flown had been augmented by eight hours in a link trainer from which you could step unharmed if things went wrong. Inside his Perspex bubble encapsulated within a treacherous grey veil, Schlieker sought to surmount the elements, but, somehow, he slid away from the reference point offered by the port wing of his leader. Perhaps 'Floogie II' felt unbalanced, maybe she malfunctioned, but, most likely, her unfortunate young pilot was overcome by the

'Floogie II' 44-14245 G4-P was usually flown by 1/Lt Otto Jenkins but had only just returned to service following this mishap on 23 December 1944. *(Merle Olmsted)*

deceit of vertigo, correcting his controls for attitudes that existed only in the confusion created by uncertainty in his mind. This illusion probably became clear only when 'Floogie II' hurtled from the cloud base. Again, it was too late. The P-51 disintegrated on impact a half mile north-east of the church in the village of Butley in Suffolk. Sadly, still further misfortune was to befall the 357FG later that day.

At Raydon, Station 157, some 25 miles south of Leiston, the 353FG were similarly struggling to get airborne in support of their 'big brothers' already bound for Mainz. For two days, bad weather had grounded the group, and conditions looked little better at 0600 that day. An air raid, 'Red' warning had already disturbed their rest, and some pilots must have harboured doubts about the sanity of senior commanders as they shuffled into briefing at 0900 for mission 212. Outside, an intermittent but icy drizzle challenged the stamina of those personnel whose duties gave them no choice as they prepared the fighters for flight. Frozen fingers gripped screwdrivers seeking to fasten in place stubborn inspection panels, while other personnel slapped their own shoulders for circulation as frozen breath accompanied further curses on England's inhospitable climate. Staff Weather Officer Wayne H. Maok had judged the cloud base at only 400ft and knew this resulted from an elongated high-pressure cell stretching from the mid Atlantic. Settling like a shroud over south-eastern England, the clouds sought to thwart effective operations. Within the stratocumulus, unpleasantly turbulent conditions allied with yet another adversary, rime ice. Malevolently, moisture on aerofoils froze easily, corrupting the finesse of balanced aerodynamics intended by designers. In minutes, an ice-laden aircraft could stall, and then tumble to oblivion. In those pre-'black box' days, no trace of the perpetrator would be found after the resulting conflagration consumed airframe and flesh alike.

Wayne Maok warned pilots about the conditions during briefing. Against a human enemy, Mustang pilots might feel they had the measure, but nature was a cheating transducer of even the best training and experience. She offered no sympathy for those souls soon to launch their puny craft heavenwards. Some pilots would, this day, continue their journey, climbing even higher to that other, more peaceful place beyond man's known realm.

2/Lt George P. Lee, flying a P-51 named 'Potchy', faced this sinister assassin, and, having successfully broken clear at 4,000ft, he might have felt some jubilation in the cerulean brilliance in that kingdom close to God. Then that old tormentor, Fate, intervened. A possible malfunction forced Lee to face an early return. Descending again into the murk from which the last tendrils had barely been shaken, 'Potchy' submerged as the other Mustangs followed Maj Blickenstaff over a solid overcast to meet Third Air Division Fortresses.

At 1245, Third Air Division Headquarters telephoned Flying Control Raydon to enquire if they had an aircraft named 'Potchy'. The Duty Officer phoned the squadrons and confirmed it belonged to the 350FS. Returning the call, they learned that wreckage of this machine had been found at Folly Farm near Sudbury. Apparently George Lee had lost control while letting down through cloud. Emerging in a fast dive, he pulled out sharply and the left wing tank detached as he levelled out. This caused a momentary loss of control and balance, causing the right wing to drop suddenly. 'Potchy''s nose fell abruptly and the P-51 plunged into a ditch, exploding on impact. Lee died instantly.

Wreckage of 44-11343 'Potchy' from the 350FS was found on Folly Farm, 4 miles from Station 174, the 486BG base at Sudbury. 2/Lt George S. Lee, of Chinese descent, had 420.45 total flying hours with 11.30 on instruments during the previous six months. *(David Wade)*

The malevolent forces of Mother Nature continued to challenge other mortals audaciously seeking to do their duty. Capt Karl K. 'Kay' Shearer knew better than most fighter pilots just how reassuring it was for bomber crews to see their 'little friends'. Kay had himself flown many flak-filled, fighter-threatened missions as a pilot in the 453BG. Impotently hunkered down when flak besmirched the surrounding blue, Shearer suffered the frustrations of inadequacy and inability to hit back. Avoiding the worst areas en route and throwing out chaff on the run-in was their only protection from anti-aircraft fire. Against Luftwaffe interceptors, they had their own ten machine guns, which, combined with close formations designed to optimise firepower, strategists originally envisaged offered adequate protection. The savage reality of air combat had shown the fallacy behind this belief, and German fighters had decimated American bomber formations before Allied fighters gained air supremacy. Even now, the enemy made punitive strikes, and their waning strength had been boosted by the advent of the Me 262 jet fighter. Sunlight glinting on silvered wings as American fighters peeled off to pursue their enemies proved inspiring for Kay. Soldiering along in his B-24, he re-avowed that, if he survived, he would one day fly fighters.

Kay did survive. Promoted to captain in August 1944, he frequently found himself in the forefront for his 732BS as Squadron Lead, Group Deputy Lead and even Group Lead on

Pilot, Capt Karl K. Shearer, had flown a full tour of Liberator operations with the 453BG before transferring to the 369FS, 359FG. His ambition had been to fly fighters and he accumulated 39.10 hours on the P-51K adding to his total of nearly 500 hours.

occasion. The operations accumulated and he continued surmounting the odds until he achieved a full tour of thirty-five missions plus a well-deserved DFC, but, ever since cavorting around in his PT19 basic trainer over Pampa, Texas, he had cherished the ambition of becoming a fighter pilot. On 18 November 1944, he bade farewell to Old Buckenham, his crew and their lumbering Liberator. In a sense, he was not leaving them – he planned still to be there – flying alongside, protecting his chums. Kay Shearer now began training to convert to his coveted role. For this ex-bomber jockey, joining the prestigious 359FG fulfilled his ambition. Although only 15 miles from Old Buckenham, their base at East Wretham on the sandy subsoil of Norfolk's brecklands seemed a world apart. Following earlier use by RAF Bomber Command, East Wretham had been home to the 359FG since October 1943 and was a grass airfield with a PSP runway. Originally equipped with Thunderbolts, the 359FG, following 8FC policy, converted to the P-51 during April 1944. Theirs was a typical fighter base of some 1,600 personnel, with both ground crew and pilots now sensing that the end of the conflict was in sight. But how long would it take finally to defeat Hitler's despicable Reich? An informal report written by Station Chaplain Capt Wilbur C. Zeigler on the morale of the 359FG during January 1945 gives an insight into Kay's new unit and is undoubtedly representative of emotions elsewhere in 8FC.

The month of January was a relatively quiet month on all fronts, except one. The excitement of the Christmas and New Year holidays was at an end. Thoughts of home were thrust back into our minds once again as we settled down to sweating the war out. If you look at Capt Platt's weather report for the month you can see there was little else we could do. Missions were few and far between. Consequently there were too many days when our men were kept inactive. However, there is one exception to the generally quiet morale front and that is the tremendous drive towards Berlin by the Russians. Most of us were over optimistic as a result of our drive through France. The great majority of our men are refusing to be too optimistic about the Russian drive ending the war. Even so as it continues day by day the optimism is mounting. I have noted this in the letters I censor, in my interviews with the men, and in the general mood of the men on this station. The average opinion seems to be that Germany will be defeated during the late spring and early summer. Some of the more cautious point to late fall, while those of the other extreme look for victory in March. As far as morale is concerned, the whole effect of the Russian drive has been to give men who had about made up their minds that they would still be fighting Germany in 1946, a new hope, that perhaps it would not be too much longer before they could return home. You can talk all you want about the aims of this war in terms of ideals, but it all boils down to one thought for the average G.I. – he wants to go home! Right now he is listening to every broadcast, reading every line in the newspaper, listening to every rumor that concerns this war and its eventual end. With every new Russian and American advance his morale is rising.

One of the greatest morale factors on any field is the mess. If the food is good and the mess clean morale is high. It varies directly with mess conditions . . . while on the subject of messes some mention should be made of the fine work being done by Sgt Benson of Officers' Mess No. 1. Under his direction the food and the manner in which it is being served has inspired many words of appreciation from our pilots.

The station theatre has been made more attractive and comfortable by the addition of six oil drum stoves. Previous to this it was quite an ordeal on a cold night to attend a show. Equipment for such a mission would include overcoat, scarf, gloves and flying boots. Then, too, the seating arrangement has been changed in such a fashion that more men are in direct line with the screen.

Speaking of the cold and inclement weather, I suppose we should remark about the snow and the frost. Much as we are tired of this countryside, we couldn't help but admire the beauty brought by a heavy frost unequalled by any we had seen in America. Words fail to describe its beauty. At least it is beyond my power of description. I only hope the photo lab will include some of the shots it took of the frost-weighted trees and shrubbery. The snow made all the New Englanders, at least, homesick and all on the snow details muscle weary. For several days in a row details were out cleaning the snow from the streets. Though there were many gripes, most of the men really liked it for it was something different and reminded many a man that he hadn't done any physical work in months.

In passing I might sound off to the effect that to me this lassitude, if you want to call it that, is one of the greatest dangers to all our men. It seems incongruous with thousands of men dying just a few miles away, but boredom is our enemy. It has ruined many of our men. How these men will ever survive the mad competition in post-war civilian life is beyond me. Everything that anyone can do is being done. The main responsibility is upon each man for his own welfare. I record it here because it is a part of our morale history and not only ours but the whole Air Force.

Contrasting with the boredom experienced by ground personnel, pilots not only faced combat with the enemy but also battled the weather, and Chaplain Ziegler officiated at several funerals during the month. Commenting on these casualties, Ziegler recorded:

To the uninitiated it seems perhaps as if the Group just forgets these men. There is no stopping in our work. There are no tears. We just go on. Those of us who have seen men go out to die know however that so long as we live they will never be forgotten. Nor will we let the world forget. They died for a dream called peace. We who live on must dedicate ourselves, our time, our interest and our wealth, to the task of making that dream a reality. To do otherwise would be a betrayal of a sacred trust.

Kay Shearer's own morale was high. Back home in Vandalia, Ohio, his parents, Alice and Karl, waited with his wife Jane and 2-year-old daughter, Suzanne Kay. Like countless others awaiting the return of the son, husband and father, they knew from press reports that Germany was collapsing and prayed for the safekeeping of their loved one during the final days of this desperate conflict. Japan, too, was retreating, but the cruel reality of casualty figures continued. Having won the Distinguished Flying Cross and Air Medal, Kay's extended service to fly fighters had fulfilled one ambition, but, after nine months overseas, Kay knew the war's conclusion would see new challenges. Before attending Ohio State University, he had worked for the Univis Lens Company, and he now considered a return to a business career developing new materials for peacetime use, but the immediate task in hand was to take one of the Group's new P-51K's into combat.

Developed from the ubiquitous P-51D, the 'K' variant featured a change of propeller from the Hamilton Standard to an Aeroproducts type. However, the adaption proved unpopular, because the electrical feathering mechanism malfunctioned more often than the earlier, hydraulically operated unit on the P-51D. Kay's aircraft was a Dallas-built machine, serial 44-11686, and carried the fuselage coding IV-N denoting the 369FS. Although Kay had over 500 hours' flying experience, his time on the Mustang was only 49 hours and, for today's mission, he was understandably assigned a relatively junior slot as 'Tinplate Blue Four'. This was the fourth man in a section of two elements. Blue Leader with Blue Two on his starboard side and Blue Three to port, with Kay on the extreme left of the section.

As elsewhere in East Anglia, conditions over East Wretham were dismal. Visibility was 'zero' and a soggy overcast, draping itself over the airfield, blended earth indivisibly into sky with no clear horizon. Thickening at 500ft, dense clouds continued to 5,000ft, making the prospects hazardous for any pilot. To assess the situation, the 359FG had earlier launched a weather ship, whose pilot offered a modicum of an improvement in visibility, reporting it as 'about one half miles ceiling 500 feet'. The wind was given as NE, strength 8–10 mph. Even so, the weather on 13 January was later described in 359FG records as 'the worst weather of the month'. The preceding week had seen no operational activity and a diarist noted: 'There was at East Wretham a somewhat helpless sense of being relegated to the position of spectators at which [sic] seemed at first to be the climax of the war.'

Kay Shearer felt this frustration keenly and waited with other pilots for an inspection of the airfield at 0900. Eighth Air Force Mission 791 needed every fighter, and, despite marginal conditions, the airfield was declared fit for operations. Using the grass NE runway 04, the Mustangs jostled out to take off in elements of four. Kay's Blue element was airborne at 1042 and formed up as planned just beneath the cloud base before warily gaining height into its embrace. Some thirteen minutes later, Blue Leader radioed East Wretham requesting news of Blue Four. Only Blue Three had surfaced with him although their No. 2 had emerged separately, after becoming detached and climbing through solo. As the Mustangs orbited over a shimmering sheet of cloud, pilots located their assigned slots and adopted Visual Formation Rendezvous techniques to form up. Operational demands and optimisation of fuel meant that the Mustangs swiftly assembled into their squadrons, with the leading four stacks higher and the next two elements stepped down astern. Group formation achieved, the 359FG soon set course leaving 1/Lt Fred P. Renkin, Duty Flying Control Officer, and Capt Donald E. Richardson, his senior, to coordinate locating the missing Mustang. No word of a crash had yet been received, but, if anything had gone wrong, Kay Shearer could have parachuted and might be lying injured somewhere in the winter countryside. The inhospitable conditions prevailing made a speedy search and rescue response paramount, but in what direction? Waiting anxiously, they now faced a worrying silence on the airwaves. Radio efforts to communicate with Tinplate 50 resulted only in the gentle hiss of static. What had befallen the popular Kay Shearer?

Airborne nearby was Tinplate 75, an AT-6 Harvard, station trainer and hack. Initial efforts even to contact him were frustrated, but, when communications were established, the aircraft was dispatched to search the battle training area and sparsely populated heath land north of the airfield. A thin dusting of snow covered the countryside, but a sweep by the Harvard found nothing untoward. At around 1130, their counterparts in the control tower on the breckland at Bodney, home of the 352FG, called to advise that a P-51 had crashed south-east of USAAF Station 143. This was North Pickenham, a B-24 base whose occupants had earlier departed as part of the Second Air Division's participation in the day's operations. Contacting the bomber base, Renkin and Richardson established that crash action had been taken and were advised to wait for further information. Forty-five frustrating minutes elapsed, then another airfield, USAAF Station 376 at Watton, called. The news was ominous: a crashed P-51 had been found at Ashill; it had nose markings believed to be yellow. The 359FG wore green, but some numbers had been found on the wreck: '1686'. This matched the last four digits on Shearer's ship, IV-N. But, more importantly, where was the pilot?

Watton had also reacted to news of the crash, and its tender had beaten North Pickenham to the scene. From the centre of a deep ugly crater, flames seared through the remains of a once sleek fighter. Radiating heat had scorched a black circle in the snow and flames

Flames seared through the remains of the once sleek fighter – had Kay Shearer escaped?

prevented close inspection of the wreckage, but nothing akin to any human form could be discerned. Kay Shearer might have parachuted clear and could be lying injured nearby in danger of death from hypothermia. Deep concern for one of their own prompted East Wretham's flying control to contact the Group Surgeon at 1230; he ordered an ambulance and Medic to be dispatched immediately.

That morning, two local farmworkers had been standing in the farmyard of Moat Farm, Ashill, undoubtedly cold and complaining about working in such atrocious weather. Overhead, other men were also working and certainly had greater reason to curse the conditions. At 1046 the two rustics heard the anguished funereal threnody of an aero engine screeching earthwards. They caught a brief glimpse of the machine plummeting vertically out of cloud, then came the sickening thud of impact. An ugly column of black smoke brewed out of a deep crater sliced into a field known as the 'Long Oris', near one of the farm cottages. The vicious emission of exploding ammunition discouraged any close approach, but the disintegration and depth of wreckage made it clear that no one could have survived if they were in the machine when it crashed. Local folk could only hope that poor visibility had prevented them from seeing a pilot's parachute drifting to earth further away.

Similar thoughts occurred at East Wretham, and, with fading winter light a consideration, a search party was detailed from the Military Police Company and Station Compliment

Squadron. They departed at 1535, still hopeful that Shearer would be found alive, but, with darkness imminent, hopes dwindled. British emergency services, including the National Fire Service, also supported the search and rescue efforts. Station Officer L.A. Pett of the East Dereham NFS noted that this was the first occasion the USAAF had used their state-of-the-art foam fire tender on a crash in the area. At the then princely sum of £10,000, it was equipment the NFS could only dream of, but the foam helped suppress the flames, allowing closer examination of the wreckage. Deep down amid the mangled smouldering remains of his cockpit, it became grimly evident the pilot had not escaped. The sad task of confirming his identity initially came from parts of the aircraft. At 1600, any hopes held by East Wretham were crushed when North Pickenham provided several serial numbers from pieces of the Mustang. Checking the number of a machine gun with 369FS, armourers confirmed the ill-fated aircraft as IV-N, 44-11686. The remains of Capt Karl K. Shearer were extricated with some difficulty and interred in the US Military Cemetery at Cambridge, where they still rest today. Circumstances of that unlucky 13 January meant his funeral service was not in isolation.

Another very experienced pilot to combat the elements that murky morning was Wendel J.A. Nelson of the 356FG at Martlesham Heath near Ipswich in Suffolk. Wendel, at 28, was older than the average pilot, and this native of Fremont, Nebraska, could draw on a tremendous

Wendel J.A. Nelson of the 356FG pictured in his P-51 during December 1944. *(Fred Vonderlage)*

depth of experience. An adventurous character, 'Wen' had been educated at the Luther Academy and Luther College in Wahoo, Nebraska, before beginning a business career in advertising, first for the *Wichita Eagle* in Kansas, then, still in the same state, for the *Pittsburgh Headlight*. Wishing to further his career, he finally went south to attend the St Austin's School of Advertising and Marketing in Houston, Texas, before taking a role with International Harvester. When he was not working, Wen's enthusiasm for sport took over. Blessed by Scandinavian origins, he was tall, with excellent physique and coordination making him a natural at sports. Blonde hair and blue eyes were a bonus accompanying his natural charm. Football, softball, tennis and athletics were challenging, but he found an even more demanding hobby – flying. Not only had the Nordic gods given this young man good looks; they had also gifted him with high intelligence and a strong sense of fair play. Fluent in Swedish, Norwegian, German and Finnish, Wen was intensely angered to see little Finland fighting for its existence against its giant Russian neighbour. Taking advantage of the non-aggression pact agreed in 1939 between the two despots, Hitler and Stalin, the communists made bullying territorial demands on Finland that October. When that plucky little country stood its ground and fought, Wen enlisted in the Finnish Air Force, hoping to challenge the aggressor during the 'Winter War' of 1939–40. However, events moved so swiftly that he was unable to contribute before the Finns were obliged to surrender land in return for peace, of a sort, during March 1940.

Meanwhile, Britain and France had declared war on Nazi Germany following Hitler's invasion of Poland during September 1939. Ill-equipped and ill-prepared, the Allies were overwhelmed in Europe within the year, and, by August 1940, Wen could see that Great Britain was fighting not only for its own life but to preserve democratic freedoms that the fascists abhorred. Like many Americans, he felt the British bastion had to stand, and he rallied to support that beleaguered little island by joining the sons of its Commonwealth also volunteering in their thousands. His parents, Lillian and John, experienced early on the anxiety soon to be felt nationwide as one of their sons left to train for aerial combat overseas. Wen made contact with the clandestine Clayton Knight recruiting organisation established by former Royal Flying Corps hero, Air Vice Marshal Billy Bishop, VC, and his erstwhile compatriot, the American Clayton Knight. This had been established to encourage enlistment and smooth the way for young American volunteer airmen and was at first tacitly accepted by the US authorities then finally blessed by President Roosevelt, who ordered that US citizens going to Canada to join the Royal Canadian Air Force or RAF be exempted from the US Draft Board. Wendel John August Nelson enlisted in the RCAF at Windsor, Ontario, on 13 August 1940 and entered the British Commonwealth Air Training Plan. This was basically an agreement between the governments of Britain and Canada for the establishment of training facilities where airmen could be taught far from the fighting zone and where there was land available to build airfields. Wen was one of the earliest into the scheme and found himself in the uncomfortably coarse blue uniform of the RCAF as the humblest of Aircraftsmen, an AC2, at $1.70 a day plus free room and board. Serving in the ranks, he endured the usual indoctrination of square bashing and boot polish before advancing to Leading Aircraftsman for a reduced dosage of the same and, more importantly, beginning his military aviation career with 2 Initial Training School and then progressing to 7 Elementary Flying Training School with its delightful Fleet Finch biplanes.

During the Christmas of 1940, Wen was allowed home on leave, and, journeying south across the border, he found himself on a bus bound for Davenport, Iowa. Sitting across the aisle was a very petite, attractive brunette and initial, introductory courtesies deepened into more meaningful discourse. Isabell Poston was travelling home to her family in Davenport for Christmas. Cupid had also purchased a ticket, because love grew as the miles shrank; it was a very different young man who determined his destiny that day. He, too, disembarked at Davenport and spent three days courting this beautiful young woman. On the third day, to the consternation of the Poston family, Wen proposed and was accepted. Concerned over this young charmer's credentials, Isabell's father, a doctor, phoned the police in Fremont. Answering this rather strange call, the Chief of Police, one Phil Nelson, was delighted to

From romance on a bus, Wen and Isabell were married in Toronto on 1 June 1941. He was now a Pilot Officer in the RCAF – she was pregnant when he left to serve overseas. *(Fred Vonderlage)*

endorse his impetuous nephew and wished the young couple well. The wedding plans went forward, as did the young aviator's career.

Things became more serious and intellectually more strenuous at 6 Service Flying Training School in Dunnville, where Wen learned the idiosyncrasies of the Harvard and its similarly styled sister, the Yale advanced Trainer. On 30 March 1941, Wen was appointed a commission as a Pilot Officer and moved to RCAF Station Trenton, where the Central Flying Establishment operated an array of training aircraft plus more serious Hudson bombers and the famous Hawker Hurricane fighter. With his departure overseas almost certain, Wen and Isabell were married in Toronto on 1 June 1941 and, following an all-too-brief honeymoon, Isabell's husband was soon drawn back to his other love – flying. He trained at 2 Bombing and Gunnery School, Mossbank, from June until August, when he finalised the Canadian element of his aviation education flying a mixture of aircraft from RCAF Mountain View. His logbook now included twin-engined experience in the Avro Anson, and, on completion of his training, Wen joined the Embarkation Pool in Halifax on 24 September 1941. He had said his farewells to his family and young bride, now a mother-to-be.

Following his arrival in the UK and transit through 3 Personnel Reception Centre, Wen was sent to 60 Operational Training Unit, which had been established to train night fighter crews for Fighter Command. Operating from East Fortune and its satellite, Macmerry, in East Lothian, the unit flew the turreted Boulton Paul Defiant single-engined fighters, outclassed and withdrawn from daylight operations, plus Airspeed Oxfords and Bristol Blenheims. The Blenheim had been a stop-gap until the advent of its later, more potent stablemate, the pugnaciously powerful Beaufighter.

Soon Wen was flying Beaufighter operations with 600 Squadron from RAF Predannock in Cornwall and wrote home of his aircraft, saying that it carried 'terrific armament and lots of scientific equipment'. With a crew of two, the Beaufighter prowled the night skies, and, carrying four 20mm cannon and six machine guns, it had devastating firepower. However, any armament is useless if it cannot be brought to bear, and the 'scientific equipment' Wen mentioned was the top-secret AI (Airborne Interception) radar used to home in on German bombers. Wen could not mention its existence when he wrote to his aunt.

We go up to intercept enemy raiders and go over to France and Germany to strafe the troops there . . . We spend our nights in the air groping blindly by instrument and radio through an impossible darkness. We have the job and are quickly getting on to it. We do an unpublicised job, get little glory but a hell of a lot of satisfaction.

A less demanding type to fly was the Miles Master III, a single-engined advance trainer with fighter-like qualities, and Wen, enjoying practically anything that flew, found himself with a non-operational, daytime task using Master W8525, and another letter home told of his misadventure.

I was sent with my kite down to a point in southern England. In the midlands, near Leeds, I had engine failure over the mountains. It was very bad weather and I was flying very low

The bedraggled remains of Master W8525 9-KT are drawn from the canal. The Form 765C noted its fate as 'Reduction To Scrap', which was hardly surprising in the circumstances. *(Via Patsy Feather)*

so I had very little time to do much. So I crash-landed in a field in a valley. The field was very small and I went through two stone fences which are so common over here. I was going very fast and my speed carried me through both fences and into a canal full of grimy water. I and what was left of my kite were completely submerged. I was slightly dazed but the cold water revived me. I got out thoroughly drenched and stood on top of my kite until some firemen took me off. It so happened that on the hill near the canal live some very nice people by the name of Vincent A. Knowles. He is a wealthy manufacturer. They took me to their home, where I had a hot bath and dry clothes. I stayed there several days with them. They have two very sweet little daughters, Patsy and Betty . . .

In fact, Vincent Knowles had dived into the canal and swum to the semi-submerged aircraft and assisted a very concussed Wendel to escape from the sunken cockpit. Meanwhile, his father, Walter, fetched a plank, which was placed to reach the wreck, and Wen was helped onto dry land. The National Fire Service also assisted, while local children took great delight in scavenging for souvenirs. Ray Mitchell, then a teenager in the 'Elland Lane Gang', had heard the sputtering engine, then seen the aircraft circling, obviously in trouble and seeking somewhere to land. They thought it was 'a Jerry', and, watching it drop down towards fields on Jaggers Farm, the youngsters immediately thought of trophies. As the plane disappeared behind the trees, Ray yelled to his chums, 'Let's get down there, quick!' and the gang took off on their quest. With a wooden fuselage and wings, the disintegrating Master had given the boys plenty of choice. Pieces of plywood were scattered across the bumpy field in its wake, and both wings had been ripped off when the aircraft crashed through the first dry-stone wall. Further pieces were floating in the canal, some coloured bright yellow, presumably from interior fittings, others were in light-grey camouflage colouring. Roy still has his coveted souvenirs.

So, too, does Patsy Feather, née Knowles, but her tiny fragment represents so many more enduring memories. Patsy, then 16, later recalled Wen's somewhat spectacular arrival. Confined indoors with whooping cough, she and Betsy did not see the crash but heard the machine splutter overhead. When the rescued aviator arrived in their home, the girls were thrilled. Pilots were like gods to young girls of that era, and the appearance of this tall, good-looking American example made an 'everlasting impression' and evoked Hollywood

Patsy (left) and Betty Knowles with their handsome hero – 'Glamour with a capital G'. *(Via Patsy Feather)*

with its handsome heroes. 'He was Glamour with a capital G, in our young lives, and Wen exemplified all that we had heard and seen at the cinema – his accent, his ease of manner, his charm.' Only this was Elland, Yorkshire, and the girls were reduced to giggles when Wen emerged from the bathroom in a pair of borrowed, bright yellow pyjamas. He joined in the laughter when they christened him 'Daffodil' – a nickname that was to endure through the following months of friendship. So excited were they by events that the whooping cough afflicting both young ladies virtually vanished overnight, much to the amazement of Dr Price, who also checked on his latest patient. Apart from slight concussion, Wen was unharmed, but the three young folks enjoyed some time recuperating. On one occasion, Wen decided to teach these young English ladies the art of baseball, and Patsy proved an adept pupil and remembers how Wen 'managed to teach me to swing a mean baseball – right through my uncle's drawing room window! We used to fall about helplessly laughing at the faces he pulled and the gyrations of his "pitching!".' Wen eventually returned to his unit, but the new roots of a young friendship had quickly grown deep between him and the Knowles family. The girls had a 'marvellous "brother"', and Vincent and Eileen Knowles 'adopted' the young American airman, who was always welcomed into Ash Grove, their family home. For Wen, the family provided fun and their house a sanctuary from the stress of combat. He spent many of his leaves with them, and the 'candy' he produced was a delight for the girls in those days of sweet rationing. Both adored 'their' pilot, but one of Patsy's plans to show him off to her chums backfired, as she recalls:

We were so proud, Betty and I, of this wonderful chap who came for his leaves, that I remember inviting several school friends to come and meet him – but he got wind of this and although we waited – and waited – no Wen arrived and I wrote a terse note which I left in his room which read, among other things, 'I am MOST annoyed' and he never let me forget and often asked if I was still 'MOST annoyed'!

Wendel was a natural with children, and his happiness with the Knowles would, he hoped, one day be mirrored in far away Fremont. Taking regular leave in America was impossible, and Wen could not even get home for the birth of his son, Richard, born on 28 February to Wen's intense pride and a damaging celebratory impact on his mess bill. More seriously, Wendel was determined that baby Richard John Lee would grow up in a world free of Nazi tyranny. Isabell was soon introduced by letter to the Knowles, and both Betty and Patsy were delighted and, no doubt, the envy of their chums when parcels of American girls' clothes began arriving at Ash Grove. The Knowles wrote to Isabell and the sisters corresponded regularly with Wen, who genuinely welcomed hearing from them, as he confirmed on one occasion: 'Have enjoyed your letters immensely girls. They have certainly been written in fine spirit and have cheered me up a lot. Of course, by that you may think I'm lonesome, well I am! So your letters really are appreciated . . .'

In letters written during the summer of 1942, Wen spoke of a pending move to the Middle East, and there was sand in his shoes by 16 September, when he joined 6 Squadron,

RAF, on the inhospitable terrain that was Landing Ground 89. This was the period of an intense Allied accumulation of resources intended finally to knock Rommel's vaunted Afrika Korps off its pedestal. A new weapon in the armoury was the ferocious Hurricane IID with its 40mm anti-tank cannon. Use of this weaponry would soon earn 6 Squadron its unofficial soubriquet of 'The Flying Can Openers'. Such was the pace of operations that squadron records are sparse and details of Wen's sorties are unknown save that his 'Particulars of Operational Duty' credit him with ten missions. It is known that pilots pressed home their attacks so tenaciously that Hurricanes were sometimes damaged in actually striking tank turrets with their tail wheels.

Wen completed just a month with 6 Squadron and was injured in action before moving to another role that literally lifted him from the sands into the heavens. This was a posting to 103 Maintenance Unit, part of 206 Group headquartered at RAF Station Aboukir near Alexandria. His purpose was to act as test pilot for the many serviced, repaired or recently reassembled aircraft processed by the unit. Another duty was to act as Flight Commander for the High Altitude Defence Flight established to counter highflying Junkers 86P twin-engined photo-reconnaissance aircraft. These flew over to spy on Allied shipping movements from 37,000ft, beyond the reach of any standard fighter then available. The ingenious technicians of 103 MU then devised their own high-altitude, highly modified Spitfire. With all excess weight removed and wearing extended wingtips, this Spitfire was capable of intercepting these annoying interlopers. Aboukir also handled some photo recce Spitfire IVs, and it was in a Spitfire that Wen set an operational high altitude record of nearly 50,000ft. He was extremely effective in his duties at Aboukir, and his Commanding Officer recorded on 6 January 1943:

> The above named officer is particularly suitable for the duties on which he is at present employed (Chief Test Pilot). He has a total of nearly 1500 hours . . . since his arrival at this unit on 17 October 1942, F/? [sic] Nelson has proved himself an officer of outstanding ability and has re-organized the flying on this station to a high pitch of efficiency . . . The high standard of general serviceability of aircraft turned out by this station . . . has been largely due to his efficiency, thoroughness and high standards of test flying . . . he is extremely popular amongst his subordinates on account of his efficiency and ability (particularly with the flying personnel).

His CO was most anxious to retain Wen's services, but Wen wanted to go home and meet his son, so he was granted leave on compassionate grounds and returned to America at the beginning of 1943.

Not only was Wen a very proud father, but his family were excited to have the young hero at home in their midst, as his nephew, Fred Vonderlage relates: 'Phil [Wen's younger brother] and two of my father's brothers were in the US Navy but Wen was clearly our hero since he was in the more romantic role of fighter pilot.' Wen introduced an admiring young Fred to the excitement of flying in a light aircraft:

My father went up with me because I was dubious about it even though I was fascinated with airplanes. My brother had no such fears and was always more like Uncle Wendel, sort of a daredevil . . . I remember that, at one point, we banked to turn and I almost came unglued and hollered, 'how come you're tipping the plane so much?' Wendel laughed and asked how he thought we were going to turn if we didn't bank. I said, 'do you have to do it so much?' Gradually I got used to it but was still glad to get down on the ground. I may have been leery because, when my brother had gone up with Uncle Wendel, I saw them swoop down and disappear momentarily behind some haystacks. He also told us one of his ambitions was to fly down under the signs stretched across Main Street between buildings. Main Street was not that wide either. He never did it but I wouldn't have been surprised if he had done it . . .

His leave complete, Wen now assumed duties in Canada, flying high-altitude mapping trips in the photo-reconnaissance Mosquito and Spitfire. He was officially commended by the

Pictured in August 1944, a happy family, Wen, Dickie Lee and Isabell. 1/Lt Wendel J.A. Nelson, proud of his new silver USAAF wings, is still honoured to wear those of the RCAF over his right pocket. Note the wings on Isabell's dress. *(Fred Vonderlage)*

National Research Council of Canada for skill shown in May 1943 when he safely landed a burning Spitfire. For several months, Wen contributed to the map-making activities of the nation whose uniform he wore with pride, but he was now missing the adrenalin of combat operations and was keen to resume his original role as a night fighter pilot. His frustration increased when, at a dance one evening, another young man called him a slacker. That individual soon had cause to regret his remark, as Fred recalls Wen 'punched the guy out and then volunteered to go back into combat'.

However, Wen's resumption of combat activities would no longer be under the King's Commission, and his RCAF Certificate of Service closes when he was 'Struck off Strength', on 29 June 1944, 'by means of Resignation upon transfer to the United States Armed Forces'. Having transferred to the USAAF, he underwent further training and indoctrination before arriving at Martlesham Heath that November. He was much older than many of his contemporaries and, in the four years since volunteering, he had accrued over 1,750 flying hours. Assigned to the 360FS, he now added a further 150 hours on Mustangs in the plethora of operational activities embraced by 8FC. These included long-range escort, dive-bombing of bridges and numerous strafing assaults on troops, tanks and trains as 356FG Mustangs were unharnessed to sweep over Europe. In a play on his name and its historical connotations, the P-51 manned by Wen was named 'Lord'. Like the warships under Admiral Lord Nelson, 356FG Mustangs took their colours proudly into battle. Each engine was bannered with a rich red cowling dressed longitudinally upon which were dark blue diamonds, and the rudder of each fighter was emboldened with the colour coding for its Squadron – yellow for the 359FS; red for 360FS; blue for 361FS. Lord's rudder was red, and Wendel's touch was delicate when he applied it to avoid the swing as his Mustang streaked down the runway on 13 January 1945. Taking off as part of the 356FG contingent under Capt Richard Rann, Wen had been ordered to furnish penetration, target and withdrawal support for bombers assaulting road and rail bridges near Mannheim. With 1,902 hours logged, he once again pitted experience against the elements as appalling cloud conditions soon swallowed the fighters from view. Wen was last witnessed making a climbing turn into the overcast.

The office of Station Surgeon at Martlesham Heath had been relatively quiet that week – seventeen patients admitted to Bracken Hall sick quarters, twelve medical examinations, including three diagnosed as venereal disease, but routine for an army anywhere. One of their more urgent requirements was to respond to crash calls and, during the late morning, they reacted swiftly to an alarm for one of their own aircraft that had crashed near Debach. At 1050, a P-51 had hurtled from cloud to explode on Bridge Farm, Grundisburgh, in Suffolk, only 3 miles from Martlesham Heath. The medical personnel were soon on the scene, but nothing could be done. Major Robert E. Nuernberger, the Station Surgeon, could only note in his weekly report: 'the pilot was killed instantly. There was a complete disintegration of both body and plane.' The courageous flying career of 1/Lt Wendel J.A. Nelson, ranging the skies by day and by night, reached this violent denouement in a simple, Suffolk meadow. The only assumption to be made was that the experienced pilot had been the victim of vertigo, but it is unlikely that the truth will ever be known. The other forty aircraft of the 356FG conducted the mission without mishap.

Patsy, now 19, was studying at a faculty of London University and was eagerly looking forward to seeing Wen again. He and his friend Bob Wallace had just spent their Christmas leave with the family, and she still recalls the merriment when Bob stood so close to the fire that he singed his 'pinks' – his best uniform. As they said their farewells at the station, Wen had arranged to take Patsy to a ball in Cambridge – she even had a new black gown for the occasion. When the phone rang, it was Bob. Wartime security handicapped the words he wanted to say, but, to prevent Patsy going to the ball and waiting for the partner who would never arrive, all Bob could utter was, 'Wen is no more'. Patsy was devastated and cried most of the night. No matter how much her loss, she knew the anguish would be multiplied when that dreaded telegram was taken to Isabell. Wen, the husband, father, son and friend, truly was no more.

Most aircraft aloft that grim morning were on operational duties to support their big friends, but new arrivals in the ETO needed indoctrination and had to encounter weather conditions typical of those they would face on a combat sortie. Like other groups, the 357FG had a training unit, irreverently referred to as 'Clobber College'. Following the departure of their operational aircraft, Capt Alvin Murphy, an experienced combat pilot, led five Mustangs away from Station 373 for a low-altitude formation flight. The aircraft used by Clobber College were typically cast-offs relegated from front-line status, and, as a tyro, Flight Officer Richard A. Anderson had been allocated a war-weary P-51B, serial 41-6987. Taunting fate, its former pilot had named the aircraft 'Satan' and rode the devil until it was usurped by a more enticingly entitled P-51D, 'Miss Satan'. Whether the age of the machine played any part in events is unknown, but it is always a possibility. Even though inexperienced on the Mustang with only seventeen hours, Richard Anderson held a creditable 407 total hours but not facing the type of weather encountered that dismal drizzly day. Low clouds were being pressed upon the countryside at 1030 as instructor Murphy took off then gathered his brood to follow. Forming into two sections, a leading formation of four with Anderson trailing astern as last man in a section of two, the six traversed the locality. Such flights did not stray far from base and helped with area familiarisation for recently arrived pilots. After some thirty minutes, Murphy tightened formation and told his fledglings he would lead them up through the overcast. He instructed the formation to uncage their gyro instruments in readiness for the ascent.

During training in America, all pilots had been taught the basics relating to the sense of position in flight. Vision was the 'all-important' sense in contact flying, but pilots were cautioned that 'it is loss of vision which makes the transition from contact to instrument flight difficult, unless you learn to trust your gyro horizon and other flight instruments with as much confidence as you do the natural horizon. In instrument flight, rely only on what you see in the cockpit.' From the Pilots' Information File issued by the Office of Flying Safety plus detailed training lectures, Anderson and other neophyte bird men were taught to understand illusory deceptions and the elements that might confuse their 'their deep sensibility'. Deep sensibility was described as the combination of sensations of pressure and tension on the skin, muscles, tendons and internal organs . . . When your feet are on the ground, sensations from your soles and the muscles of your legs tell you what position your feet are in. This deep sensibility is an important factor in helping you maintain your bodily balance. In flight you get the effect of deep sensibility in the seat of your pants, since gravity and centrifugal force exert their action there. Changes in the position of your plane make you feel heavier or lighter, or as if you are being forced sideways in your seat. When you can't check your position by visual reference, you rely mainly on your inner ear. The inner ear has two parts. The semicircular canals, which are placed in three different planes, are responsible for the sensation of rotation or turning, pitching and rolling. The static organ tells you the position of your head in relation to the ground. The sensations provided by deep sensibility and the inner ear lead to confusion when you are flying on instruments. Never trust your feel or sense of position when you are flying on instruments or at night; if you do you'll get into trouble since the sensations from the seat of your pants and your inner ear do not indicate the true position of your airplane. You often get false impressions when on instruments even during straight and level flight and especially in turns. If your airplane tilts or tips suddenly in rough air and recovers slowly, you may not know when recovery is complete. Your inner ear retains the impression that your aircraft is still tipped or tilted. This impression may be so strong that you may lean to one side in an attempt to remain upright. 'The Leans' is one of the most common sensations experienced during instrument flight. If you don't check your instrument readings every few minutes, your airplane may turn from the desired heading so slowly that you won't notice it. Then when you check with your instruments and correct your heading and position, you'll feel that you are continuing your turn in the opposite direction. The greatest single danger to an inexperienced pilot flying at night or on instruments is the 'Graveyard Spiral'. This is a diving spiral which gets progressively tighter and steeper, and which is accompanied by a rapid loss of altitude. Such a spiral results directly from relying too much on your sensations and too little on the instruments which indicate bank and turn. The spiral starts when the airplane gradually enters the turn without your realizing it. In such an involuntary turn the angle of bank and the rate of turn both increase so slowly that you have no sensation to warn you that the position of your airplane has changed. You retain the positive impression that you are still flying straight and level. Your first indication that anything is wrong is a change of noise, an increase in airspeed or a loss of altitude. Under these circumstances, unless you look at and believe the instruments which indicate turn and bank, you may merely pull back on the stick, under the impression that by so doing you are recovering from a straight dive. If you do, this impression of being in a straight dive increases, since pulling back on the stick gives you the same feeling you have in a normal straight pullout from a dive. Once you start to pull back on the stick, the turn gets tighter, the nose drops lower, and there is a great increase in airspeed and the rate of descent. After a few seconds the airplane may have more than doubled its original speed, and the rate of descent may have increased to several thousand feet per minute. You can recover easily and quickly from such a spiral. *Remember: when anything seems to be going wrong, when the airplane is starting to lose altitude and gain speed, first look at the instruments* *which indicate bank and turn.* In all probability the airplane is banked and is turning, although your sensations make you feel it is in straight and level flight. Don't act according to your sensations. *Check and cross-check your instruments.*

Anderson would have relied on visual contact with his leader, but, if he became separated, reliance on flight instruments would be his salvation. These instruments used air pressure to give readings. Mounted on the Mustang's starboard wing was a pitot-static tube that provided measurements of airflow to determine airspeed through the airspeed indicator. It also gave static pressure readings for the altimeter and rate of climb indicator. The rate of climb indicator would have been relatively useless in turbulence, and the altimeters of the day were set before take-off by use of a barometric scale to provide altitude above sea level for that particular airfield. Altitude and the prevailing air temperatures and pressures could seriously affect the instrument. Low air temperatures and reduced barometric pressure could mean the aircraft was lower in reality than the reading on the altimeter. Obviously, this could be very dangerous, and pilots were taught to be aware of it and to reset the altimeter in flight if necessary. The instruction for Anderson to uncage the gyro instruments referred to his gyro horizon indicator and directional gyro. These two key instruments were next to one another, centrally positioned on his instrument panel. The artificial horizon had a horizontal bar representing the wings of his machine over horizontal segments symbolising the horizon with markings indicating angle of bank, plus climb and descent. However, this instrument could 'tumble' beyond 100 degrees bank or 70 degrees climb and dive. It would be caged – locked – during aerobatics and uncaged in stable flight beneath cloud to be used during a blind ascent. The directional indicator gave a course heading for use with the aircraft's magnetic compass, but it, too, could tumble beyond 55 degrees of bank, climb or dive. Another key player in the process of flying on instruments was the turn and bank indicator, which was a combination of two instruments, a bank indicator and turn indicator both housed in the one case and prominently positioned lower centre of the instrument panel. The bank indicator was a ball enclosed in a curved glass tube full of a non-freezing liquid. When straight and level, the ball sat neatly between two vertical bars in the centre of the curve's saucer. Above it was a needle pinioned to point vertically down at the ball with 'L' and 'R' to either side for indicating left or right bank. This instrument gave the relationship between angle of bank and rate of turn. In a precisely positioned turn, the needle moved but the ball sat centrally. If the ball drifted low, the aircraft was slipping downwards – if it went high, you were skidding upwards. In an ascent through cloud, the needle and ball could help determine your attitude. These instruments were basic to any aircraft and it was vital for a pilot to rely on them in cloud if he had no visual reference point such as the horizon or his leader's wing.

During training, Anderson had received his instrument rating on 9 May 1944. Since then he had accrued only twelve hours on instruments, bolstered by five hours beneath the hood of a link trainer. It must have been intimidating for the young pilot peering up into those looming dark clouds. Climbing gently, the six Mustangs slid into the murk. A short time after entry, Anderson called agitatedly to his element leader, 'check your needle and ball' – 'check your needle and ball!' He was clearly in trouble, probably owing to vertigo. Moments later, his P-51 fell out of the formation and went down out of control.

On 14 January Police Sgt R.W. Ruffles reported from Stradbroke Station to Superintendent Rumsey:

I beg to report that on Saturday 13th January 1945 at 11:10 AM a Mustang single seater fighter came out of the clouds and appeared to make a landing in the fields on Sancroft Manor Farm, Laxfield. One wingtip was seen to catch the ground and the machine crashed breaking up into a hundred pieces. The petrol caught fire and many parts of the machine were burnt out. On arrival I found the pilot's body on fire and with PWR Mills I put this out and found the identity disc around his neck. He was dressed in American uniform and the name shown on the disc was Richard A. Anderson with numbers T 63210 T43-44A. The machine carried G4 on the fuselage and two numbers on the wing, 693 and 987W. The machine crashed in a field on Sancroft Manor Farm and pieces travelled onto Gatehouse Farm, both are in the parish of Laxfield. The map reading I gave as M77/723905. Horham aerodrome control was informed and took over at 12 noon sameday. The Stradbroke Fire Brigade also attended.

Poor Anderson had not entered combat with any mortal enemy but became a casualty of senses confused by a foe just as deadly in a half-lit, swirling grey world that would continue to test other, more experienced pilots that morning.

Not only were military lives at risk. In a semi-detached cottage in the country town of Melbourn, three families were about to be embroiled in the tragic events triggered by such appalling weather. The ancient wattle-and-daub dwelling stood next to an orchard on Rose Lane and comprised two homes. Mr and Mrs Walter Waldock lived in one half, but Walter was abroad fighting his way through Europe with the British Army. His wife Daisy and his 2½-year-old daughter Brenda were generously sharing their tiny home with Daisy's elder sister, Alice Beech, and her three children, Jack, aged 11, and twins David and Arthur at 3 years 5 months. Their father, Charles, was serving in the Royal Navy, and his family had left their own home in the frequently bombed naval town of Portsmouth for the apparent sanctuary of a rural community. That morning, domestic duties were being shared between the sisters, and Daisy climbed the stairs to remake the beds and tidy up. Meanwhile, Alice was busy in the tiny kitchen to the front of the house. There were only two rooms downstairs, including the kitchen, so the children, usually in the garden, were indoors because of the cold weather and amusing themselves in the living room.

Next door, Mrs Alice Cooper also set about her morning chores and debated whether to put her baby daughter, Pauline, outside in the pram as usual. Like any young mother, Alice knew the benefits of fresh air and the 18-month-old baby seemed to thrive on it. Her ruddy, chubby cheeks often glowed with freshness from the clean Cambridgeshire air as, chortling from the attention, she was hoisted into the air for a cuddle with her father. On other

Walter and Daisy Waldock with their daughter Brenda. Walter was abroad with the British Army when the P-51 crash endangered the lives of his wife and child. (Arthur Beech)

occasions, snugly wrapped with a breeze gently joggling the pram springs, she slept in the front garden, undisturbed and undisturbing as her busy mother tidied house and prepared food in those days of rationed, pre-convenience food. That Saturday, one of Alice's apple pies seemed in order, and her husband, Harold, set off for the nearby orchard. Peering through a scattering of snowflakes, Alice decided against putting Pauline outside and placed her daughter in her playpen beneath the front parlour window while she returned to the kitchen and began peeling potatoes.

A few miles further west, the prospects of home-made apple pie were the stuff of dreams for ground crew and pilots of the 355FG, now in its eighteenth month of operations from

Station 122 Steeple Morden. For 1/Lt Thomas A. Ksanznak, the prospects of Mom's apple pie were tantalisingly closer than for many of his comrades. Having arrived during June 1944 and flown his first mission on 19 July, Tommy was close to the completion of his tour. This might even be the last sortie for 'Sad Sack' – the nickname this popular young Pennsylvanian had acquired since the early days. Tommy was a serious young man in his Christian beliefs but balanced this with the exuberance and confidence required to make an effective fighter pilot. Tommy, like many of his contemporaries, did not regard himself as essentially military, and that unruly crop of curly hair creeping from beneath his flying helmet characterised his style and charm. An avid aviation enthusiast since childhood, Tommy had set his sights on achieving that coveted, elite role of fighter pilot, but there was no hint of arrogance in this miner's son from West Hazleton; just the burning ambition to fly fighters. His father,

Charles and Alice Beech with their sons (from left to right) David, Jack and Arthur. The exploding P-51 left an image imprinted on young Arthur's mind that was the earliest he could remember. *(Arthur Beech)*

Thomas, and mother, Barbara, were understandably proud of their son gaining a commission in the Army Air Force. At 23, Tommy was one of seven children, and his brothers and sisters were proud to have a handsome young flier for a brother. He was an inspiration to them all, and his eloquence, charm and patience with his young brothers and sisters gained their lifelong adoration. Tommy helped his mother and taught his young brother, Larry, which snakes were dangerous. The pair spent memorable moments with the boy gazing heavenwards – to the sky – Tommy dreaming of his pursuit plane, as fighters were known then, winging between clouds in a world beyond the coal mine or, at night, teaching Larry of the stars and sharing the wonder of what lay beyond. Cherishing these moments, Larry would one day inspire other children as a teacher, but, for now, Tommy himself had to become a pupil, and he proudly inscribed his first Pilot Log, 'Ksanznak, Thomas A Jr . . . April 27 1943.'

Harold and Alice Cooper with baby Pauline. Alice found the child face down in her play pen amid shards of glass, debris and soil blown in by the explosion.
(Pauline Bird)

1/Lt Thomas A. Ksanznak entered service to do his duty and embrace the opportunity of becoming a pilot. The unruly crop of curly hair creeping from beneath his flying helmet and the charm of that big smile endeared him to members of the opposite sex. *(L. Ksanznak)*

That memorable day he had made his first flight from Jones Field in the humble, bumbling Fairchild PT19A twin-seat primary trainer, but he was on his way and, on 14 May, went solo – an unforgettable occasion. Over the ensuing weeks and months Tommy trod a path towards the stars as he gained proficiency and experience. In June he graduated to the more powerful Consolidated Vultee BT13A Valiant at Perrin Field and had barely a day's respite from the rattling, low wing monoplane. He well understood the reason for its nickname 'Vibrator' after twenty-seven flights during July alone. These included night flying and hours 'beneath the hood', where Tommy's cockpit was covered, and he learned in the darkness beneath that he must trust his instruments. During August he added six more such sessions and, by 27 August, could proudly record over 88 hours accrued at Perrin. In September Tommy transitioned to the even more challenging AT6 Harvard and then added solo time in a real fighter, the Merlin-engined variant of the Curtiss P-40, a type still in operational service. Gaining in expertise, December found him handling the P-47D, very much a front-line fighter, but he also punted the air in an A-24, a training derivative of the Douglas Dauntless dive-bomber and then got to grips with an A-36, the Allison-engined Mustang. He was by now at Abilene AAF Base in Texas and close to the conclusion of his training. Formation, cross-country flights and aerial gunnery using a camera feature appeared in his log. His marksmanship against ground targets would be needed in Europe, and his first effort on 27 January 1944 produced a creditable 25 hits with 6 bull's-eyes from 200 rounds. Less than two weeks later, bullets from his A-36 savaged the target – 67 hits, 17 bull's-eyes, again from 200 rounds. He proved just as adept flying the P-40N and spent hours now on cross-country and navigational training flights from De Ridder Army Air Base and, less enthusiastically, more hours in the diminutive but necessary Link Trainer, still 'flying' for miles but on the same spot. On departure from the USA, he had nearly fifty hours in this unsung 'aircraft' of the Second World War.

Tommy had also tackled other matters in life with similar enthusiasm and gusto, and, when the time came to part, his girlfriend, Elsie Yannis, gave him a wistful portrait and, for the times, a racier reminder of what he would miss by way of a bikini-clad image as his personal pin-up. Elsie had become part of the family and would be even more so while her beau was abroad. All were heartbroken when the handsome young aviator hoisted his kitbag for the last time and journeyed into the uncertainties of aerial warfare. His plans to marry were on hold, his career aspirations stalled; there was a war to be won, and Tommy Ksanznak, of Polish descent, had a sense of justice such that his personal life was secondary to the struggle for democracy.

Now, nearing the end of his tour, Tommy had made a valuable contribution since his first mission on 19 July. Coincidentally, this had also seen the P-51's debut with the 355FG, which had converted from the P-47. That day, Tommy witnessed the devastation wrought when German fighters broke like a pack of wolves on a batch of unescorted B-17s. His 358FS diarist noted:

The Group furnished Penetration, Target and withdrawal support to a bomber task force attacking targets in the Munich area. Rendezvous with the bombers was made at 0837

Elsie gave Tommy a wistful portrait and a slightly racier reminder of what he would be missing. She noted on the swim-suit shot, 'May I be your Pin Up Girl?' *(Larry Ksanznak)*

hours at 21,000 feet. The target was reached at approximately 0930. The bombers were bounced by 15 plus Me 109s and FW190s. The Luftwaffe used the tactics of having one gaggle draw off the fighter escort, and then another gaggle would hit the bombers. The other two squadrons of this Group, escorting the forward Combat Wings, were jumped this way. This Squadron (Bentley), which had been escorting the rear Combat Wings, arrived too late to be drawn off by this ruse. At the time this squadron arrived, the bombers had been attacked and several bombers were seen going down in flames. This Squadron bounced the enemy at approx. 0945 hours at 25,000 feet. In the ensuing combat this squadron claims a score of 4-0-1 . . . After the combat, the Squadron resumed bomber escort until 1200 hours at 24,000 feet near Antwerp. All pilots returned safely to home base.

In truth, the Luftwaffe's strength was waning, and the squadron encountered enemy fighters on only four more occasions during the next thirty missions flown by Tommy, but the very presence of the P-51s served as a deterrent. Foraging for their foe at floor level had long been a philosophy for 8FC and Tommy participated in numerous strafing attacks on enemy aerodromes as well as hunting along roads and railways for other prey. Trucks, trains, troops – all were machine-gunned, and Tommy's prowess from his training days paid back some of Uncle Sam's investment. His first attempt at dive-bombing was thwarted when the fin fell off one of his 500lb bombs, forcing an early return to base. On 23 December, Tommy flew a Ramrod mission before being given furlough to a rest house, cheerfully dubbed a 'Flak Home'. In these establishments, aircrew were given time for rest and relaxation and the

Tommy taxiing back past the control tower. The only time he flew YF-N in combat was on 30 September 1944 when radio failure prompted an early return, which might explain the emptiness of the airfield. Note signal square with aerodrome identification letters. *(Larry Ksanznak)*

facilities available – sports, reading, walking or simply lazing – undoubtedly rested nerves taut with the terror of facing flak, fighters and that accursed weather. Tommy's own morale had also been boosted by the understanding and friendship of an attractive English lass, Mary Lee, who found herself beguiled by his mischievous spirit and boisterous behaviour. He returned from R&R early in January. At close to 200 operational hours, Tommy was now a veteran, with an Air Medal and Oak Leaf Cluster awarded for his 'courage, coolness and skill in action'. The family were mighty proud when a picture of Tommy accepting the award appeared in the local *Standard Sentinel*. He eschewed any glamour; he knew how little of it there was in ruthless combat, with bullets tearing into running men below; raking railway trucks or flak cutting comrades from the air; then the tiring reality of long hours strapped into his P-51. This weariness is reflected in remarks made in his last letter home dated 9 January 1945.

Dear Mom: Well here I am again. I just got back from the flak home last night and I had 25 letters waiting here for me. That sure did make me feel good. About 5 were from you alone. I'm glad you received my package okay. I got your letter with the picture of Jo Jo [his brother – also in the military] in it. He sure looked good. He looks as if he's gotten a lot heavier, and that tan, sure wish I had one like it. I did when I was in the Cadets, but that seems as though it was about 10 or 15 years ago . . . You think that you have a bum handwriting, well some of the fellows mothers are even worse, and besides, they don't have to read your letters. We all get a laugh at some of the dumb questions our mothers write. Of course it isn't their fault that they don't know as much about combat flying as we do, but it is funny. Bart Magazine sent me a card with a calendar on it, and a World Mass Directory. All you have to do is find out the time and then see in what country mass is being celebrated then say a prayer that it has on there, and it's the same as going to Mass. Have you seen one of them? I got a letter from Jo Jo also. I sure would like to see him again. He was wondering what we were going to do after the war. He said he was going to get a car, if he never gets anything else. I don't blame him, cause I'm going to get one also. Well, I guess that's enough for today. I'll write again tomorrow or the next day. Love, Tommy.

The young man piloting a powerful aircraft dreamt of going home: of owning his own automobile; of the open road; of his girl; maybe of marriage, kids? Who knows?

Four days later, Tommy settled into the seat of a machine – not a fondly thought of car but his familiar fighter, Mustang YF-O, serial 44-13319. It was his preferred mount, even though it had occasionally proved troublesome. Tommy had flown YF-O on twenty-four combat missions but been obliged to return early four times with engine trouble. Manufacturers and maintenance personnel took great care, but the likelihood of mechanical failure was an ever-present threat, and you could not simply pull over to fix it. That far-from-home morning, Tommy had been assigned call sign 'Bentley 47', flying as a spare. He and Lt Tolby, another spare, would follow the group up through the overcast and fill in for any pilot who aborted. This way, the 355FG kept its strength at maximum.

The 355FG briefing included a dismal discourse on the strong high-pressure belt laying east-north-east across Scotland with anti-cyclonic circulation over England. A very weak cold front lay across southern England paralleling the isobars on the weather map. For the pilots, this translated into the predominance of haze, fog, drizzle and snow showers. Sensing some anxiety, ground crews gave the Perspex a reassuring extra polish, then, nearing 1100, the first of forty-two Merlins rasped into life. Soon Mustangs jostled from their panhandled concrete hard stands, snaking along the perimeter track. Steeple Morden lay on a gently sloping landscape, and all pilots were aware of their close proximity to the 91BG base at Bassingbourne. This demanded some fine tuning in air traffic control, but their neighbours were not operational that day and the fighters' focus would be on ascent and assembly under Maj Graham for completion of Field Order 1513A. This was a Ramrod to rendezvous at 1230 with Liberators of the Second Air Division. The B-24s were pounding tactical targets – railway bridges and marshalling yards in the region of Worms, Kaiserslautern and Rudesheim.

Tommy's 358FS was commanded by Capt Gresham and for this, its 278th sortie, it comprised the customary Red, Yellow and Blue flights of four aircraft each, with Tolby and Tommy taking off in the spare slots. Tommy's P-51 lifted neatly off the turf and slid into cloud at some 700ft. The group's course would be south to depart near Dover and across the Channel at its narrowest point, but, before then, was the hazardous climb to assemble.

Life in Rose Lane moved peacefully towards lunchtime, and the sound of aircraft in the gloom above went unheeded because it was so common. Local residents were oblivious of the tribulations being faced by men whose aircraft now swam upwards, striving for the sunlight. Sitting on a couch next to the window, young Arthur Beech might have been fascinated by the snowflakes, but he was about to register an image from the heavens much more violent, an image that would be forever imprinted on his mind. His first-ever memory, when later articulated, could only be described as 'a ball of fire' heading straight at him. In that instant before disintegration and chaos, Arthur did shout, but he was too young to warn, and it was already too late. The very next moment, he was being thrown across the room in a maelstrom of glass and debris blasted in from an enormous explosion in the garden. He has no recollection of the noise and simply recalls the ball of fire one moment and then being tossed like a discarded toy towards the rear of the house. Upstairs, Daisy had been startled by a loud noise and her glance outside froze into an expression of horror. In the split second before it exploded, she saw a burning aeroplane plummeting towards the house.

Next door, Alice Cooper had continued peeling potatoes for the midday meal. One glimpse of the lazily descending snowflakes confirmed the wisdom of placing Pauline in her playpen. Warm as her pram might be, it was just too cold for the child's usual routine. Years later, Alice could not recall hearing the approaching aircraft, but the weekend domesticity suddenly shattered in a terrifying explosion. The entire cottage shook as the kitchen seemed to erupt around her in a storm of glass and broken crockery. The windows vanished and her curtains shot horizontally inwards amidst a deafening roar and the seemingly endless cacophony of splintering glass. In those milliseconds of pure terror, Alice thought only of baby Pauline. Racing into the front room, she confronted every mother's nightmare. There, face down and deathly still, lay her tiny daughter amid shards of glass, debris and soil blasted in from the garden. Fear for her child rose in her throat as she scooped the limp form from the playpen. Please God, let her baby be safe.

Events moved so swiftly that Harold Cooper barely understood what had happened. An explosion then a pall of smoke plumed up from the cottage. A bomb? Plane crash? Harold raced from the orchard, running the longest emotional distance of his life.

Baby Pauline drooped limply in her mother's arms. There were no visual injuries, and, frightened beyond reason, Alice instinctively shook her daughter and was desperately relieved when the baby began crying. Outside, flames scorched the front door and exploding bullets zinged dangerously from the debris of a burning aircraft. Racing upstairs, Alice snatched what little money they had from their wardrobe and noticed that a wicker chair and cushion by the shattered window were already ablaze. The flames, flashing upwards in a window-framed view of hell itself, seemed poised to devour the rest of the bedroom, and her home seemed lost. There was no rear door and escape through the front door was clearly impossible so Alice hastened downstairs to a rear window farthest from the blaze.

The Waldock and Beech families had also struggled to escape. They had a rear door, but it was jammed, probably because the frame had twisted. Use of the front door was impossible, because of the spread of burning aviation fuel, so they all clambered from a rear window. They soon realised the predicament faced by Alice Cooper, who was potentially trapped, but, to the relief of all, she appeared at a broken rear window and was assisted out of the house. Together, mothers and children fled along a path to the rear of the property until they reached the safety of Miss Gilbey's cottage at the top of Rose Lane. Harold Cooper appeared moments later, thankful to find both his wife and daughter shaken but miraculously unscathed. Had the weather not been so bad, their child and the children from next door would have been directly beneath the crashing aircraft, but none realised how the weather had both saved and taken lives. In different weather conditions, with no risk of vertigo, it is unlikely Tommy Ksanznak would have crashed. There had been no emergency call from Bentley 47 – the aircraft's engine had 446 hours on it that morning and Tommy's final flight added only a further 15 minutes, but the Merlin might have malfunctioned. Daisy Waldock thought it was on fire in the air, as did little Arthur Beech, but the eruption of flames might have been from the aircraft striking the chimney stack of the property opposite just before impact. Maybe the malevolence of ice, or instrument failure, played a part, but total disintegration of the aircraft destroyed any evidence.

In wartime, the daily drama enacted overhead fascinated many schoolboys, and those in Melbourn were no exception. The chance of seeing their favourite aircraft close up or of acquiring souvenirs for playground bartering was an opportunity not to be missed. Living in the High Street, 14-year-old Graham Goldthorp had heard the fighter screeching into the village and later visited the scene. The devastation in the garden was horrific. Barely 6ft from the Cooper's front door was a shallow crater some 15ft across now smothered in foam. Countless fragments from the fallen fighter littered the garden, and a gaping hole had been blown through the dwelling's upper story, creating a large gap in the roof pantiles and blasting one window from the Waldock home with large chunks of plaster into the garden.

Barely 6ft from the Cooper's front door was a shallow crater some 15ft across and smothered in foam. A member of the British National Fire Service stands half-hidden at the corner of the property. *(David Wade)*

Tommy's aircraft had completely disintegrated, and the devastation can clearly be seen in this photograph. One local account relates how the concrete bird bath was blasted completely over the cottage roof to be found in one piece some distance away in the direction of the church. *(David Wade)*

Damage to both the Cooper and the Waldock dwellings is clearly visible. Furniture was taken from the Waldock homestead for storage in the Salvation Army Chapel, while the Beech and Waldock families moved into temporary accommodation with other family members nearby. *(David Wade)*

This exposed the ancient weave of wattle and daub, now splattered with soil, as was the brick-built house opposite. Like most youngsters, Graham regarded death as something distant and remote. Youth enamelled emotions as he observed American airmen carrying out the grim task of retrieving the pilot's body. Damage to the property in Rose Lane had been substantial, as witnessed by a letter to Mrs Waldock, from Maj Russell Stompler, the Claims Officer from Station 122:

A report of the damage to your cottages on Rose Lane on 13 January 1945, caused by the crash of American Mustang aircraft type P-51 number 44-13319, has been made to The Damage Officer, No. 54 Maintenance Unit, RAF, Newmarket Road, Cambridge, Cambs. The report read 'the damage here was very extensive. The building itself was deemed unsafe by the ARP Warden and the occupants moved out. There was much loss to the personal things of the occupants from the blast and shower of burning petrol from the crash. Five sets of curtains were burned from the window, the charred remains of a raincoat, three women's coats, and a child's Macintosh were examined. There were numerous children's clothes damaged by fire as well as a bed, blankets, eiderdown, and bedroom things, all burned beyond use. There was a large hole in the wall two yards by two yards. All the windows [five] were broken as well as the frames being smashed and burned. There was severe damage to the roof and walls, a hole in the roof one and a half by two yards. Aside from the hole in the wall, the outside plaster was torn off on an area three by five yards. There was much damage to the interior of the house as well as loss of personal items of the occupants. The accident occurred in connection with a combat operation and you can expect representatives of both the War Damage Commission and the RAF Claims to call upon you shortly.'

Alice Cooper was soon allowed home, but her neighbours were obliged to reside with Alice Beech's parents in Meeting Lane until repairs were effected. The claims of all involved were eventually honoured by the Assistance Board under rules for compensation in the War Damage Act. There could never be adequate compensation for the loss of a son and brother.

Upwards of a week after the crash, in another kitchen, another mother – hands dusty with flour – was peacefully baking for those of her family not taken away by war. There was a knock at the door. Barbara Ksanznak glanced at her hands and dishevelled apron before telling 14-year-old Larry to answer. He opened the door. Uniforms. Two men. His mother screamed and collapsed.

Larry learnt that his big brother had been buried in England at the Cambridge American Cemetery and Memorial. Even after the war, his parents could never afford such a trip.

Heartbroken, Barbara Ksanznak collapsed upon receiving news of her son's death. *(Larry Ksanznak)*

A simple wooden cross was later replaced with proud, white marble after the family's decision to leave their boy in the constant care of The American Battle Monuments Commission. Tommy still rests in this beautiful site on land donated by Cambridge University, where many other headstones and a Wall of the Missing remind visitors of the loss of so much youth – young men and women whose chance of a future was selflessly sacrificed for others.

The cruelty of weather conditions that dark day in January 1945 continued to take a toll, although there was one loss that was fortunately material only and not attributable to the weather when engine failure forced 2/Lt Raymond J. Kensik of the 55FS, 20FG, to parachute from his P-51 over Thrixendale in Yorkshire. His group was not required operationally that day and Kensik had the good fortune to survive his mishap.

Those operational groups of Eighth Fighter Command had paid a high price just getting into combat. Their very presence frequently proved a deterrent, and reaction from the enemy that day was muted. Most fighter groups failed to encounter the Luftwaffe, and bomber casualties were low. Only one fighter group received any reward for the risks taken getting airborne. Thirty-seven Mustangs of the 55FG were on a freelance sweep between Bad Nauheim and Mannheim. Arriving at 1255, they patrolled uneventfully for an hour before being recalled, but their ever-combative ace, Lt Col Elwyn G. Righetti, enthusiastically sought some excitement and recalled events in his Consolidated Encounter Report:

We had conducted an uneventful area patrol east of the Second Air Division targets between Bad Nauheim and Mannheim. At 1330 we were released by the Group Leader to conduct a sweep. At this time there were nine planes in the squadron. I was leading White Flight with Capt McGill No. 2, Lt Miller No. 3 and Lt Henry No. 4. Red Flight was led by Capt Brooks with Lt Sharp No. 2, Lt Konantz No. 3 and Lt Schneider No. 4. The ninth pilot, Lieut Eastman, was tucked on to Red Flight as a fifth man.

We took a heading toward Nurnburg, and as we approached Giebelstadt aerodrome, which we had strafed a few days previously, I observed several twin engined aircraft dispersed thereon. We let down, and I instructed Red Flight to attack the field while I covered with White Flight. As Capt Brooks approached on the deck with his flight, a twin engined [aircraft] took off from the field and Red Flight gave chase; the destruction of this enemy aircraft is covered in a separate report. As the airdrome was clear I sent Lieut Miller and Lieut Henry down for an attack. They made a pass from south to north. Lieut Miller saw an Me 262 parked on the south side of the runway too late to fire so continued on firing into an open hangar containing several more Me 262s. He made a shallow left turn and fired on a Ju 88 parked north of the runway near its west end, securing good hits, but no fire, and claims this enemy aircraft as damaged. Lt Henry had no targets on this pass and only fired at the hangar. They circled the aerodrome and approached again from the south. This time Lt Miller secured an excellent concentration of hits and good fire on the Me 262 seen on his first pass. This aircraft burst into flames under the cockpit and is claimed as destroyed. Both pilots again fired into the hanger with unobserved results.

By the time these two attacks had been completed Capt Brooks' flight attacked the aerodrome going from north to south and then reversing directions for the second pass. Both Capt Brooks and Lt Sharp secured good hits on a Do 217, and the enemy aircraft burst into flames as Capt Brooks passed over it. It is believed that Lt Eastman clobbered two or three enemy aircraft also, as he later had to bail out as the result of a flak hit, and his last words over the r/t were, 'tell my wife I'm OK and I got three of them'. Lt Eastman was seen to make strafing passes at the aerodrome and was heard over the r/t, but was not seen thereafter. It is not known whether the claims he mentioned were air or ground, but it is presumed they were ground, as there were five or six fires on the aerodrome at the completion of our attack. We have not included claims for Lt Eastman in this report as no one saw his actual strikes on the enemy aircraft. If we can assume the actual fires observed were his, at least two and probably three planes should be credited to Lt Eastman.

Captain McGill and myself were the last to strafe the field, and we made two passes, the first from NW to SE and the second from SE to NW. On the first pass I placed a 4-second burst in the engines and fuselage of a Ju 88 and saw it blaze up as I pulled away.

Claims: Lt Col Elwyn G. Righetti, 1 Ju 88 destroyed. Ammunition expended 1,700 [rounds]; Capt Philip Brooks [and] 2/Lt Francis R. Sharp, 1 Do 217 destroyed. Ammunition expended 1500 [and] 540; 1/Lt Roy D. Miller, 1 Me 262 destroyed, 1 Ju 88 damaged. Ammunition expended 1,700. 1/Lt Phillips Eastman Jr (MIA) 2 or 3 unidentified twin engined aircraft destroyed.

The separate report referenced by Righetti was a Pilot's Personal Encounter Report submitted by 1/Lt Walter J. Konantz, who wrote:

I was flying Red 3 as we approached Giebelstadt aerodrome about 1330. We observed three or four aircraft taxiing along their long runway and circled for a few minutes to position ourselves for a strafing attack. One of the aircraft took off on the long runway from east to west and made a climbing port turn and came back east at about 1,000 feet just south of the aerodrome. I was on the same side of the field, above him and going the opposite direction. I made a very tight 180-degree turn and identified him as an Me 262. I caught him easily as he was in a medium turn and got a long burst into him from about 200 yards. He caught fire near the port jet unit and made a diving turn straight into the ground about a half-mile from the aerodrome. He exploded with a big flash of flames when he hit. The pilot did not get out. The Me 262 was a silvered one and had no markings or insignia of any kind. My radio went out immediately after this so I did not hear what the rest of the squadron was going to do. I made one pass at a parked enemy aircraft on the field but it must have been hit by our squadron a few days before as it was already burned-out and I did not fire at it. I strafed some very small tin sheds later which seem to contain ammunition as there were a few small explosions and fires started there. I shot a locomotive near Giebelstadt also but had only three guns out on one side and couldn't hit much in that condition. I started out [home] but became lost because both my radio and compass were out. I later joined formation with a 9th AF P-47 and he took me to St Trond where I spent the night and returned to base the next day, after repairs were made to my aircraft. I claim one Me 262 destroyed and the pilot killed.

The unfortunate German vanquished that day was Unteroffizier Alfred Farber of 1KGJ 51 piloting Me 262 werke number 110601. The take-off speed for the Me 262 was some 120 mph so Konantz had easily caught his adversary and these claims helped redress the non-combat losses suffered by 8FC although 'non-combat' is simply a relative term. How they died would not alleviate the grief suffered by families on either side of the conflict.

As those Mustangs of the 55FG that did make the return to Wormingford settled into their circuit for landing, the nearby airfield of Wattisham anxiously awaited another pair of P-51s seeking sanctuary earlier than their main 479FG force. One of the aircraft, Bison 53, flown by Lt Fred Zellman, had experienced engine trouble, and its pilot was seriously sweating out the last few miles to landfall. Forced below cloud, he was now only 200ft over the North Sea's

Happy days. Ray King earns extra by working at the soda fountain in his local drugstore. *(East Essex Aviation Society)*

Flight Officer Raymond E. King pictured with a PT-17 biplane during training. *(East Essex Aviation Society)*

deadly embrace and was thankful for the comforting companionship of the nearby Bison 54, 'Little Zippie', flown by Flight Officer Raymond E. King. Fred knew that prolonged survival would be impossible in the sea's icy grasp. The notorious ditching characteristics of the P-51 might make his demise even swifter and he was too low to jump. Fred had already nursed the troublesome fighter from the area of Worms, where, after overcoming adverse conditions on take off, the 38 Mustangs of his group had rendezvoused in surprisingly clear conditions with Second Air Division Liberators attacking railway bridges. Until his engine misbehaved, Fred's only distraction had been observing some superb bombing by the B-24s, with one fellow pilot noting both ends of a bridge being 'well clobbered'. Few fighter pilots were jealous of their 'big friends', but Fred's malfunctioning engine gave him rueful occasion to envy the advantages of more than one motor. Over the target, a concerned call to his leader, Captain Claire Duffie, released Zellman, with Ray King being ordered to act as escort. Leaving their 436FS formation, the two P-51s turned for home. That had been 350 miles and many harrowing minutes ago, but now they were almost home. Only a mile or two to reach the English coastal resort of Clacton then a short flight inland to Wattisham, some 20 miles beyond. Suddenly and without warning, Ray King's engine quit.

Ray had little time to react and insufficient power to climb and bail out or reach land, even though the sea front of Clacton was now less than a mile away. Events happened so rapidly there was no time to transmit a distress call, but Ray knew Fred would do this, and, if he were lucky enough to survive the ditching, help should rapidly be on hand. Raymond King, at 22, was a determined and very fit young man – he would need to be. Their roles suddenly reversed, Fred Zellman circled back transmitting a desperate Mayday call as 'Little Zippie' dropped into the waves. The signal was picked up and, aligning on the direction and strength of his transmissions, a good fix on his position was obtained. Four air sea rescue Thunderbolts of the 5th Emergency Rescue Squadron, already aloft for just such an emergency, were hastily diverted to the location. Specially adapted, they carried under-wing dinghies and smoke marker bombs to confirm wind direction so precious dinghies could be released upwind and blown towards survivors. In addition, a Walrus amphibian and its later stable mate, the Seagull, were also sent, plus a twin-engined Warwick carrying an airborne lifeboat. While awaiting this support, Fred courageously risked his own engine failing completely and loyally circled overhead.

Despite limited combat experience, Ray King 'rode the ship down as a veteran'. He barely had time to release the canopy, and, judging the waves as best he could, he smacked 'Little Zippie' down in a perfect ditching. Although it was in only 15 feet of water, the temperature was near, if not below, zero and the shock to his system was tremendous. Bitterly cold water engulfed him and, struggling in near darkness, Ray released his harness, kicking free as the Mustang vanished beneath the grey water. Using his CO2 cylinders, Ray inflated his Mae West and bobbed to the surface only a few hundred yards west of Clacton pier.

Ray had ditched at 1505 and Ed continued his vigil until the four 'Teamwork' Thunderbolts arrived at 1515 and he was ordered to leave. Below, there was no sign of his buddy, only an ominous oil slick staining the sea. The P-47 pilots radioed this grim fact in as they orbited the smudge that marked the passing of 'Little Zippie' and possibly her pilot.

Five minutes elapsed with pilots peering anxiously at the seemingly empty waters below, then new hope arose when Teamwork 64 sighted the tiny yellow speck of Ray's Mae West. By now, the Walrus was preparing to land, but additional assistance was on hand in the welcome form of the Clacton lifeboat, *The Edward Z Dresden*, a veteran of many rescues, including troops from Dunkirk.

Barely had the lifeboat slapped into the sea from its steep ramp when coxswain Charles Ellis commanded a course towards the scene. Bitter experience from nearly thirty occasions during six years of war dealing with downed aircraft had taught him not to expect a rescue. But this time, the crew prayed for success, as the aircraft was so close.

Spluttering to the surface, Ray fought to remain conscious, but the sea's icy fingers clutched hard at his chest. It was cold, bitterly, bitterly cold. Within minutes, darkness had overwhelmed his senses, but Mae West was doing her job. He floated limply in the swell completely unaware of the lifeboat sliding alongside. In seconds, Crewman Cross hauled the inert form of Raymond King on board and, opening his own jacket to impart warmth, he worked feverishly to resuscitate the young pilot. Holding him close and rubbing hard on the airman's back, he was rewarded with slight signs of breathing, but, he knew it would take too long to return to their boat shed, so Ray was transferred, his breathing almost imperceptible, to a nearby rowing boat, which pulled sturdily shoreward.

On the sandy beach, a small crowd had gathered, including a number of local children, who often frequented vantage points on the shoreline to observe naval activities or aircraft returning from combat. Occasionally the youngsters were rewarded with a victory roll from an exuberant fighter pilot, but, more often, it was a distressed bomber struggling homewards. Today, the drama was prolonged, with several aircraft circling low overhead, and 14-year-old Albert Scott watched with mounting excitement as the squat form of the 45ft *Edward Z Dresden* swung inshore, then slowed to allow a small boat alongside. The lifeboat was too large to get any closer and it was difficult to discern details, but a bustle of activity was followed by a small boat cutting quickly away from the larger vessel and coming hard for the shore. As soon as it grounded, the boatmen leapt clear, rapidly dragging their small craft to rest against the sea wall near the pier. Lying limply in the boat's stern was the sodden form of a fighter pilot. Looking at the unconscious airman, Albert realised this youthful hero was barely much older than himself. He never forgot the tableau – the bright yellow Mae West lifejacket on the pilot's chest seemed grotesquely cheerful against the ashen pallor of his skin, and his saturated flying suit – an American one – had offered no protection against such bitter conditions. Was he dead? Albert did not know, but the speed of transferral to a nearby ambulance told him the adults still hoped to save him. Only later did he learn that the young pilot had been pronounced dead on arrival in Clacton Hospital. 13 January 1945 had claimed its last fighter pilot fatality from 8FC.

That day was but a microcosm of the many misadventures visited on aerial operations by the elements, and events might well have vanished into the background of the dramatically vast panorama of The Second World War. However, for almost all the incidents described, there would be an aftermath that rescued them from historical anonymity.

Becky Barnard, Ray's girlfriend. Her love was lost beneath the bitterly cold waves of the North Sea. *(East Essex Aviation Society)*

My friend, the late Ron Buxton, took the first steps on this path when he investigated the crash site of Wendel Nelson's Mustang in 1972. Interest in aviation archaeology was strengthening, and Ron's success with Count Czernin's Hurricane and other sites – see my book *Final Flights* – prompted him to check out the tale of a Mustang buried on Bridge Farm, Grundisburgh, in Suffolk. During excavations in August that year, the Packard Merlin from 'Lord' was retrieved, but, in their enthusiasm to recover the engine, many interesting items were overlooked or, for reasons now unknown, returned to the crater. It was two decades before another team rectified matters. Led by Jeff Carless and David Wade, the East Anglian Aircraft Research Group (EAARG) returned to the site. As will be described, both men had developed a dedicated interest in events of 13 January 1945 and diligently tracked down almost every site with some amazing results. Their rewards for reopening Wendel's crash site surprised them both, as Jeff later related:

Re-digs are proving very successful these days, with recoveries profiting from the early 'alloy-rush' digs and also, I believe, altered values. This is not only true of Battle of Britain sites in the UK. Of all the 13 January 1945 P-51 Mustang losses in this country, there was only one that had not been checked out, either by David Wade – who has done a lot of research into the losses in bad weather this date – or myself, both separately and together. This aircraft was the 356FG P-51D crash at Grundisburgh, Suffolk. It had been the subject of a recovery in the early 1970s by a team of East Anglian enthusiasts. Both David Wade and I had been told that – everything had been taken – it was not worth doing.

Nevertheless, we decided to locate the site and try to recover a few representative pieces. In due course the impact point was located, and according to the Fisher detector, something remained in the ground. The new Forster deep-scan device agreed. Having obtained permission, a hole was opened up. The reading that the Forster had picked up turned out to be the radio and dynamotor, both in 'manky' condition. However, the engine primer also emerged and this was in good order. Then the stainless cowling section from above the exhaust stubs [port side] emerged, almost straight. We returned, intending to enlarge the hole, but not expecting to find much. In the event we recovered: the other stainless cowling from below the exhaust stubs; the remains of a few instruments – the face from the climb and descent indicator; the carburettor cold air door; ammunition track; a rudder pedal bar; sections of fire wall armour; glycol tank armour – this had traces of blue paint

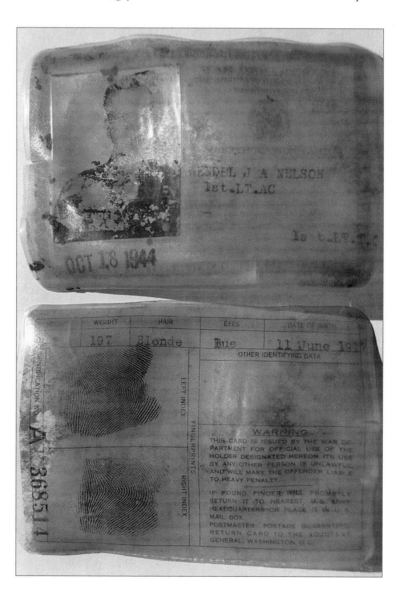

The remains of Wendel Nelson's identification card found during excavations on the crash site in 1972. *(David Wade)*

from the 356FG nose markings – and a two foot square fuselage section where the aircraft data plate should have been. These were the mundane bits. From within the hole came items of a more personal nature – the remains of the pilot's 'G' trousers, his Mae West life preserver, his flying helmet and his goggles. Another surprise find was the control column – minus the pistol grip. Finally came a complete – unbroken – instrument panel, with the aircraft call-signed plate attached confirming the identity of the P-51 beyond all doubt. P-51D-15-NA 44-15365 of the 360FS from Martlesham.

It angered Jeff that such remarkable items had been discarded or overlooked by the original team, yet his predecessors had recovered one item that had puzzled them, and Jeff now explained the mystery. In 1972, a Commando dagger had been recovered, and it was assumed this had belonged personally to Wendel Nelson. Now, research by the EAARG established that, following an incident where, to the pilot's consternation, a dinghy had inflated in the cockpit, one 356FG custom had been to tape a dagger to the control column for use by the pilot should he face this predicament. This was confirmed when close scrutiny of the control column showed evidence of tape still on the shaft.

That re-dig was the EAARG's fifth on an aircraft lost that day and I had the privilege in sharing three of these, although, during excavations on one site in August 1986, we did not realize it was a crash that had occurred on 13 January 1945. The invitation from Jeff Carless to 'knock the rust off my spade' for the 16th and meet on land belonging to Boyton Hall Farms near Monks Eleigh was, we thought, in pursuit of a P-51, serial 44-14366, lost on 2 June 1945. A wartime picture in my possession looked remarkably like the location. Local accounts told of a collision and both pilots parachuting to safety.

The site lay in a ditch at the foot of a sloping harvest-stubbled field, and we focused our efforts on an apparent break in the hedge line. As I dug, I noticed a young oak growing from the burnt remains of an earlier tree. Nearby, fragments of fighter were soon found, including, ominously, several parachute buckles indicating that the aircraft had not been empty on impact. This was soon supported by another local account, relayed second-hand, claiming the aircraft had crashed on a foggy Saturday morning. The unfortunate pilot had been 'shredded in the wreckage', which would explain the presence of parachute buckles. Jeff's hopes for more substantial remains, deeply buried, were based on the previous discovery of the Merlin's Stromberg mixture control. As the JCB cut into the ditch, these hopes seemed well founded. The usual detritus of a dig soon appeared – exploded ammunition, pieces of Perspex and clusters of unrecognisable fragments all bagged for later inspection. Scraping into the ditch, metallic-seeming sounds frequently revealed only flint embedded in clay. Amidst these, however, we did discover pieces of engine casing and the remains of the generator or starter motor. Doubts about anything deeper soon arose, although some interesting finds emerged near the surface, including a broken rudder pedal, a tangible connection with the pilot, but who was he? Fragments of engine cowling found carried a clue – yellow–black–yellow squares, the 353FG. The only item of substance was located in the side of the ditch, a single sorely corroded propeller blade. Judging from this and other pieces, we deduced the Mustang had hit at a shallow angle and exploded, scattering pieces over the landscape and burning

The broken rudder pedal. Its full inscription is 'depress pedal to release parking brake'. It would be many years before research revealed the pilot to be the hapless George S. Lee.

furiously. There were signs of a shallow crater created on impact, and we felt most of the machine had been removed. One further clue to its identity was found, a piece of red nose-art. Only later did research tie this in with 'Potchy', serial 44-11343, flown by the unfortunate George S. Lee.

Meanwhile, unbeknownst to the EAARG, reminders of events on that unlucky 13 January 1945 surfaced, literally, elsewhere. In 1978, Ken Marks, a member of the lifeboat crew and local fisherman, was trawling for plaice off Clacton, eastwards of the pier, when his nets snagged something on the seabed. Ken had heard of a Spitfire thereabouts but thought he had allowed a wide enough berth to avoid the wreck. Clearly, his nets had caught on something heavy. Not wishing to lose expensive gear, he was able slowly to haul his find on board and found, soundly ensnared, the remains of an aeroplane wing containing two hefty machine guns and belts of shiny bright brass ammunition. Preferring fish, Ken soon dumped his unwelcome catch on the beach, much to the consternation of beach inspector, Ernie Lister. Alarmed by the quantity of still-live ordnance shimmering on the shore, he hastily called the police, and Ken, concerned only for his nets, soon found them cordoned off, pending the arrival of explosives disposal experts from RAF Wittering. Eventually the weaponry was disentangled and Ken retrieved his nets, promising himself he would avoid that spot in future. Examination of the guns found American electrics fitted and identified the ammunition as .5 calibre, precluding a Spitfire.

Ken's unwelcome catch was almost forgotten until, six years later, Bill Gadd, chairman of the East Essex Aviation Society, heard the story of his find. Bill's curiosity was aroused and he initiated a quest that would take several years to complete. Bill commenced his research at the lifeboat station, and then used his powers of persuasion to charm information from the understandably reticent hospital authorities, and soon he had the bare facts about the loss of young Raymond King. A fellow member of the EEAS was Albert Scott, whose memory of the young pilot's deathly pallor had haunted him down the years. Together the two men determined to honour his memory, and, with the help of aviation historian and author Danny Morris, established contact with Alvin Stuart, a cousin of Raymond King. The story became even more poignant when Alvin revealed that Ray's brother had perished only three months later while flying a Mustang on combat operations in the Pacific Theatre. Heartbroken over the loss of both his sons, Ray's father had died soon after. Anything exhibited from 'Little Zippie' would honour the sacrifices made by both boys and the price paid by a grief-stricken father.

At first it seemed impossible that a deliberate and careful recovery of the lost fighter could be achieved. But Bill Gadd and other local enthusiasts had now combined their efforts and, by 1985–6, had established the EEAS. Further developments ensued when they secured an artefact from a much earlier conflict – an enormous Martello Tower, built on Point Clear during the Napoleonic Wars to command the Colne Estuary. Many hours of work would be necessary, but, if 'Little Zippie' could be lifted, it now had a home.

Two local divers, David Buxton and Robert Bradbrook, surveying the wreck whenever conditions and time allowed, commented on its remarkable state of preservation and even recovered one of the main undercarriage tyres. Manufactured by Goodyear, it had been home to a crab for some time, but the crustacean was evicted and the tyre retrieved for the museum. More exciting finds would soon follow. Bill Gadd had observed a large barge and floating crane engaged on sea defence works, and an approach to the owner, Peter Horlock from Mistley, gained a favourable response. Peter calculated that the barge would sail right over the wreck when it returned to its moorings. Bill anxiously awaited developments, then, in August 1987, the barge was ready and weather conditions were perfect. Anchoring close to the sunken Mustang, the barge master positioned the boom of his crane for the best lift. Waiting divers took charge of the descending chains as they rattled into the sea. Disappearing into the murky water, the divers descended gently onto the P-51 to shackle the fighter for its first 'flight' in more than forty years. It took over thirty minutes before all was pronounced ready, and the clank of retreating chains told anxious onlookers that the lift had commenced. Taut now, the barge listing slightly, dripping chain links clacked slowly upwards, as those nearest peered into the sea. Nothing at first, then a shadow was followed by barnacle-encrusted propeller blades breaking the surface accompanied by loud cheers. Water poured clear as the tattered remnants were raised. Snagged around the propeller were several lines and pieces of lost netting. Once clear of the water, the aircraft's engine and forward fuselage were swung gently to the deck, before divers descended to shackle another large section of the aircraft still on the seabed. Soon, the forlorn remains of the once sleek fighter were moving slowly to Mistley Quay. Once the barge was ashore, the sand and seaweed were hosed away

Right: The only picture of 'Little Zippie' located so far with Lt Hans Grasshoff. *(East Essex Aviation Society)*

Above: The tattered remnants of the once-proud P-51 are lifted from the sea bed. That Ray ditched with minimal impact and a dead engine is evident from the lack of distortion on the propeller blades. *(East Essex Aviation Society)*

Right: 'Little Zippie' crashed into the sea just before 3.30 p.m. The clock on the instrument panel stopped just over 10 minutes later, when seawater penetrated themechanism. *(East Essex Aviation Society)*

'Little Zippie' was lovingly restored by members of the East Essex Aviation Society and has pride of place in their collection.

A display board dedicated to the lost pilot. Included are: 479FG insignia; a dog tag; cap badge; silver wings; silver identity bracelet and his Purple Heart. *(East Essex Aviation Society)*

before the remains were taken to the recently acquired Martello Tower and the enthusiastic embrace of EEAS members for whom the work was just beginning.

For the next few years, 'Little Zippie' received countless hours of cleaning and restoration, while Bill pursued another ambition associated with the recovered fighter. By 1995, the aircraft had pride of place at Point Clear. Displayed nearby were mementos donated by Alvin Stuart – Ray's silver wings and identity bracelet, with a prominently positioned portrait of the smiling young pilot, parachute attached, posing in front of a Boeing Stearman biplane trainer during his early service days. Ray had so nearly made it home, and Bill felt that there was one further gesture to make. On 13 January 1995, fifty years to the very hour, Alvin Stuart attended a ceremony on Marine Parade, Clacton, to unveil a memorial tablet honouring his lost cousin. Deliberately positioned, the plaque was only a few hundred yards from where 'Little Zippie' went down. The inscription read:

In memory of Flight Officer Raymond E. King of the 436th Fighter Squadron, 479th Fighter Group, US 8th Air Force, whose aircraft crashed into the sea near this spot on 13th January 1945 after developing engine trouble. F/O King was returning to base after a combat mission and never survived his ordeal in the bitterly cold sea.

Fifty years to the very hour, Alvin Stuart unveils a memorial to his lost cousin. The Stars and Stripes used in the ceremony had previously been flown over the White House as a salute to the young pilot who perished so far away defending freedom. *(East Essex Aviation Society/Essex County Newspapers)*

Bill Gadd was proud of the museum's P-51 centrepiece, and, despite failing health, he continued his work for the EEAS. Delighted on hearing of my research, he unhesitatingly volunteered his material for inclusion in this chapter. Sadly, Bill died in 1996, and, in recognition of his achievements, Alvin requested that 'Little Zippie' be dedicated to the EEAS Chairman. Now, the Mustang is exhibited in tribute to its pilot and the man who preserved its remains in his honour.

Further north, the dedication of David Wade would see others lost that day given historical recognition. A year after the raising of 'Little Zippie', the search was on to see if substantial remains of Kay Shearer's rare P-51K still existed beneath the soil of an enormous field, now the combined acreage of Long Oris and Top Oris. As we stood in a sea of harvest stubble, there seemed little chance of locating our quarry – not a trace of that cruel cut in the countryside remained. As in 1945, a vast expanse of cloud covered the landscape, but it was high and gentle, with a strong warm wind from the south-west urging its departure. A dozen of us had disembarked from vehicles including an optimistic Range Rover and trailer. We were in the approximate location, but now needed technology to pinpoint the precise spot. Detachments of small detectors were supported by the heavy artillery of Jeff's expensive investment in a Fisher II capable of reading to some 20ft. Fisher or not, we first needed a clue, and it was my favoured C-Scope that gave the first signal, a few scraps of aluminium

August 1988. Standing in a sea of stubble, there seemed little chance of finding the rare P-51K, but my favoured C-Scope soon provided our first clue and the team then focused where signals from the deeper-detecting Fisher were at maximum strength.

near the surface. Sharp eyes soon supported these with some tiny pieces of Perspex, but morsels like this were easily carried by ploughing and could be some distance from the point of impact. We still needed a song from the Fisher to confirm whether the USAAF recovery crew had both removed the remains of the courageous Capt Shearer – now buried at Madingley – and cleared his aircraft or, hopefully, abandoned the aircraft as beyond retrieval. The landowner, Mr Pickering, had related a tale of American heavy recovery vehicles breaking through the surface of Moat Farm Drive as they endeavoured to reach the site. Compensation had been paid for repairs but had they fulfilled their task?

Patiently, Jeff paced the terrain, gradually drifting further from the few fragments found and taking our hopes with him. With silence from the Fisher, apprehension increased, then, at 0945, and over 30yd from the surface scraps, it gave a resoundingly strong signal. Tweaking the controls, Jeff traversed the spot from another direction. Same result. And again. We were onto something, maybe 10ft down. Our friend and contractor, Pat Ramm, had generously trundled the miles from his home at Old Buckenham in his brand new Massey Ferguson digger. His journey now had a purpose, and Pat cut the first swathe at 1000. As he was grinding and scraping through flint-ridden soil, we were treated to a dance of sparks and our first signs of 'daz'. This is digger parlance for the washing-powder blue of aluminium corroding into crystals. Discovering daz was disappointing and indicated the remains might be in poor condition but could, hopefully, simply signify exposure to air for parts near the surface. A further colourful accompaniment of purple soil was suspected of being chemical discolouration caused by the foam jetted onto the fiercely burning wreck.

As the machine bit more deeply, we clearly saw the line of the original crater slanting downwards and our spoil heap now yielded oddments of domestic detritus discarded to help in-fill. Forty-year-old sauce bottles might have excited bottle prospectors, but we found the hazard of broken glass a nuisance. Studying the burnt scar line from the original crater, Pat carefully skimmed the surface, exposing more of its outline and gradually uncovering more finds. Anything revealed by scraping triggered a signal to halt the machine while hand removal was attempted or the line of approach adjusted to avoid further damage. Every bucketful was carefully sifted as we set a deliberately slow pace. Experience had shown that haste meant harm, and smaller but still significant finds could so easily get overlooked as more soil spilled over them. Only when okayed by those scouring the spoil heap would Pat thinly spread the next load so that trowel work would be easier. Scrutiny of the deepening crater now frequently interrupted Pat's progress as many parts were carefully extricated by hand. An intriguing array of artefacts emerged: the radio antenna from atop the rear fuselage; radio equipment from behind the cockpit and the top of the aileron trim tab with, as always, rounds of exploded ammunition. These were followed by sections of broken armour plating that had once protected Kay Shearer's back and, now we were deeper, there were no signs of rust on the heavy steel, and aluminium fittings shone brightly in the sunlight. Removing the armour plating enabled work to commence on remains of the cockpit now crushed into the rear of the engine. Use of the Massey Ferguson all but ceased as delicate handwork picked pieces from a crater now nearly 6ft deep. Some parts would need cleaning to confirm their identity, but there was no mistaking the shredded remains of Shearer's flying helmet, a personal reminder that had somehow survived the intense conflagration. Despite that fire and the passage of time, the stench of high-octane fuel now hung heavily in the crater. It was also evident that the debris had been thoroughly jumbled when the pilot's body had been removed by the wartime recovery crew, and some, perhaps more, scattered pieces had been picked up and thrown in before back filling. The discovery of two Handa manufactured electric gun heaters in the core of cockpit debris confirmed this theory – they would have been with the wing-mounted guns. Other finds, deeper than work required to remove the pilot, must have been undisturbed since the crash, and we felt this applied to remains of the instrument panel embedded into the rear of the engine. Its frame had been broken in three but still held many of the shattered instruments whose combination of delicate balances had possibly been doubted by the pilot. Had he trusted them, he might have lived unless some other dreadful unrecorded catastrophe had overwhelmed him. Among the instruments was his artificial horizon, now mockingly horizontal. Close to this we discovered the rudder pedals that he must have operated, desperately trying to recover in those last, agonising

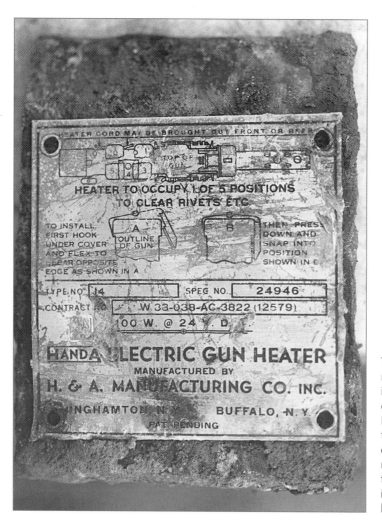

The instruction and manufacturer's identification plate for one of two Handa Electric gun heaters found amid the cockpit debris indicated that the recovery crew had thrown scattered debris into the crater before back filling.

Many instruments were recovered including this Gyro Horizon Indicator or artificial horizon. This was one of the key flight instruments used by Shearer, but it could 'tumble' beyond 100 degrees of bank or 70 degrees climb and dive. Even the experienced Shearer might have slipped into a trap with fatal consequences where his senses were deceived and he doubted his instruments.

seconds before oblivion. One of the aluminium footplates had folded backwards, and still trapped in its grip was Shearer's right flying boot. His remains had been pulled clear, leaving this macabre reminder of war's horrific brutality.

At the very moment we removed this sad relic, a 42 Squadron Nimrod from RAF Marham whined low overhead in unwitting salute, en route to the "Wings of Liberty" display being held on the nearby USAF base at Lakenheath. The warrior whose wings had folded on this very spot had died defending liberty – our liberty – and those present paused, silently, before placing the boot gently aside.

Removing the final items associated with the cockpit now exposed the supercharger which had broken away from the engine. At a depth of eight feet, the team now confronted the bulk of the Packard Merlin rammed firmly into the ground almost vertically. Clutched firmly by the heavy brown loam, we found the task of hand digging very difficult so Pat dexterously worked on the peripherals, easing earth away to create a column of soil enclosing the engine. Once this had been achieved, space restrictions meant working by hand in relays to remove earth still encrusting the engine until enough had been exposed to attach chains without further damaging the find. After an hour, it was poised precariously on its nose and those working alongside moved cautiously in case the almost perpendicular power plant tilted to crush someone against the wall of the crater. Soon, only Jeff Carless and Nigel Beckett were left to attach the chains – a final adjustment and they were hooked to the digger bucket. At 1405, Pat gently increased power, took up the strain, and then lifted. There was an instant of resistance then the engine came free leaving a perfect mould of its forward extremity in the compacted earth. The propeller boss was still attached but there were no blades from the Aeroproducts unit and detectors checks confirmed the crater devoid of metal.

As the Merlin was lowered onto a trailer, the team began back filling to leave the site to the landowner's satisfaction. Pleased with events, our hoped-for bonus of six machine guns

The Packard Merlin was almost perpendicular and firmly embedded in the flint-ridden soil. Here the team work by hand preparing the engine to be lifted.

turned to disappointment when only a few rounds of ammunition were recovered from the places where the guns should have been. It was felt that the wartime team had understandably focused on removing Shearer's remains then cleared the surface debris, possibly including wings sheared off on impact. By 1600, the land had been levelled off and only a dark patch in the bright straw stubble remained. We always endeavour to leave our workings tidy even if they are in a vast field like Long Oris.

The next site to be investigated was 'Floogie II' in July 1989. The EAARG team did not expect any major finds because of the police report from Sergeant Leslie Dunnett forty-five years earlier. However, detector readings taken earlier that year indicated some wreckage still extant. The search conducted that summer proved disappointing because the debris petered out at only 3–4ft and most of the aluminium had corroded into 'daz'. They did recover a part of the K-14 gun sight with range and wingspan criteria for sighting on enemy aircraft. Three sixpenny pieces also emerged, and a trail of smaller fragments indicated the path of total destruction. Once more, they tidied up to ensure their reputation with local landowners.

Never would landowner's satisfaction be so important as on the next dig David arranged – a search for Tommy Ksanznak's aircraft. Locating the crash site was easier than on some enormous field, but it was with some trepidation that David duly knocked on the door of 'Pantiles', 14 Rose Lane, Melbourn. The houses had been renumbered in the intervening years because the orchard had vanished beneath further buildings. David's nervous knock on the door set in motion an extraordinary sequence of events. Fortunately for David, the current occupants of the now two-into-one conversion were very interested in the history that had

One of R.L. Schlieker's dog tags was found by Geoff Barker when hand-sifting a sandy spoil heap during a search of the crash site in 1989. 'T43-44' confirms receipt of anti-tetanus jabs. The 'A' denotes blood group and the 'P' is for Protestant.

occurred literally on their doorstep. Elizabeth Crow was a primary schoolteacher and felt there might be not just excitement but an educational aspect for her pupils in hearing about the recovery of the crashed aeroplane. Happily for David, Lawrence Crow also endorsed his activities; he could search their garden for the lost fighter. Mr Crow had found evidence of the tragedy himself: having the garden level lowered had revealed metal fragments and several rounds of ammunition. With the family's curiosity aroused, David hoped a few more pieces might be found for museum display to honour the young pilot. Permission granted, David strolled over the lawn doubting if the Fisher would register anything with its sensitivity levels low. To his astonishment, the needle swung sturdily across the dial as the machine emitted a resoundingly audible burst of encouragement − unless it was a drain cover! This was discounted as the steady tone continued, only weakening when he was some 16ft from the house.

A week or so later, on 24 March 1991, I joined David in the cottage garden and appreciated a warming brew from Mrs Crow to alleviate the early morning chills. The strongest signals were no more than 6ft from the front of the cottage, and the Crow family had consented to careful removal of turf from their beautifully maintained front lawn. They were, understandably, reluctant to see excavations undermining the concrete driveway or their homestead itself. David had carefully paced the reading pattern and taped out the target area. No sooner had the first square of spring-green grass been removed than we picked up fragments of aircraft immediately underneath. Within minutes, the usual clusters of ammunition emerged intermingled with patches of unwelcome daz and odd pieces from the instrument panel. A few shovels later, David's keen eyes spotted a fragment of black plastic with evidence of a handgrip pattern and which he immediately recognised as a part from the control stick top. It needed little imagination to envisage the young pilot pulling hard on this, willing the Mustang to respond in those last desperate moments. A tiny broken fragment symbolising so much induced a few moments of sad speculation; Tommy had probably been frantically attempting to pull out, his hand around the control column − this very fragment – at the instant his life and dreams were savagely stolen. Today, a bright, benign, March morning, Mother Nature wore a coat so different from that of forty-four years earlier. True, her capriciousness had spared those children, now adult with children of their own. Baby Pauline's pram was regularly parked where our first trench sliced across the garden, but, in a real sense, Tommy's own future had been given for those succeeding generations. We felt this very keenly as we looked at other debris describing the ferocity of impact – strong armour plating shattered; a fragment of main wheel; shards of armoured glass and crushed, exploded rounds of ammunition. Beneath thin topsoil we found chalk and began what was almost a mining process to a depth of 4ft where we uncovered a chunk of supercharger. Close by, chiselling deeper into the chalk, we revealed the propeller boss, but, with daylight now fading, we tarpaulined our efforts and gratefully accepted a final cuppa from Mrs Crow.

Circumstances prevented my further attendance, but David and other supporters continued throughout that week – 'bloody hard work' – to carve further in and retrieve additional finds, including Tommy's crushed cigarette lighter and, close by, a scarred silver florin, presumably from his pocket, and a 4in length of his identity disc chain. Of the Mustang, they found four instrument faces, the cockpit cold air on/off switch, a fuel cap and additional assorted fragments. Surprisingly, considering its proximity to property, they revealed the shattered, chalk-encrusted carcase of the once-powerful Packard Merlin. It lay on its side with one solitary propeller blade alongside. Even with one cylinder bank missing, the

David Wade and young Rowan McLachlan measure out the crash site at 14 Rose Lane, Melbourn. The proximity of strong detector readings close to the house and driveway can be clearly seen.

No sooner had the turf been lifted than fragments of aircraft and rounds of ammunition appeared.

David Wade – foreground – holding remains of the altimeter, while the author readies his C-Scope for another sweep. *(Ian Miles – Mid Anglia Newspapers Ltd)*

Impact damage is evident on this florin found amid the cockpit debris. For the now elderly Larry Ksanznak, the return of this and other relics were reminders of the big brother who had not grown old but remained forever as the handsome young fighter pilot.

V12 engine was some 5ft long and too heavy to shift manually, so a local farmer assisted by fitting forks to his tractor and lifting it into the waiting pick-up truck. This and other finds from an unusually urban excavation project are now displayed in the 93BG Museum at Hardwick. The propeller blade was presented to the Crow family for retention in the cottage as a tribute to the pilot, although this has since moved on. Perhaps the most poignant presentation relating to this site occurred some thirteen years later when David Wade gave me the two-shilling coin and some additional parts for a special purpose. David Crow, the 355FG historian – no relative of the family owning the cottage – had put me in touch with the Ksanznak family.

An exchange of correspondence soon established that my wife Sue and I would be close to Larry's home when visiting New York in October 2004. Plans were made to present the coin, an engine exhaust stub and some other fragments to the family. For some, this might seem insensitive or inappropriate, but, for Larry and his sister Patsy, these finds were welcomed as a link to that long-lost brother, his place still in their hearts sixty years on. They now had grandchildren, just as Tommy would almost certainly have done had he come home; that gap in their family could never be filled.

When I opened the door to our hotel room, any apprehension I felt about the wisdom of this gesture vanished in the warmest of embraces from Larry Ksanznak, now a sprightly 73. As I handed the items over, his eyes filled with tears, an emotional cocktail of pleasure and tremendous sadness at the story these broken parts represented. Words were superfluous; tears rolled silently down the elderly cheeks of the young boy within; his big brother had gone to war and never came home. Now, in a sense, he had; these relics were for the Ksanznak family, for Larry to share and use as a key. After some moments, more was unlocked, as Larry described his brother and how much these pieces meant, the closure they helped achieve. Tommy had been a spiritual member of the family for a long time – Larry told me that he wanted to 'humanise him and share this with my grandchildren. I want them to know who the real heroes are in life. It's not someone who gets a million dollar contract to wear baseball shoes.' The parts that went home will hopefully speak to Tommy's family for generations to come.

Amazed by the finds from Tommy Ksanznak's Mustang, David Wade continued his research and site surveys. A sortie to Sancroft Manor Farm, Laxfield, corroborated

An empty bill fold and a cache of coins found on the Elin crash site. The coins, a mixture of British and American currency, trailed in the path of wreckage for a depth of several feet. Fate had dealt a cruel hand the morning after Elin's win at poker and the young pilot's luck ran out. *(David Wade)*

Sgt Ruffles's description of Anderson's loss. David later recalled following the 'longest trail of bits' he had ever seen. Ascertaining the point of impact, he then picked up tiny, inconsequential fragments of aluminium along a path that went through a hedge, all the way across the next field, through another hedge and most of the way over the next field. The tiny pieces told a tale of total devastation, but David knew that, if displayed well with the story, even these fragments would at lease serve to recall the tragedy of trainee Anderson's final flight.

In August 1991, the EAARG located Elin's crash at Walpole and met more success. A long, undulating field produced several readings on the Fisher from beneath the harvest stubble. Using a somewhat ancient Ford digger, they soon recovered a propeller blade and other parts that had lain undisturbed since the crash. These indicated that Elin had hit the earth in a shallow dive and must have been close to recovering but did not have quite enough height. Trailing at the bottom of a shallow crater they found a cache of coins and Elin's empty, silver billfold – presumably the paper currency had been consumed in the conflagration, leaving only these sad reminders of a poker game and a pilot's fate.

For Elin and the others lost that day, fortune had not favoured the brave. Eighth Fighter Command had launched some 469 sorties and the combat casualties attributed to weather represented a sustainable loss ratio of some 1 per cent, but these figures camouflage the truth of young men seeking to do their duty. Each man, whether operational or training, faced appalling weather conditions and confronted an implacable enemy from the very moment his wheels left terra firma. Those *ab initio* young men flying training missions faced the same foe with far less experience to draw upon. It may also be that other elements contributed to the downfall of more than one – the full truth will never be known – but it is fitting that their loss should be recalled by the various artefacts recovered and restored.

CHAPTER NINE

Sally's Last Sortie

It is not widely appreciated that several USAAF bomber groups had fighters on strength. These were often war-weary birds retired from front-line tasks and used to check weather conditions or aid assembly of the bomber formations. They were also used for the more exuberant pilots to enjoy the additional thrill of aerobatics – not recommended in a B-17 or B-24!

One such machine was 'Sally', a veteran P-47D used by the 466BG Liberator Group base at Attlebridge in Norfolk. Sally had performed her duties as a formation monitor well and was proudly adorned with the 466BG tail markings, red with a white horizontal bar. These markings overpainted the original stencilling of her serial number, 42-75513, but 466BG personnel simply shifted the last six digits to her rear fuselage and more-or-less achieved compliance with regulations.

'Sally', a veteran P-47D, serial 42-75513, used by the 466BG to check weather condition or to monitor the group during assembly. The aircraft call-letter is P as marked on the fin, but there is what appears to be the remains of a V on the rear fuselage, from her days as a front-line fighter with the 352FG (see Chapter One). *(Michael J.G. Harris)*

Capt Everett R. Jones's decision to take an afternoon hop would have serious consequences. *(Michael J.G. Harris)*

With the cessation of hostilities on 8 May 1945, a lot of pilots found time on their hands, and one such, Capt Everett R. Jones Jr, decided on an afternoon's sortie in 'Sally'. It was to be a fateful decision. Everett had experienced a number of close calls during his career as a bomber pilot. His first seven missions had been flown with the 458BG from Horsham St Faith, where his exceptional talent as a pilot had been noted. This resulted in his selection for training in a Lead Crew School run by the 44BG from their base at Shipdham, and successful completion of the course saw him assigned to the 466BG. Lead Crews were chosen for their abilities and to lead their less experienced brethren on operations. As such, they were rotated with other Lead Crews to conserve their skills and did not fly every mission, so a Lead Crew's tour might take longer. Everett's operational record shows he commenced operations with the 466BG on 27 May 1944 when they attacked railway marshalling yards at Neunkirchen, Germany. His first mission as Deputy Lead for the 96 Combat Wing occurred on 21 July 1944. Every mission was hazardous, but there were occasions when fate tapped him on the shoulder as a reminder of his own mortality. On 11 September, flying Deputy Lead for the 458BG to Magdeburg attacking industrial targets, his aircraft was only two minutes away from bomb release and surrounded by bursting flak when one shell hit the bomb-bay. The explosion ignited their smoke marker bombs and frightened the crew into thinking they were on fire, and several were anxious to bale out. Stifling his own fears, Everett swiftly assessed the situation, and his 'gallant example and skilful piloting inspired his crew to remain at their posts'. Not only this, Everett had to contend with severed control cables to the starboard aileron and flap plus a broken hydraulic line. Maintaining both formation and control, his crew released on the lead ship and returned successfully to base after a remarkable feat of teamwork.

Further testimony to Everett's talents came on 26 October, when leading the 466BG low left squadron to Bottrop, again assaulting the enemy's industrial and communications systems. During assembly, he discovered his No. 1 engine's electronic supercharger control was malfunctioning. Everett was flying a GH aircraft, one capable of using its radar for effective blind bombing. Knowing there were not enough of these aircraft in the formation, he increased power on his three good engines to compensate and successfully guided his squadron to the target. Almost a week later, on 1 November, flying a B-24 named 'Shamrock', he again lost a supercharger and once more continued leading his squadron for a strike on a synthetic oil installation at Gelsenkirchen. The following day he could be forgiven

Everett's operational tour with the 466BG lasted throughout the summer of 1944. A representative aircraft, B-24H 42-51138 from the 784BS, is undergoing repairs on 27 August after landing at Woodbridge. Many crippled machines sought sanctuary on this Suffolk airbase, where extra-long runways allowed greater margin for error. *(Ray Zorn)*

for feeling persecuted by fate when his No. 1 engine failed and had to be feathered. Only his prowess as a pilot once more enabled him to continue leading his squadron for a GH precision run on an oil refinery at Castrup-Rauxel in the heavily defended Ruhr. He was cited for his leadership on 16 November during an attack on enemy gun installations near Aachen preparatory to an Allied ground offensive, and 1/Lt Martin H. Kern, an Intelligence Officer, commented in his report:

> Special note should be made of the coordinated teamwork of the GH crew of 1/Lt E.R. Jones (aircraft 503) which took over the 466th Group lead at IP. Clouds were slightly less than 10/10s at the IP and from this point the target was not visible. Accordingly the run was being made on GH. Approximately 2 miles W of Aachen, clouds dissipated to 2/10 – 3/10s and the target became visual through ground haze. Course was good here and no corrections were necessary. In the short time still available, the bombardier [1/Lt R.J. Blumenfeld] picked up the target in the sight, made necessary last minute corrections for rate and bombed visually with good results.

This resulted in a recommendation for the Distinguished Flying Cross for Everett, and Maj Norman R. Crosson, CO of the 784BS, endorsed it, noting of Everett's operational record:

> He has flown lead positions for Second Division, 96 Combat Wing and for three different groups on twenty-two occasions. His sound judgement, skilful flying and inspiring leadership have enabled his squadron to complete their missions . . . His magnificent example has raised the morale of his fellow officers and Enlisted Men and the Squadron as a whole. I recommend the award . . . to Captain Jones without reservation.

More important to Everett on the 16 November mission was the fact that the bombs had hit the target and not strayed on to American troops close by. A Commendation to Everett from the 466BG CO, Col William H. Cleveland, stated:

Reconnaissance and ground forces reports affirm that all bombs were in the target area and that they greatly assisted the advancing infantry. Following the attack, Major General Terry Allen, commanding the 104th Infantry Division, wired Lt Gen James H. Doolittle, CO of the Eighth Air Force, 'Doughboys thank you for a fine job . . .'

This pleased Everett as much as the Commendation itself, because the accolade continued: 'By your presence of mind, judgement, decision, coolness and skill you contributed greatly to the success of this highly important operational mission and behaved in the finest tradition of the United States Army Air Forces.'

Everett had completed his tour of operations on 30 December 1944, but remained with the 466BG as Assistant Group Operations Officer. During the course of his duties he had taken 'Sally' on the occasional non-operational sortie, so was familiar with the P-47 as he strolled over for another flight during the afternoon of 4 June 1945. He might have recalled another summer's evening two years earlier during his training at Lakeland in Florida. He was then still a novice and had made a cross-wind landing but failed to make sufficient correction for drift. The PT-17 biplane had ground looped and cracked a rear spar, quite apart from denting the young airman's pride. This and all the missions since had taught him never to take anything for granted when it came to flying, but he little knew that events would soon require as much 'presence of mind' as any combat operation.

Even though this was a pleasure flight, Everett conducted a careful pre-flight check on the elderly P-47. Slap-happy pilots soon became deceased pilots, but his inspection could not ascertain the detailed condition of the big 2000HP Pratt and Whitney radial. The motor was an R-2800-63, serial 42-57116, and the brass plate affixed to its grey casing behind the propeller identified it as part of a production batch subcontracted for manufacture by the Ford Motor Company, famous for its cars. The engine had received its last overhaul at Base Air Depot 1, Burtonwood, Lancashire, and was ground tested for an hour without adverse comment on its record card. Since then it had taken 'Sally' aloft for 106 hours and 40 minutes with an oil consumption rate of 2 quarts per hour causing no concern.

His external checks complete, Everett clambered into the cockpit and settled in. The seat could be adjusted, as in any automobile, and the cockpit had an airplane aroma so familiar to fliers – a mixture of aviation fuel, oil and military paintwork. In 'Sally''s case, there were the scratches, scuffs and nicks acquired through use – scuffed rudder pedals and paintwork told of many hours doing her duty and created a gentle air of war-weariness. Her job, like many of the machines used by the mighty Eighth, was done and her fate uncertain – most probably conversion into raw materials required for peacetime production, a new fridge perhaps?

Everett scanned the cockpit confirming that the ignition and master battery switches were off, then he initiated his pre-flight checks. Landing gear handle in the DOWN position; flaps UP; flap equalizer CLOSED; generator switch ON. He now moved the master battery switch to

ON and confirmed neutral settings for the shutters on the intercooler and oil cooler. Preparations proceeded meticulously through checks on the propeller switch, fuel booster pumps, fuel pressure gauges and so on, until Everett decided that life should be instilled into the dormant bird. Ground personnel had pulled the propeller through by hand so that oil and fuel accumulations were shifted and the risk of fire reduced. Everett now rotated the ignition switch to ON, confirmed the fuel selector valve was set for his main tank and cracked the throttle open an inch or so before continuing his checklist into mixture control, propeller and pumps, and so on, until 'Sally' was ready to energise. A few strokes on the priming pump prepared her, and a quick check with the crew chief confirmed there were no personnel near the massive propeller. With the ignition switch set to BOTH, Everett energised the electric starter motor and allowed some fifteen seconds for the initial whine to become a shrill squeal before he engaged the engine. Pressing firmly on the starter switch, he held it and felt the airframe shudder as the big Curtiss Electric propeller first stirred. With a cough from the exhaust system, the powerful Double Wasp cleared its throat then caught and crackled with energy as Everett adjusted the fuel mixture to auto-rich. Setting the throttle to an easy 900 rpm, Everett waved away the external battery, which was soon disconnected by ground staff who fastened the access panel and then pulled away the chocks. 'Sally' chortled happily as Everett noted a satisfactory oil pressure already beyond the minimum of 25 pounds required within the first thirty seconds. She seemed eager for the off, but a few more instrument readings were taken before he released the parking brake and unlocked the tail wheel.

Nearby, Herman Laubrich had undertaken an identical process in the 466BG's second P-47 and he was also cleared for take off. A burst of power saw 'Sally' shift easily forward, and Everett commenced taxiing to the runway, weaving slightly to obtain forward vision otherwise blocked beyond the bulk of the engine. 'Sally' swung gently from side to side in the tail-dragger's familiar shimmy, as Everett manoeuvred to his take-off position. Reaching the main runway, he ran through his pre-flight routine. The trim tabs were set for take-off, fuel was on auto rich, propeller settings were established and the engine cowl flaps open. Another burst of power ran 'Sally' forward a short distance to straighten the aircraft so her tail wheel could be locked. This reduced the risk of an embarrassing swing on take-off. Holding 'Sally' on her brakes, Everett increased power to check the manifold pressure. Satisfied with the reading and all other checks, he cleared himself with the control tower and firmly advanced the throttle. 'Sally' surged ahead, the tail soon lifted, and, with some correction on the rudder, Everett aimed the P-47 straight down the runway as his speed increased. A touch back on the control column and 'Sally' broke away from the inelegance of her landbound posture, climbing powerfully into the afternoon sky. A dab on the brakes, and Everett retracted the undercarriage as he climbed away at over 150mph. Unburdened from the drag, 'Sally' soared enthusiastically into the heavens on her final flight. Puffs of summer cumulus drifted gently at 2,500ft, adding to the beauty and tranquillity in skies so recently dense with fully laden bombers and fighters bearing men into the terror and uncertainty of combat. Everett now had the freedom to cavort and enjoy the sheer beauty of being airborne alone. Herman had headed off elsewhere, so 'Sally' went skipping alone over the clouds in the freedom of peace, although Everett, like any experienced pilot, remained vigilant for other aircraft in his vicinity.

Beneath her wings, 'Sally''s shadow danced across the landscape. Nearby, the spire of Norwich cathedral and the tower of its ancient castle were surrounded by rural communities now converting to peace. Many servicemen from the region were still fighting in the Far East, but some were coming home, and home was where Everett himself hoped to be soon. Plans were under way for the 466BG to join the Eighth Air Force exodus from East Anglia on 9 June. Everett knew this might be his last opportunity for a flight in a fighter, even an elderly machine such as 'Sally'. Cruising over the coastline and countryside, he was enjoying the view from 4,500ft, and with its power setting at 32–21, the big radial was barely being taxed.

The first hint of trouble came when Everett detected some discomfort in the engine's rhythm. Thinking it no more than a temporary wheeze, he increased power, hoping to clear the engine. Instead of the engine responding with a spurt of acceleration, there was no noticeable improvement in 'Sally''s performance, and matters in the cockpit now commanded Everett's full attention. Getting no reaction from the increase in throttle, he was further disconcerted when the motor cut out completely – only momentarily, but enough for the deceleration to remove the 'arm chair comfort' of his cruising speed and throw him forward against his seat harness. Concerned in case it was a fuel blockage or, perhaps, a fault with the main tank gauge meaning the indicated 150 gallons was an error, Everett switched his fuel selector to the auxiliary tank and noted it read 50 gallons. He was sure there was no fuel shortage because the quantity indicators were fine, the fuel pressure warning lamp had not illuminated and the fuel pressure gauge indicated a healthy 17–18 on its scale. These checks and adjustments had taken only seconds, and he noted no adverse readings on any of the instrumentation until he read the oil temperature and pressure gauge on the right-hand side of his instrument panel. The split dial had a temperature indicator on its top right segment, and the needle was advancing unhealthily beyond the normal 40 degrees.

From the first indication of trouble, Everett had turned instinctively towards Attlebridge and looked capable of reaching it. Less than thirty seconds had elapsed since the engine's first splutter, and it seemed to have recovered, but he was taking no chances and intended to land as soon as possible. Then the engine cut out again. He was now less than 2 miles from Station 120, with hopefully enough height in hand for a dead stick landing. This second cough caused a rapid reassessment of his instruments and another change on the fuel selector valve from reserve back to his main tank. It made no difference, even when he increased fuel boost to 20 pounds. 'Sally' stubbornly rejected his attentions, and his predicament worsened decisively when the engine quit completely and the black propeller blades froze into sharp relief against the skyline. Everett could now even read the curving letters on the Curtiss Electric decal and knew for certain nothing else could be done to 'start the little jewel'.

He was now racing time, distance and altitude. The runway seemed so close, but the four propeller blades stood out like the flat facing palms of a traffic cop and their resistance to the airflow was remorselessly dragging 'Sally' to destruction. Everett knew the powerless P-47 had 'the glide angle of a brick' when the propeller was not windmilling. He was now so close to Attlebridge he could discern the markings on the threshold of runway 22, but altitude was rapidly being robbed from beneath his wings. He now set himself a mental marker, a point at which it would be obvious he would be unable to stretch the glide and below which he lacked the height to bail out. Once there, he would jump and leave the troublesome 'Sally' to her own devices.

Having released the canopy lock, he slid the frame easily back on its runners, noting the increasing amount of detail becoming apparent on the landscape of Norfolk. A comparison between rate of descent and distance now clearly determined that 'Sally' would never reach the runway. He would inevitably crash-land short, and there were too many trees between himself and the threshold, quite apart from the community of Weston Longville. With the canopy fully back, Everett decided to follow through with the remaining procedure for parachuting from the P-47. His glide angle was as flat as he could make it – one further tweak on the trim controls and he was ready.

Reasoning that there was – hopefully – little likelihood of a repeat experience, Everett decided to extract what he could from this, his first and last parachute descent. Having undone his harness and disconnected himself from the radio, he pulled himself upright into the slipstream with 'Sally' sliding steadily earthwards. His trim adjustment apparently compensated for his body interrupting the airflow and 'Sally' remained level as he climbed almost nonchalantly out on to the port wing. Stencilled on the wing's trailing edge were the words 'No Step', but that would not matter now. Balancing a moment, Everett took one short but very long step off the wing and into space.

Curiosity can be a killer, whether for a cat or for a miscalculating pilot. Everett had paused on the wing and decided that, as this was the first time he had jumped, and, furthermore, by choice and desire, it would be his last, he ought to experiment with a little free fall.

Peering through the glass atop the control tower at Attlebridge, 1/Lt Earle H. Brehemer, the Duty Flying Control Officer. would later record:

At approximately 1625 hours on 4 June 1945, a fighter aircraft was seen to be diving straight toward ground approximately a mile and a half northeast of field, with a man with unopened chute also falling to the ground. Chute opened just as objects passed behind section of trees. Crash trucks and ambulance immediately drove to the scene . . .

Whether Everett had lived was unknown. Personnel playing softball were convinced of his demise having witnessed him disappear behind the tree line, his parachute unopened.

Presumably 'Sally' had nosedived following Everett's departure. Her pilot had survived, but only just, and later felt the eyewitness accounts were accurate when he wrote:

I do not remember too much about my contact with the ground. I must have been in that moment of black-out resulting from the chute opening followed promptly by impact upon mother earth. I was probably unconscious at the moment of impact or I might have been seriously injured. Luckily I was not hurt in any way other than being sore all over my body for the next few days. I came down in what must have been the middle of an oat field not over 300 yards from a very nice English home. When I got up, I noted that I was within a 100 yards or so of a large hole in the ground with a tail of smoke and dust rising out thereof and my first thought was . . . someone else has crashed too. I was wrong on this

The wreckage of 'Sally' at Weston Longville. The troublesome engine is on the edge of the crater to the right of the inverted and crumpled rear fuselage. The propeller looks deeply embedded – one blade can be seen in the centre, left of the tyre, and it might still rest today beneath the sixth green of Weston Longville golf course. *(Chris Gotts)*

assumption as that was the remains of 'Sally', the ole girl I had just left somewhere below 4,000 feet up. At this moment, an Englishman was running towards me calling out, 'Are you all right, Mate?' Then, within just minutes, Doc Elliott's ambulance pulled up with the Protestant Chaplain alighting therefrom . . .

Luckily, Everett kept the chaplain unemployed, and the medics were so pleased that they detained him in hospital as he later recalled, 'drenching me with spirits which could only be had in their stores and all was well the next few days . . .'. His mishap had occurred on the Monday, and, when Everett departed for America on the following Saturday, he put his co-pilot, Earl Beitler, in charge, because he himself was not feeling too well, possibly from the 'treatment' meted out by the medics, profoundly pleased to have a live pilot on their hands.

'Sally' had gouged a sizeable scar on the landscape, and her forlorn remains were handed over to 3 Strategic Air Depot at nearby Watton. A report by Engineering Officer Jay C. Evans noted that 'Examination of oil screen recovered from the wreckage showed evidence of metal filings'. This demonstrated a serious internal failure of the engine. Clearly 'Sally' was one fighter reluctant for an ignoble ending in the salvage yard, and her downfall would at least merit a mention in Norfolk's archives, as a police message on file relates:

It has come to notice that at about 3.15pm on Monday, 4th June, a USAAF Thunderbolt Fighter, number not known, from Attlebridge Aerodrome, crashed in the Park, Weston Longville, map reference G.573350, and was completely wrecked. The pilot baled out prior to the crash and was slightly injured. About two acres of growing barley was spoiled.

'Sally' might also occasionally prompt comment at the nineteenth hole of Weston Longville Golf Course, because a few pieces were found during the creation of the sixth green, and some fragments undoubtedly still exist as buried reminders of '"Sally"'s Last Sortie'.

CHAPTER TEN

Strategy and Tactics

A merican fighter pilots during the Second World War are sometimes portrayed in films as individualistic flouters of authority whose rebellious flamboyance eventually wins the day. True, there were those with these characteristics, but the achievements of USAAF fighter pilots were primarily based on good training, effective leadership and teamwork. These were overseen by sound strategy and tactics plus effective aircraft with skilled ground personnel and equipment. None of these would have been of any value without the tenacity and courage of the airmen themselves.

This chapter explores the strategy and tactics using the words of none other than the former Commanding Officer of Eighth Air Force Fighter Command, Lt Gen W.E. Kepner DSC CB DSM, to illustrate how they defeated an enemy whose courage might have been equal but was squandered supporting a corrupt cause crippled from within by internecine squabbles. The German hierarchy often sought to maintain personal prestige with their Führer, who, losing touch with reality, interfered in military decisions and undermined or replaced those officers who could have been effective but who disagreed with him. An example was Generalleutnant Adolf Galland, a

'Big Dog One' was the call sign for the diminutive but feisty and determined commander of 8 FC (technically VIII FC) Lt Gen William E. Kepner. His vision of the strategy and tactics to be employed to increase the offensive potency of his fighter force made a valuable contribution to the war effort.

most capable fighter commander who was eventually relieved as General in Charge of Fighters after his outspoken criticism of German High Command put him in conflict with Reichsmarschall Hermann Goering, Commander in Chief of the Luftwaffe. The inability of the Luftwaffe's leadership to establish and assert their own sound strategy and tactics ultimately contributed to their defeat. That there were doubts and disagreements within the Allied camp is evidenced by a letter, never previously published, from Bill Kepner to my old friend, the late Charlie Gallagher. As the then Chairman of Friends of the Eighth (FOTE), Charlie was our own 'gentle dictator' when FOTE was founded in 1972. Established to perpetuate the memory of the Eighth Air Force, FOTE was, and still is, a loose arrangement whereby those of us researching different aspects of 8 AF history could meet and exchange information. During those early days, our quarterly meetings saw help given across many and varied projects under way beneath the broad banner of FOTE. We often heard from veterans themselves, either directly because they attended the meetings or indirectly by correspondence or audiotape in those pre-VCR and DVD days. The letter from Bill Kepner is dated 31 May 1977 and follows, with my own explanatory interjections where necessary. The chapter concludes with additional contributions from men at the sharp end in the 357 FG who recorded their own strategy and tactics at the time.

Mr C Gallagher
F.O.T.E.
Dear Sir
I am sorry I could not make the tape. As I told you, I am pretty much restricted to my house in taking care of my wife. I am glad to forward a message of greeting and that is probably too long? A discussion of what I consider pertinent and I hope interesting facts concerning the 8th Fighter Command. Than which there is none greater. Or was during WWII in the USAF. It is hand written, I hope you can read it. You may wish to cut out the first four and a half pages or select out some of the items yet I see these as important from history's standpoint . . . Good luck and regards. W E Kepner DSC CB DSM Lt Gen USAF Ret.

Bill Kepner was born in Miami, Indiana, in 1893 and served in the US Army during the First World War. He transferred to the Air Service during 1920 and made his mark in lighter-than-air aviation, winning records and races as a skilled balloonist. During the early 1930s, he trained on conventional aircraft and by 1932 was a Major at Wright Field in charge of the Purchase Branch so understood more than most the difficulties the young aviation branch of the Army had in achieving funding. With the political climate darkening during the Depression, dictators and despots – Hitler, Mussolini, Franco, Stalin – were in or achieving positions of power and the Japanese were savagely asserting military supremacy in the Far East. Meanwhile, America remained isolationist, her head in the sand, despite the endeavours of Roosevelt and other politicians to offer some counterbalance. Several neutrality laws sought to segregate America from the darkness brooding elsewhere. As Germany rearmed, American military expenditure languished, and her inwardly facing posture, plus the appeasement policies of European countries, including Britain and France, emboldened the aggressor nations. Bill graduated from the Command and General Staff School in June 1937 and was posted to Langley Field in charge of the 8 Pursuit Group. Foreign aircraft such as the Spitfire and Me 109 already outclassed US fighters of the period, including the recently received Curtiss P-36. Bill was aware of inadequacies in indigenous designs when commanding defending aviation forces during American military manoeuvres in 1938. By 1940, when war had broken out in Europe, he was a Colonel in the Air Defense Command, and, although operational American fighters still lagged behind the performance of potential adversaries, new designs including the P-38, P-47 and the superlative P-51 were catching up.

It has to be borne in mind that thirty years had elapsed since the end of the Second World War and Bill's letter to FOTE has some minor inaccuracies. However, it offers a vista of events beneath which are to be found the details of a daily struggle for aerial supremacy over Europe.

From: Big Dog One (my code name) to Friends of the Eighth. It is a pleasure to greet FOTE in any manner possible. I wish it could be in person, but 'Father Time' and illness in the family prevents. It is a temptation to talk of combat actions in WWII that are engraved on my memories . . . However . . . I will try to tell what happened in getting prepared for the action . . . in what to me was, and still is, the greatest fighter command of the USAF. My memories of fighter aircraft, plans, developments and policies go back to the '30s, when almost every one seemed to be interested in following up General Billy Mitchell's tactics, when he sank the German battleships [targets] off our Atlantic Coast. In the minds of many people, the only weapon worth very much seems to have been bigger and more bombers, with better bombs to drop. It took lots of money for bomber types. There was not much left for pursuit [fighters] attack, recon or transport types. Without money there was not enough drive to get very much development. When I was Chief Contracting Officer in 1932 we had 3 million dollars. One bomber contract for 10 Martin bombers cost one million dollars, one-third of the whole account. Bomber people, many in high positions of authority, advocated cutting down on all other types, and use the money for bombers who, they said, were capable of taking care of themselves with the 10 machine guns on each bomber. They did not see much use for fighters. Of course, some of us disagreed and were equally loud in claiming great future development of fighters. It was a tight situation. Then Winston Churchill spoke. F.D. Roosevelt listened. The Japs foolishly bombed Pearl Harbor, and we were in a WWII. The USAAC expanded 4,000 percent. We got ready for the forecasted war by the writer Gray in 1730 when he wrote: 'The time will come when thou shalt lift thine eyes; to behold a long drawn battle in the skies. While the aged peasant, too amazed for work, stares at the flying fleets of honored birds.' With time we produced thousands of airplanes. After a few 'drawn battles in the skies' the bombers were convinced they needed lots of fighters, and wanted them always around to protect them against a German Air Force that did not know bombers were invulnerable. The Germans had learned the lesson in the London blitz, when RAF Hurricanes, Spitfires, Tempests [sic] had stopped the German Luftwaffe. Even Herman Goering admitted it.

The American Eighth FC had to come from a way behind in types and quantities. They had to use the machines, planes and equipment that could be made available, in limited quantities, month by month, and grow up to a total of 15 combat groups in the Eighth FC, while protecting American B-17s and B-24s, also B-26s, in the presence of a great and experienced German Air Force, in the years of combat in air warfare before the Americans even started. Somehow we did it with the help of Providence, American production lines and RAF advice and equipment that could be made available at the start. In the beginning a good motto would have been 'the difficult we do at once, the impossible takes a little longer'. Sometimes it did. But in the end, the Eighth FC with 1,500 young pilots, age averaging 23 years, Group Commanders, aged 23 to 29, and Squadron and combat leaders in between: with 1,500 airplanes, fighter types, P-51 Mustang, P-47 Thunderbolt and P-38 Lightning, they pretty generally controlled the skies with lots of help from RAF and The Ninth FC. We escorted bombers to Poznan 750 miles; Berlin 600 miles and back by way of the Baltic Sea to English bases, and believe me those English bases were beautiful to return to. We also had many friends of the Eighth at that time. Let's keep it going!

In the year of 1939, while in command of one of our three pursuit groups at Langley Field, Virginia, we were being equipped with new P-36 type airplanes. I persuaded the factory to hang a 50-gallon belly tank on one plane, without cost to the USA AC. Washington heard of it and I was told to drop the idea. It was not approved for combat manoeuvres of a fighter type. Of course I cancelled my request for an extra belly drop tank, but I did not forget the idea. In 1943 [month of June] General Arnold [General of the Air Force Henry Harley 'Hap' Arnold] sent for me to come to his office. He had a job for me.

The Lockheed P-38 Lightning had a shorter tenure as a top-line, high-altitude escort fighter in the ETO because of deficiencies in its promised performance. Introduced in 1942, it suffered a series of problems including turbo-supercharger inter-cooler inadequacies.

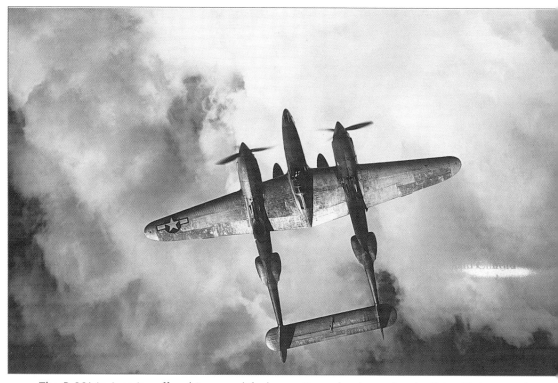

The P-38J to L series offered increased fuel capacity and enhanced potential with improved engine performance from the twin Allison engines. However, other difficulties – oil haemorrhaging at altitude; high oil consumption; turbine failures and lack of cockpit heating – caused senior 8FC commanders to lose faith in the product and set about standardisation on the P-51, ultimately eliminating the P-38 from front-line inventory. In other combat theatres, the P-38 enjoyed a more auspicious service record. *(Mike Bailey)*

He talked of the escort problem, particularly the loss of B-17 and B-24 bombers on missions over Germany. He said, 'I am sending you to the Eighth Air Force where General Eaker [Lt Gen Ira C. Eaker, CO of the Eighth Air Force] wants you to take command of the Eighth FC, and I want you to escort our bombers all the way to Berlin, even to Poznan eventually. They have got to bomb and you have to protect them. That is 600 miles to Berlin.' After I nodded my head he said, 'How are you going to do it?' I suspected he remembered my P-36 and its belly tank but I said very seriously 'I think it is time we hung extra fuel tanks on fighters'. His face flushed, then he said, banging his fist on the desk, 'I don't care how you do it, but get going.' And out I went to visit the three factories turning out P-47s, P-51s and P-38s. I explained the absolute requirement that we not only hang fuel tanks on each, but we had to have 60 gallons extra inside the fuselage so we could be sure to have fuel to return after 15 minutes combat over target 750 miles distant from English bases. After some discussion, all three, Ralph Domen, P-47, Dutch Kindelberger, P-51 and Bob Gross, P-38, agreed to do it. Of course the Procurement Department of the Pentagon knew about it at once. When I was stopping for fuel at Bolling AFB, Wash. DC, I received a telephone call from Lt Gen Barney Giles, General Arnold's deputy assistant, who had probably recommended me for the 8th FC command in the first place. He said, 'Come to my office at once.' Of course I complied at once. As I walked in, he said, 'Bill, you are in trouble.' 'Yes,' I replied, 'I was in trouble when I left here the other day'. He said, 'Seriously, you'd better read this letter.' It was real trouble. The letter was signed by the Chief of Procurement. The letter stated officially that Maj Gen W.E. Kepner had, without authority, and without going through the regular channel of procurement, ordered aircraft manufacturers to make changes in airplane design. It further recommended an official investigation, with a view to preferring charges if appropriate, etc. etc. I re-read the letter while I tried to think of my reply, which was certainly expected. I decided to face it. I said, 'Gen Giles, you heard Gen Arnold say he didn't care how I got escort fighters to Berlin, but to get going. This is the way I started. What do I do now?' Gen Giles took the letter, tore it up, laughed and said, 'That is about what Gen Arnold said.' Then he laughed and said, 'Gen Arnold also said, "I think maybe Kepner is going to Berlin."' 'Bill, you go on to London, we will handle this end.' So I left for the UK and the 8th AF.

I took a month to visit all the bomber bases. It was wonderful to see the courage of those bomber crews. But I was a man of mystery, and rumors followed me because I probably asked a lot of questions about fighter escort, tho my official title was Vice Command 8th AF. Many, including Air Chief Marshall Sir Trafford Leigh Mallory RAF, openly questioned my interest in fighter escort. Leigh Mallory, in a friendly challenge one night, said, 'I hope you are going to tell us how to win this war. Don't you think we have learned something?' Certainly, the man credited with stopping the German Blitz knew more about it than I did. Then he said, 'how far can you escort bombers? We have found that 275 miles is the practical limit.' While he waited for my reply, I said, 'A man by the name of Arnold in Washington thinks it ought to be as far as Berlin.' He snorted, said, 'I never heard of such a possibility', and walked away. Three months later he came to me and congratulated 8 FC. When I told him we were going out over 400 miles, but we would be going to Berlin, he laughed, said, 'Damned if I don't believe you won't.' I said, 'it will be Poznan.' Then he said, 'let's have a drink.' And we did, plus many more as time went on we became good friends throughout the balance of WWII.

Incidentally, our first 400+ miles range was possible because old men and women of London made us our first drop tanks for extra fuel. They made them 6 to 8 at each place by laminating paper together with glue, shaped and wrapped around a frame that could be hung on P-47 Thunderbolts. They were sometimes made with newspapers. We sent a truck around to the various places and generally picked up enough to equip one group of planes. First they held about 60 gallons then were increased to 108 gals. They worked but were good for only one trip . . .These emergency tanks handled us until our American drop tanks arrived. If any of these elderly citizens are still around, I would like to pass on my own, and the thanks of our 8 FC, for being an outstanding asset to the 8 FC. Theirs was indeed a job well done and I so wish to pass it on to all of them, or their descendants.

The tanks Bill mentions were made by the then Bowater Company, now absorbed into Rexam PLC, although, in fact, there were over forty UK companies involved in the

Kepner's reference to the 'old men and women of London' has a touch of mythology about it. The fifteen personnel pictured in this view of the Bowater factory are predominantly young women, with one male, possibly the foreman, top right near the tanks stored vertically. These 108 US gallon paper composite tanks work-in-progress are being hand painted, some olive drab, some silver. The odour must have been overpowering, but the workers seem happy enough. (Rexam PLC)

production of components for the tanks or the tanks themselves. Bowater, a renowned paper merchant since 1881, was principal among these. Restrictions on the use of newsprint obliged its paper mill at Sittingbourne in Kent to diversify into making containers for munitions. The idea of laminated paper expendable petrol tanks for aeroplanes was an entirely new use for paper, but Bowater's expertise aided design and development of a fuel tank capable of use at high altitude and able to stand a strain of 9G. The early days described by Bill burgeoned into production output of nearly 8,000 45-gallon tanks and a recorded 253,432 90-gallon tanks. The concept of carrying extra fuel on externally hung tanks is commonplace on combat aircraft today, but this simple expedient was one that enabled advanced strategy and tactics ultimately to wrest aerial supremacy from the Luftwaffe.

Bill's letter continues:

In the beginning, when we had only three–four groups and generally 75 planes on a mission, in order to be sure we would have enough planes for another day, it was our policy to save about 10 minutes combat time, ammunition, and fuel, so all planes in one group [or each group] could fight their way back to England. I always thought the Germans would jump our fighters returning, and would possibly destroy the entire mission, so we would be stopped from the next day's missions. Apparently, General Galland, of the Luftwaffe, thought about it, but gave up after six attempts . . .He says Reichsmarshall Goering ordered him to stop trying, after six missions – he won the first two; then we took four victories in a row. For this I thank Reichsmarshall Goering.

In this situation Col Jim Stone CO of the 78 FG phoned me to request I talk to two of his pilots who would not stop combat in order to return with the group. He said they were outstanding combat pilots. He had fined them and now wanted me to talk to them. I agreed and waited for them in my office. In they came, perhaps a little awkward, but not a sign of fear, and very little remorse. One, a stropping 6' officer . . . The other about my size, 5'7". I said, 'Gentlemen, be seated.' They sat down, looked at each other in surprise, then at me. I liked them. I asked why they did not believe in teamwork. The big chap said, 'We believe in teamwork and I know the Colonel is right but when I am in a fight about to

Drop tanks awaiting use by the 359FG at East Wretham. The concept of jettisonable tanks added leagues to the already long-striding Mustang and saw bombers escorted to objectives once thought impossible. Bill Kepner achieved his ambition. *(C. Baldridge)*

get a German, I guess I am not a good soldier. I just have to get him, I can't seem to stop. I don't blame the Colonel, guess I would think as he does.' When I started talking, I had no plan but as I looked at these two young Americans, I thought of some others who had also been doing well in combat and sometimes on their own. Then my plans emerged in a rush. I said, 'Well, you are not the only ones like that. I think you all have a good chance to get killed. However I want you to kill as many Germans as possible before you go. I am going to collect all of you in one squadron, where you can fight any way you want, except that you must kill lots of German pilots before you get it. I am going to call for volunteers for that squadron. They straightened up with fire in their eyes said, 'Gee that's great when do we start?' I said, 'Go back to your outfits until I ask for volunteers for this squadron that will raise hell with German pilots wherever they find them. Good day gentlemen.' They grinned and walked out.

Thirty-seven pilots volunteered. We put all in one squadron attached to Colonel Duncan's Group [353FG]. He led the squadron on three missions, selected a squadron commander and they really went to town. They wanted to name the squadron 'Bill's Buzz Boys' and [I] became proud of them. However, the groups copied them and we had a 'FC' of really tough killers. It was time to send them back to their groups. They nearly all became outstanding as leaders in their respective organizations. I was sincere when I congratulated them on having developed new tactics for individuals throughout the 8 FC. It was one of those things that paid dividends, in that we had discipline, with a great fighting spirit intact.

Bill's Buzz Boys comprised officers from several groups. 353FG: 1/Lts Kenneth Chetwood, Charles O. Durant, Francis Edwards and John A. Sullivan. 355FG: Capt Albert B. Starr, 1/Lts Norman J. Fortier, Kenneth R. Williams and 2/Lt Gilbert S. Wright. 359FG: Capt Charles Ettlesen, 1/Lts Clifford E. Carter, Robert L. Thacker and 2/Lt John W. Oliphint. 361FG: 1/Lts Eugene W. Kinnard, Martin H. Johnson, Joseph Kelly and 2/Lt Johnny C. Wright. From reporting to Col Duncan at Metfield on 15 March 1944 until they disbanded on 12 April 1944, Bill's Buzz Boys made a significant tactical contribution to the development of an 8FC strategy that saw increased aggression against the Luftwaffe wherever it could be found. If the Germans refused to come up and fight, seeking to conserve their diminishing resources by remaining earthbound, the USAAF would take the war to them. Capt Charles C. Ettlesen wrote a report of their activities on his return to the 359FG.

In order to insure the success of the invasion the Eighth Air Force had as its objective the destruction of the Luftwaffe. The German Air Force was not to be found in the air, and therefore had to be sought out and destroyed on the ground at its airdromes . . . It was up to this squadron to discover a means of attacking airdromes that would insure success yet cut casualties to the minimum. In the days to follow every form of attack that had been heard of, and many that hadn't, were tested and discussed. Dive bombing was discarded as inaccurate, glide bombing as suicide, low altitude navigation as impossible, and so on. It became apparent that the P-47's eight machine guns must be brought to bear in order to destroy an enemy aircraft, and, in order to do this without being shot out of the air by the enemy's ground defences, Surprise, Cover and Evasive action must be utilized to the utmost. At length a form of attack encompassing these elements was hit upon and practised to perfection. The squadron would enter enemy territory properly briefed on specific enemy airdromes as to installations, cover, routes of approach and withdrawal, flak, dispersal areas, etc. On reaching an initial point some 20 miles from the airdrome one flight would split-ess from 15,000 feet, pick up some 400 or 500MPH and hit the deck about five miles from the airdrome. With some excellent check point such as a road leading to the airdrome the flight in line abreast would hit the installations, etc. exactly as briefed. Dropping down so that props were cutting the grass, the flight would proceed to shoot up everything in sight. Only by the time the ships had reached the far side of the enemy airdrome were the ground defences alerted and for a few seconds as the ships pulled up to clear hangars, etc. they were the center of converging 20mm fire. Dropping down behind some form of cover, as briefed, the attack was finished and the flight was safe. Arriving at a flak free area the flight would regain its altitude or strafe other ground targets such as locomotives, tugboats etc. . .

Methods of assaulting aerodromes used by Bill's Buzz Boys were honed and refined by individual 8 and 9 FC Groups. The strategy of seeking out the enemy offered no respite or refuge, and the advent of the P-51 extended the long reach of 8 and 9FC into their farthest boltholes. Bill congratulated Bill's Buzz Boys at the time: 'The Commanding General expresses his sincere appreciation to each pilot and to those supervisory personnel contributing to the successful development of new fighter tactics.'

His letter to FOTE continues:

In August of 1943, the Eighth AF dispatched a double mission to Schweinfurt: one Wing and one Wing to Regensberg. The 3rd Wing, Gen Curtis LeMay [General Curtis Emerson LeMay, Commanding General, 3 Bombardment Division] had heavy losses but got by fairly well. They missed most of the German fighters, who seemed to be late, and flew on south to the Mediterranean area. However, the 1st Wing, Gen Bob Williams commanding [Brig Gen Robert B. Williams], seemed to fly directly in to the first assembly of German fighters who, having missed the 3rd Wing of LeMay, now attacked Gen Williams' 1st Wing and shot down about a quarter of the B-17s attacking Schweinfurt. It was our biggest loss of the war. We thereafter tailored the ranges of the bombers so they could have 8FC escort. That was the correct measure to take and fighter escort with longer range became a key to the range of bomber missions. I don't remember that we ever flew a mission of longer range than the range of the escort. Fortunately we began to get the metal drop tanks and soon Berlin was in sight as a possible target, to be followed by Poznan and the shuttle raids on to Russia.

I recall one mission to Poznan and beyond when we had P-51s over the target then bombers would fly north and be met by P-38's over the Baltic sea leaving 100 miles in question. I solved it by talking to Gen Doolittle and recommending we allow one squadron of the 4th Group to take musette bags with toilet articles. They would escort the 100-mile gap to the Baltic then if unable to return to England; in emergency could land and be interned in Sweden somewhere. I gave instructions to Don Blakeslee (Col. CO 4FG). He said, 'You won't object if we all take them to the Baltic, will you?' I said, 'Yes and don't lose your whole group.' 'OK!' said he, 'I will bring them all back'. I said, 'OK. But promise me, that except for one squadron, you be darn sure to leave with fuel to get home.' He took his whole group to the Baltic where the P-38's met them. Then only one of the 4FG had to land. I asked Don Blakeslee, 'How in the devil did you do it?' He said, 'We came home on our spark plugs.' They explained, they slowed down flight to save fuel over Poznan and it worked. Fortunately we had 15 such groups, all dedicated to getting the job done no matter what happened. We were close knit and any information known to one individual or organization was freely passed on for the benefit of the whole 15 groups.

Poznan (Posen) was in Poland and the bombers were targeting factories in the aviation industry on 13 May 1944. This was the P-51's deepest penetration to date at some 1,470 miles and over six hours in the cockpit for many pilots.

Bill continues:

On our first shuttle to Kiev, the 4FG, with one extra squadron, was to rendezvous near 'Leipzig'. Two minutes before rendezvous, the Bomb Wing commander called the 355 FG Col Cummings [Col William J. Cummings Jr] and said, 'Have you contacted the 4FG?' 'No,' replied Cummings, 'but we have our musette bags and will go with you if the 4FG doesn't show up.' Of course, the [Bomb] Group Wing Commander said thanks with a sigh of great relief. Then immediately, Col Blakeslee with the 4FG said over radio, 'It is OK, Bill, I have you in sight, you can leave.' We could really be proud of that combination of help and coordination; with probably, at that time, 25 to 30 aces in each group.

This was a prestigious mission for the Eighth Air Force on 21 June 1944 and took its aircraft, via an attack on synthetic oil plants near Ruhland, to Russia, where the display of power was not solely intended to impress the Germans. Over 1,200 bombers were launched, followed by a similar number of fighters, including five groups from the Ninth Air Force. Those aircraft shuttling into Russia used three airfields provided by their allies – Poltava, Mirgorod and Piryatin. The arrival of the Americans had been noted by the enemy, who successfully raided Poltava that night and destroyed many aircraft on the ground. It was a costly exercise for the Eighth and over 100 bombers and fighters were lost during either the mission or the later assault on Poltava.

Returning to Bill's letter:

Late in the year of 1943, when we had seven or eight fighter groups doing well and eager to take on the Germans, I went to Gen Eaker and recommended we spread out from the bombers and try to knock down more German airplanes. I thought we could still protect the bombers and pay extra dividends. He listened seriously then said, 'No. It is better to stay close to the bombers.' Of course, he was right in his decision. At that particular time, he knew best. Many important things began to happen in later 1943. Development and production began to show results of planning. We got P-51 airplanes, our first of the type. The 4FG that had been born of the old 'Eagle Squadrons' was getting the first P-51 replacement. Every pilot had checked out in the one plane they had. They were enthusiastic, when out of a clear sky and without warning, we were informed the P-51 would go to the newly formed 9th AF. That was a discouraging blow that brought gloom to the 4FG and other groups due to get P-51s. I went into General Eaker three separate times to plead for the Mustang, that I had gotten into near trouble over demanding extra fuel for long range escort. Moreover we who had flown the Mustang knew it was a good escort plane. Probably more manoeuvrable with more range than any plane in the Luftwaffe. On my last futile request Gen Eaker said, 'A decision has been made by high authority which must be accepted. Don't come back again to request a change of course.' I had to accept it as a command decision. But I was depressed to blue over the result.

Then General Spaatz [Maj Gen Carl Spaatz] came to England to organize for the final big battle to end the war. On his first appearance at General Eaker's farewell before leaving for the Mediterranean Theatre, I met him ten feet inside the door. He said, 'Hello, how are things going?' I said, 'Pretty poor.' He laughed and said, 'I thought you were doing all right.' I said, 'General Spaatz, a big mistake has been made in assigning P-51s to the 9th Air Force. They are ideal, and made for long range escort. They won't exist on the deck in my opinion.' Then a crowd formed and Spaatz said, 'Kepner, we will talk some more later, I am not so sure but that a mistake may have been made.'

Sure enough, three days later he phoned me to meet him for a meeting in London. I was there. He said, 'Bill, you had better defend the P-51 if you want it.' And we did. I also pointed out that the P-47 could take the punishment on the deck in the 9FC. That it could dive bomb, because during the previous month, we had flown 16 dive bombing missions in addition to the escort for 20 missions, and I offered to demonstrate both the Thunderbolt and the P-51 for the missions required. Finally in late afternoon General Spaatz said to the presiding officer, 'Air Chief Marshal, I am going wire the Joint Chiefs of Staff that I can't carry out my strategic bombing missions without satisfactory and adequate escort and need the P-51.' The presiding officer said, 'wait a minute General Spaatz, don't do that.' Then he said to Gen Louis [sic] Brereton 9th AF [Maj Gen Lewis H. Brereton, CO 9AF], 'I have decided to vote for the P-51 to the 8 AF.' That clinched the deal and a most critical decision had been possible through General Spaatz' decisive action. We got the P-51 back for the 8FC. The 9FC kept two P-51 groups. But six weeks after the invasion General Quesada [Brig Gen Elwood R. Quesada, CO 9FC] told me he had decided to use his two P-51 groups primarily for reconnaissance. They suffered too much on the deck. So it was a good decision for all concerned.

Goering was to say the P-51 swung the tide in favor of the Americans. They considered it ten miles faster and more manoeuvrable than their best fighter in combat. However, the Germans could not justifiably low rate either of the three [sic] American type fighters. They each did well. Yet the P-51 made us sure of our long range escort where it was

Rugged, reliable and more capable of absorbing small arms and light anti-aircraft fire, P-47s were more suited to 9FC operations. This example pictured from a 385BG B-17 is 44-32754 of the 48FG.

P-47D Thunderbolt, 'Doogan' 42-26041, 3T-A, of the 36FG taxiing out from its base in Belgium for another raid supporting ground forces during the Battle of the Bulge. Bitter conditions prevailed – pity the poor maintenance crew working on the aircraft in the background. *(Tom Glenn)*

critical. With long-range fuel tanks on each type of fighter we could protect our bombers of every part of the enemy's territory.

In the summer of 1943 we needed some way to get pertinent combat information to new pilots. They had all the will required to do the job but they needed contact with experienced pilots. We kept them around the base for two weeks to try and absorb knowledge required for successful air combat. It was hoped they could talk to older pilots who returned from missions each day, also to become familiar with their own air bases in case they came back from missions in poor weather or a crippled airplane. I decided to write a combat manual to assist each new pilot. We wound up, after considering 400 combat reports, with 20 standard problems that seemed common to all combats. We send a copy of these 20 questions to each Group and Squadron commander and one to each ace and well-recognized combat pilot. They were required to answer these questions as to how to solve each problem. Then we took the written sponsors with the combat pilot, leader or ace's picture printed on each answer list and bound all together in a manual form. Then had these distributed equally among all the Groups, to be given to the new pilots. They could and did immediately look at the pictures and answers of some pilot in their own Group. They were encouraged to pick out one list whose answers appealed to them and ask questions. Of course where they just stopped and looked at some leader or ace, that pilot was told to speak to them and get them asking questions. The ace often suggested they fly with him. It worked out fine. We called the combat manual 'The Long Reach'. It certainly paid big dividends. Washington had hundreds of copies made and distributed to other commands.

Shortly after General Spaatz arrived General Jimmy Doolittle arrived to take over and organize the Eighth Air Force. There was lots of speculation as to just who would be reorganized and where. The morning following Jimmy's arrival he showed up at the Operations room of the 8FC. We had a rather complicated mission on the table together with living maps. He came in unannounced and insisted of course that we pay no attention to him while the mission moved pretty much as planned. He did express to me that he thought it most impossible for fighters to navigate our long ranges successfully. I said, 'Jimmy, let's you and I fly with them and see it, as I believe it happens.' He looked at me grinning and nodded okay.

About that time the map showed the Germans reporting a Wing of bombers and escorts well off course, and not where the bombers were scheduled. After three consecutive reports showed them with the correct speeds and a logical track, I asked the Fighter Wing HQ, who were in radio contact with the fighters, to find out if the Fighter Group CO, Col Duncan, was with his bombers. He reported 'affirmative'. Next I asked if he was on his scheduled track. Duncan reported 'negative'. That satisfied Doolittle that the fighter knew where he was. At the same time we heard a fighter pilot over clear radio exclaim, 'There is [the] Eiffel Tower!' Duncan said firmly, 'Shut up!'. I gave orders for Col Duncan to use his own judgment but try to get home okay. Shortly we heard Duncan say to the Wing CO, 'I am changing course for home.' The Bomb Wing CO said, 'Yes, so am I.' Duncan left shortly then the Germans appeared and the Bomb Wing asked for help. Duncan did not reply. Jimmy asked, 'What will Duncan do?' I said, 'he will come back but we won't hear him say so.' And pretty shortly the bombers radioed and thanked Duncan for helping drive off the Germans. Then Duncan said, 'I am going to have to swim partway, but I am leaving.' 'Okay,' said the Wing CO. 'We can manage, thanks.'

Jimmy said, 'That is interesting, the fighters knew where they were.' He seemed favorably impressed. Then we went to my office. He saw a motto, 'Our mission is to bring the bombers back.' Jimmy said very seriously, 'That is changed. Your mission is to destroy the German Air Force.' I was delighted, and said so. Jimmy [later] said I also remarked, 'Now we can act like fighters.' I guess I did say that because we were ready and it was time to go all out after the German Air Force. We roamed the German skies, but when our bombers were under attack, tried always to help by shooting down the enemy. And at times a Group would leave one squadron with bombers while they took the Group's two other squadrons to attack any Germans in the area.

Contrails curving overhead are from escorting fighters but the 'little friends' could do nothing to assist when it came too flak. Ever present, ever deadly – bursts surround this 490BG formation on its bomb run.

The bombers did not like it at first but realized we were destroying the German Luftwaffe. Then, on one occasion, we covered all Germany with fighter patrols, while the bombers moved freely all over the enemy territory without a single loss. That proved we were right.

In Feb. 1944, we went to Berlin. Our P-38s were over Leipzig the first day, we reported it as a reconnaissance. But a couple of days later, everything, bombers and fighters, were over Berlin dropping bombs and, of course, German fighters rose to defend the air. The *scores* of downed enemy aircraft were truly great from our angle. As I remember, the first day of the battle of Berlin, 8FC downed 67, the next day 83. Then the fourth [means third] day no Germans showed up – probably reorganizing. The fourth day we got 97. The fifth day we got as I recall 130 enemy aircraft. This battle turned out to be decisive, and thereafter we had to hunt the German aircraft. They had learned their lesson. When we couldn't find them in the air we went down to the deck, over their airfields, along roads, open spaces and at times even in – over – woods destroying hundreds. Over all, several groups would report with pictures to prove it, 40 and once over 50 airplanes destroyed. This was after our ground forces were working across Western Europe.

Another point of Gen Doolittle's fighting character, we were attending a combined meeting of all ground and air commanders just prior to the invasion. Jimmy asked the British General, 'I guess it's going to be tough over that beach. How long do you need help against German air attack before you will feel secure?' The British General said, 'Yes, we will need help. Particularly the first day. We will be vulnerable – give us 48 hours and we have a 50/50 chance. Give us 72 hours and all hell won't throw us off that beach.' Jimmy turned to me and said, 'Bill, they will get 72 hours secure from German air [attack] or there won't be any 8th FC left.' The British General almost jumped for joy, his eyes glistened. He said, 'Gentlemen, that is the best encouragement I have had on this whole business.' Well, they had it. We had about 3,000 fighters available in 8th and 9th air forces. The British had about the same. We estimated the Germans had about 900 fighter aircraft available. We hoped they would show so we could finish them off. They did not show up.

I was present at Rheims, France, when the Germans surrendered. General Spaatz was in the main room while we were in an adjacent room. Afterwards, Spaatz came to me and said, 'Bill, I have a compliment for you and the Command. I talked to Air Marshall Goering. I asked him, "When did you realize the jig was up?" Goering answered, "When I saw your American fighters over Berlin shooting down our fighters. I realized you could protect your bombers, and we could be bombed out of the war."' General Spaatz said, 'I want to pass the compliment to you because I know you had some trouble getting the fighters to Berlin,' and he smiled knowingly.

I believe the 8FC pilots to be a great example of the type of the American 'Man at Arms', in the air, on the ground and at sea, who writes his own eulogy on his enemy's breast in blood. Bless them and keep them together with all our true friends. We shall need their type when our liberty is again at stake. 'Big Dog One' signing off. W.E. Kepner DSC CB DSM Lt General USAF Ret.

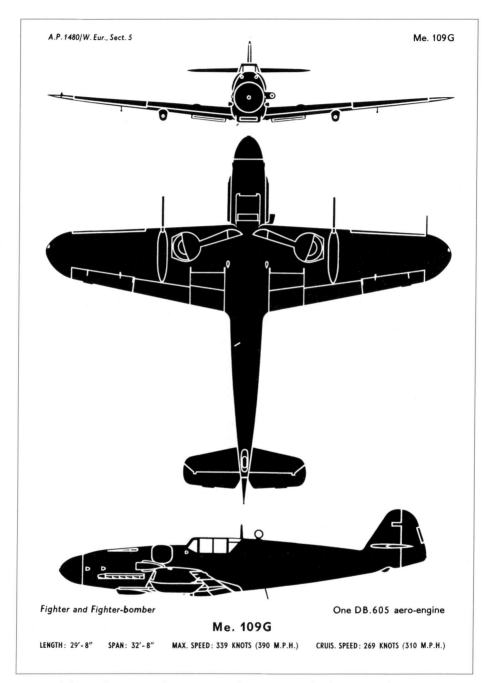

A.P. 1480/W. Eur., Sect. 5   Me. 109G

Fighter and Fighter-bomber   One DB.605 aero-engine

Me. 109G

LENGTH: 29'-8"   SPAN: 32'-8"   MAX. SPEED: 339 KNOTS (390 M.P.H.)   CRUIS. SPEED: 269 KNOTS (310 M.P.H.)

USAAF fighter pilots primarily encountered two principal adversaries, the Messerscmitt 109 and the Focke Wulf, and both were dangerous when flown by skilled opponents. The Me 109 served in front-line combat throughout the war, and captured examples were tested against Allied fighters. The Mustang was faster at all heights but the Me109 could outclimb the P-51 below 20,000 feet. If diving away from danger, the P-51 could outrun the Me 109 or, alternatively, catch up. In dogfights, the P-51 had a much better turning circle but the rate of roll was comparable. In summary, the Messerschmitt was outclassed by its principal American contemporary but victory could not be taken for granted.

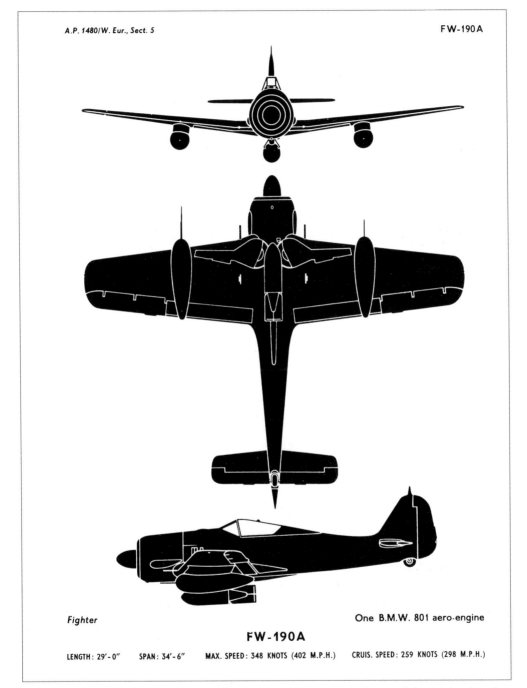

FW-190A

Fighter

One B.M.W. 801 aero-engine

FW-190A

LENGTH: 29'-0"   SPAN: 34'-6"   MAX. SPEED: 348 KNOTS (402 M.P.H.)   CRUIS. SPEED: 259 KNOTS (298 M.P.H.)

Throughout the war a game of technological leapfrog occurred with aircraft being developed to counter advances achieved by their enemies. The FW 190 entered service in 1941 and was, like its US contemporaries, equipped with drop tanks and adapted to carry bombs. In pure fighter mode, the FW 190 was slower than the P-51 at all heights, they climbed comparably but the Mustang could outdive the Focke Wulf. The FW 190 totally outperformed the P-51 in its rate of roll and was only slightly inferior in its turning circle. Victory, either way, so often depended on the element of surprise or the advantage of height, sun and speed.

P-51 GENERAL GROUP TACTICS

By Maj Thomas L. Gates, Asst Group Operations Officer, 357 Fighter Group

The Group leader is the quarterback of the team. But before the Group leader takes over we must prepare the field for play. There is essential work, which it is well to mention at this time. We will take only the action in which this Group participates. Immediately upon receipt of a field order, the teletype operator notifies the Duty S3 Officer and the Duty Intelligence Officer. The Duty S3 Officer plots the course on the operations map to target, or R/V [rendezvous], whichever the case maybe and computes the time for set course, take-off, start engines and briefing. He then notifies the Squadron Operations giving the number of aircraft required, start engine time, fuel required and armament required: the squadron orderly room giving the number of pilots required and the briefing time; the mess hall to have meals served at a certain time; the weather section time of briefing, flying control the time of take-off; the Group leader 90 minutes before briefing, the time of briefing and makes any immediate decision necessary. He can now study more closely the field order and plot the entire course from base to target and return. He also plots any other activity on the operations map. The Duty IO works very close with the Duty S3 Officer. He plots the courses and targets with pertinent information on the briefing map and flak map; prepares maps for the Group and Squadron leaders and briefs the pilots on pertinent intelligence information.

The Group leader by now has arrived at the briefing room. He studies the Field Order, checks the route and timings of all bomber and fighter forces, studies the flak maps and consults the Weather Officer and the Intelligence Officer. If it is felt necessary he gives a preliminary briefing to the Squadron leaders.

It is now the designated briefing time and all pilots scheduled for the mission have copied from the mission data board the route courses, distances, times, calls, minimum gas, average course home, etc. The Group leader now begins his quarterbacking. He briefly but thoroughly reviews the operation, giving the strength, type and identification markings of our bomber force (if it is an escort mission); the route timings and type of target; our R/V point, time and box or boxes, of the force we are to escort; the distribution of the Group for escort and the formation to be flown; the locations and times of other escort fighter groups; the probably and possible E/A [enemy aircraft] reaction with their type, strength and tactics; and an overall picture of all forces involved in the day's operation. He now assigns the runway for take-off by squadrons; and the formation to be flown, i.e. high, middle and low squadrons. The Weather Officer and S2 Officer are called on for their respective briefing and after they have finished, watches are synchronised and pilots are dismissed.

It is well to add here that the manner in which a Group leader briefs his pilots is rather important. He should impart confidence and aggressiveness. The right amount of humour is never out of place. Overconfidence, indifference and negligence must be avoided.

To develop the role of the Group leader the formation and tactics employed by this Group are briefly described.

The Group flies the standard three-squadron formation. Each of the three squadrons is composed of four, four ship flights and two spares. Each squadron is divided into two sections of two flights. En route to R/V flights within the squadrons fly rather close formation. The down sun squadron flys from 2,000 to 3,000 feet above the lead squadron and up-sun squadron about 1,000 feet below the lead squadron. Each squadron flies approximately 3,000 feet horizontally from the lead squadron.

P-51 FORMATION COMBAT TACTICS

By Lt Col Irwin H. Dregne, Group Operations Officer, 357 Fighter Group

The group flies as three sixteen-ship squadrons with the down-sun squadron 1,000ft above the lead squadron and the up-sun squadron from 3,000 to 5,000 ft above the lead squadron. Climbing out to the enemy coast, the flights are flown abreast in a compact

Lt Col Irwin H. Dregne, Group Operations Officer 357 FFG. He commanded the 357FG from December 1944 until July 1945. (Merle Olmsted)

formation with the three squadrons stepped up line abreast. Upon reaching the enemy coast the individual flights loosen up.

En route to rendezvous we fly to get mutual protection rather than manoeuvrability. The flights within the squadron give cross cover rather than individual in the flight. Keeping the group in a compact unit makes it easier to avoid heavy flak positions. It also makes it simple to spot bandits and prevents mixing with friendly units en route.

The disposition of the squadrons after contact with the bombers depends on how big a force of bombers we must cover, the type of formation the bombers are flying and the size of enemy force that we can expect to encounter. On a mission deep into Germany where heavy enemy resistance is expected the squadrons will stay intact and the three squadrons will remain in the same area in contact by radio.

If there are two or three boxes of bombers to cover, the Group leader will place his squadron about 1,000ft above and in front of the bombers giving them close escort. The middle squadron will be above the second box from 1,500ft to 3,000ft above the bombers. The increase in altitude gives them a chance to dive to the front if they are needed. The top squadron will stay about 5,000ft above the bomber force, taking care of any top cover the enemy fighters might send in or catching any enemy aircraft coming in high. At this altitude the high squadron can dive to any place along the bomber force that might need help.

If there are more than three boxes to cover, the squadrons will be placed in the same position on the bomber force, depending on fighter–bomber inter-communication to warn them of trouble on the rear of the force. One can get from the front to the rear of the force in a very short time, but if you are in the rear and the front gets hit by the enemy aircraft it is very hard to get up there in time to break up the attack.

To give good escort, it is essential that the bombers fly a good compact formation. During the escort the flights fly a finger formation, loose enough so each pilot can look around. The two flights in each section fly in trail, with the blue section giving top cover to the red section. With this type of escort formation we have a strong enough force to meet anything the enemy has put up to date and we are able to make a good killing when the Germans hit in large numbers at our bomber force. All bandits or bogies are called into the squadron, section or flight leader. If the squadron leader fails to spot the 'called-in' aircraft immediately, the supporting flight leader or the pilot calling in the aircraft will lead the flight down for the bounce.

After combat the squadrons will reform at a point designated by R/T in relation to the bomber force. Any flights or individual ships getting separated in combat will immediately climb back to the bombers, where they can find friendly fighters to join. When the enemy aircraft are sighted, the squadron having the most advantageous position goes in for the bounce. The other squadrons will join the fight if they are needed. If the enemy force is large enough the whole group will engage it. The Germans have been hitting one box of bombers in a large concentrated force and if the escorting group can engage this force and destroy a large number of them, it has done a good day's work.

P-51 SQUADRON TACTICS

By Capt John B. England, Acting Commanding Officer, 362 Fighter Squadron, 357 Fighter Group

1 Offensive

Most perfect bounce would be made from out of the sun and from 3,000 to 5,000ft above the enemy. A pilot making a bounce should always instinctively have the advantage in speed or altitude, since one can be converted to the other. Flights should fly close formation relying on mutual support between flights or for protection. Jerry will think twice before he jumps eighteen planes in good formation. This has been proven many times by our experience.

2 Defensive

The best defensive manoeuvre for the P-51 against the common enemy fighter plane is just a simple tight turn. I have never seen one of our fighters shot down in a tight turn, but I have seen our fighters shot down while trying to evade Jerry by diving to the deck or pulling some fancy manoeuvres. I say never be on the defensive list; if you are on the defensive, turn it into an offensive situation immediately. Always let the Hun know you're after him from the beginning.

3 Flak Evasion

Best method I have found for evading heavy flak at high altitude is a climbing turn of not over 15 degrees. If you are leading a flight, your evasive action can be more acute. The best insurance against light flak is speed.

Capt John B. England, 362FS, 357FG, is pictured with his ground crew. Crew Chief S/Sgt Currie (L); Assistant Crew Chief Sgt Highland peers over the cowling and armourer, Cpl Hamilton sits with a belt of .50s draped over his shoulders. The nose of the P-51 is a busy piece of artwork with mission and victory tallies plus the aircraft's name. (Merle Olmsted)

P-51 SQUADRON TACTICS

By Maj Edwin W. Hiro, Commanding Officer, 363 Fighter Squadron, 357 Fighter Group

1 Offensive

The squadron is made up of four flights, red, white, blue and green, divided into two sections with red and white flights in the 'A' section and blue and green in the 'B' section. Red flight leads, with white flight on the up-sun side and about 500ft below red flight. 'B' section acts as top cover about 1,000ft above and on the side away from the sun, with green flight the furthest out in the formation. By staggering the flights by altitude it brings the whole squadron together for mutual support both defensively and offensively.

The ideal squadron attack is to come into the enemy force from above and out of the sun in a surprise attack and level off into a stern approach with speed enough to overtake but not over-run the enemy aircraft. 'A' section makes the attack while 'B' section stays above and acts as top cover, keeping a watch out for a trap or any enemy top cover. The same

Maj Edwin W. Hiro, Commanding Officer 363FS, 357FG. His aircraft was named 'Horse's Itch'. *(Merle Olmsted)*

holds true in ground strafing and low altitude bombing. As 'A' section goes down for the attack; 'B' section stays up for top cover and when the 'B' section goes down 'A' section does top cover.

2   Defensive

Referring to the basic information in para. 1, 'B' section acting as top cover can get into position with 'A' section by diving down and warding off the attack. In a surprise bounce by the enemy, a quick break away is essential into the attacking planes thus giving them only a short burst, if any, and deflection shooting. The Lufberry [*sic*] is then formed as tight as possible, each guarding the other's tail. Draw the attack to the rest of the squadron for their mutual support, using such natural aids as climbing into the sun, cloud cover and your best performance altitude. [The Lufbery was a defensive tactic of aircraft forming a circle, turning tightly, with each fighter protecting the one in front. The tactic is accredited to the First World War ace Raoul Lufbery, but there is no proven provenance.]

3   Flak Evasion

The best evasive action, of course, is to avoid flak-infested areas and large cities, going around them if they are spotted on the ground or if flak is already being shot up ahead. In heavy meagre flak, the squadron leader can call a turn to the right or left and all four flights can still stay in formation well abreast. If the flak is intense, an immediate change of altitude and course, adding throttle and continuing to weave, is effective, then diving and climbing until clear. It is possible here to keep flights together; at least individual flights can stay together. The greatest error in flak evasion is to fly in trail.

P-51 INDIVIDUAL COMBAT TACTICS

By Maj John A. Storch, Commanding Officer, 364 Fighter Squadron

1   Defensive

The basic defensive manoeuvre is to turn into the attacking enemy. Often this will automatically turn a defensive situation into an offensive one. If the German turns with you, the P-51 should be on the tail of the average enemy plane in short order. If, as we have found to be more often the case, the German split-esses for the deck, without top cover, you can split-ess after him. He may outdive you on the way down and outmanoeuvre you during this dive, but when you level out on the deck you will probably be able to catch him.

We have found at times that clouds can be life savers for us, but more often they serve as life savers for the German. If you are alone, as you never should be, and are jumped by superior numbers of Germans and all else fails, there is nothing nicer than a big thick blanket of clouds to get into and fly instruments in for a while. During my limited experience, our Air Force has managed most of the time to have sufficient planes at the right place at the right time to enable us to be on the offensive. Therefore, the German, eager as he is, has been able to rob us of possible kills by diving away into the clouds.

Capt – later Maj – John A. Storch, Commanding Officer 364FS, 357FG with Assistant Crew Chief Sgt Joe Kubarek and 'The Shillelagh'. *(Merle Olmsted)*

When attacked by superior numbers, if no cloud cover of help is available, about the only thing you can do is to keep turning into his attacks and take such shots as you can get, hoping to even things up. You should, under such circumstances, continue to watch all the time for an opportunity to make a break for home; however, it does not pay to straighten out on a course unless you are very sure you will be out of accurate firing range. My own opinion is that the best way to make the break is a shallow dive with everything full forward. If the enemy starts to overhaul you again and gets within accurate range, about the only thing to do is to turn again and give him a deflection shot at you. When attacked I like to have my wingman stay close enough that he can take a plane off my tail and I can do the same for him. He is of no help, however, if he stays in so tight that we cannot manoeuvre and are practically one target.

The preceding and following statements are completely dependent upon circumstances and no hard and fast rules can be set down.

2   Offensive

When attacking an enemy aircraft, the leader should go in for the first shot while his wingman drops out and back far enough that he can watch the sky and clear his own and his leader's tail. If the leader overshoots or has to break off his attack, his wingman will be in position to start firing with the leader covering him. If you have to break off combat but want another shot later, break up and either turn to right or left but not in a turn of 360 degrees as you probably will be unable to catch the enemy aircraft after you complete it.

The main enemy evasive tactics we have noticed are: split-essing for the deck, going to cloud cover, rolling, sliding, slipping or bailing out. In any case, except the last, the only thing to do is to follow him shooting or if you think he will be unable to get away, wait until he straightens out and gives you a decent target.

If the German has superior numbers in a large gaggle formation, you can usually get on a straggler or take one of the top outside planes of the formation and try to separate him from the others. The others may not miss him. If the enemy aircraft is flying in a gaggle-type formation, there isn't a lot they can do about it. Of course, you must have altitude on the German so you will have superior speed to break away should you get into trouble. Flaps can be used to avoid overshooting, but once you put them down you will have lost your speed advantage and perhaps become vulnerable to attack.

The best shooting method for us seems to be to get in as close as you can and still avoid hitting his plane or any pieces that by chance may fall off it and let 'er rip. Anyone will do his best shooting when he is so close that he cannot miss.

The men of the 357FG were representative of the many under Bill Kepner's command and this premier fighter group typified the spirit shown by USAAF fighter pilots.

Bill Kepner died on 3 July 1982 and the years since have seen many more of his command awarded their final set of wings, joining the comrades who already, as the old Air Force song has it, 'Fly with Pete and his angels sweet'. The multitudes of aircraft they flew – Thunderbolts, Lightnings and Mustangs – are a rare sight in the skies, just a few examples lovingly maintained as living memorials. A few more rest with silent pride in museums. Of others, only a handful of shattered parts exist to tell the story. For most aircraft and their pilots all that remains are fading photographs, dog-eared documents and letters echoing love and friendships lost defending democratic freedoms. We should honour that inheritance and never forget the fighters – machines and men – plus the courage, strategy and tactics that bequeathed us this legacy.

Bibliography

Caldwell, Donald L. *JG26 Tops Guns of the Luftwaffe*. New York: Orion, 1991

Freeman, Roger A., *The Mighty Eighth*. London: Macdonald, 1970

Freeman, Roger A., *Mighty Eighth War Diary*. New York: Jane's, 1981

Freeman, Roger A., *Mighty Eighth War Manual*. New York: Jane's, 1984

Morris, Danny, *Aces and Wingmen*. London: Neville Spearman, 1972

McLachlan, Ian, *Final Flights*. Sparkford. Haynes Publishing, 1989.

McLachlan, Ian, *USAAF Fighter Stories*. Sparkford. Haynes Publishing, 1997

O'Leary, Michael, *VIII Fighter Command at War 'Long Reach'*. Oxford: Osprey, 2000

Spick, Mike. *Allied Fighter Aces*. London: Greenhill Books, 1997.

Index